MIND VIRUSES

MIND VIRUSES

AMERICA'S IRRATIONAL OBSESSIONS

JOHN LEAKE

NEW YORK TIMES BESTSELLING AUTHOR

Skyhorse Publishing

Skyhorse Publishing books may be purchased in bulk at special discounts for sales promotion, corporate gifts, fund-raising, or educational purposes. Special editions can also be created to specifications. For details, contact the Special Sales Department, Skyhorse Publishing, 307 Fifth Avenue, 4th Floor, New York, NY 10016 or info@skyhorsepublishing.com.

Visit our website at www.skyhorsepublishing.com.
Please follow our publisher Tony Lyons on Instagram @tonylyonsisuncertain.

10 9 8 7 6 5 4 3 2 1

Library of Congress Cataloging-in-Publication Data is available on file.

Cover design by David Ter-Avanesyan

Hardcover ISBN: 978-1-5107-8680-6
Ebook ISBN: 978-1-5107-8681-3

Printed in the United States of America

CONTENTS

PREFACE

The whole aim of practical politics is to keep the populace alarmed (and hence clamorous to be led to safety) by an endless series of hobgoblins, most of them imaginary.

—H. L. Mencken

Since 2001, the American people have been subjected to a series of crises, emergencies, foreign wars, moral panics, and purported threats to public safety and health. We have been frequently told the world is full of hostile foreign actors who "hate our freedom" and that our homeland is a racist country built on the repression of Blacks, women, gays, and transgender people. We regularly hear alarms that the earth will soon become uninhabitable due to human-induced "climate change." Psychiatrists assert that a large percentage of American children suffer from gender dysphoria. Since Donald Trump announced he was running for president on June 16, 2015, scarcely a day has passed without melodrama in the public forum. This steady stream of disturbances has produced a host of negative emotions, demoralized and divided us, and undermined our trust in our institutions. In the vacuum of positive and unifying ideas, several morbid and irrational obsessions have emerged.

For me and my fellow members of Generation X, it's often tempting to feel nostalgic for the relative harmony and stability of the 1990s, and to wonder what happened to it. The decade began shortly after the Berlin Wall fell on November 9, 1989. On December 26, 1991, the Soviet Union dissolved, thereby ending the Cold War that began in 1947. Out of this protracted struggle, the United States emerged as the victor and world's sole superpower, animated with confidence and optimism. In 1992, Francis Fukuyama, a distinguished political science professor at Johns-Hopkins

University, published *The End of History and the Last Man,* proclaiming the triumph of liberal democracy and the market economy. James Madison's Enlightenment vision of a free citizenry had bested all ideological rivals. The American way of life reigned supreme and was destined to be universally emulated in the final stage of humanity's development.

In 1997, the Supreme Court (*Reno v. ACLU*) ruled that the internet is entitled to the highest level of First Amendment protection. The *United States v. Microsoft* in 1998 signaled that even the richest corporations and men still had to play by the rules. The highest paid American athletes in 1999 were Michael Jordan and Tiger Woods. Oprah Winfrey, Sean "Diddy" Combs, and Will Smith were in the top twenty of *Forbes* magazine's "Celebrity 100" list. The biggest scandal of the era was President Bill Clinton's dalliance with White House intern Monica Lewinsky. Despite this unsavory episode, the decade ended with budget surpluses, a booming stock market, and roaring good spirits. *Shakespeare in Love*—a charming celebration of our English literary heritage—won Best Picture at the 1999 Academy Awards ceremony, while *Saving Private Ryan*—a celebration of American valor and virtue during World War II—won five Oscars, including Best Director for Steven Spielberg.

This book is a brief history and exposition of how the American Republic went from being a strong, unified, and confident nation in 1999 to the basket case that it is today. Like other great powers in history, the United States has declined not from the depredations of foreign adversaries—as much as our politicians like to rail about them—but from our internal divisions that are incited and stoked by various interests. Divisions are created through the interplay of three essential elements:

1. Propagating fear and loathing of a purported threat to public health and safety
2. Presenting a purported solution whose implementation is characterized as a sacred mission.
3. Scapegoating the purported enemies or opponents of this mission.

Recent missions have included reducing greenhouse gas emissions and getting all humanity vaccinated against SARS-CoV-2, the causative agent of COVID-19. Here at the outset, it should be noted that, in each of these missions, the threat is grossly overstated and oversimplified, and the efficacy of the championed solution cannot be measured, tested, or falsified. The rational observer eventually suspects that the point of the sacred mission is to keep it going, because the interested parties would be out of business as soon as the problem is solved.

Millions of people may become preoccupied with a mission and develop burning hostility to its purported enemies. Fear and loathing of the threat disable critical reasoning and trigger extreme and even violent behavior. Because of man's imitative nature and his strong inclination to exert peer pressure and to engage in groupthink, false beliefs and irrational behavior may spread like a viral contagion. Preoccupation with the mission is therefore aptly (albeit metaphorically) characterized as a mind virus.

The evidence that mind viruses are largely the fabrications of powerful interest groups is not difficult to find or understand. Most of it is hidden in plain sight. People struggle to recognize and comprehend it because they believe that the US government is acting in their interest, because they are bombarded with propaganda, and because of their mistaken belief that large-scale fraud must be concealed in a subtle and sophisticated way. Once the mind fully realizes that our "scientific-technological elite" (as President Dwight D. Eisenhower called it) and mainstream media are captured by interests, it becomes easy to spot the clear pattern of how they manipulate the public.

The objective of this book is to show how mind viruses are produced and transmitted to the public, and to illuminate the qualities that make some people susceptible to them while others are resistant to their spell. I hope that revealing the anatomy of this diabolical phenomenon will immunize readers against the next mind virus that is unleashed on us.

PROLOGUE

A MURDER IN MOSCOW

On the night of November 21, 1869, Ivan Ivanov, a student at the Petrovsky Academy of Agriculture in Moscow, was brutally murdered in the academy's park. The perpetrators tried to conceal the body by lashing bricks to it and sinking it in a shallow pond near the murder scene, but a couple of peasants strolling in the park a few days later spotted it, looming below a thin layer of ice that had formed on the pond's surface. The Moscow police quickly ascertained the identity of the murder victim. Chief of the Moscow gendarme directorate, Colonel Slezkin, described the body as follows:

> The corpse of Academy student Ivan Ivanovich Ivanov has been found with all the indications of violent death – head smashed and, in addition, was penetrated from behind by a bullet that exited in the left eye; neck strangled by a scarf, to which was attached a brick; legs at the knees and near the feet tied by a whip, to which also a brick had been attached. No robbery.[1]

Detectives discovered that Ivanov had been a member of a revolutionary group called the People's Reprisal, led by a young man named Sergey Nechayev. Further investigation revealed that Ivanov had become disillusioned with the group and was trying to distance himself from it just before his death. Fearing that Ivanov might become an informant for the Tsar's secret police, Nechayev decided to murder him. Though four accomplices assisted with the crime, it was Nechayev who fired the pistol shot into the back of Ivanov's head. Realizing the police were on his trail, he fled to Geneva, Switzerland, where he was finally arrested in 1872 and extradited back to Russia, where he was found guilty of murder and spent the rest of his life in the Peter and Paul Fortress in St. Petersburg.

The savagery of the murder—as well as the remarkable personality of the culprit and his political motive—generated much newspaper coverage. Among those who were engrossed by the story was the Russian novelist, Fyodor Dostoevsky, who had, in his youth, been a member of the Petrashevsky Circle that advocated free speech, the abolition of serfdom, and other social reforms that were proscribed by the regime of Alexander I.[2] In 1849, Dostoevsky was arrested for distributing a letter that was critical of the government and the Orthodox Church. He spent six months in solitary confinement in the Peter and Paul Fortress and was sentenced to death. Seconds before he was to be shot by a firing squad, he was told that his sentence had been commuted to four years hard labor in Siberia, followed by six years of military service.

From his own hard experience, Dostoevsky understood the harsh authoritarianism of the Tsarist regime in Russia and the desirability of liberal values such as free speech. However, he also knew that, though the pace of social reform in Russia was slow, it did happen. After all, Tsar Nicholas II abolished serfdom in 1861, which is what Dostoevsky's circle advocated in 1849. When he read about Nechayev's bestial murder of Ivanov, he perceived in it a terrifying absolutism and nihilism. As Nechayev himself had put in his pamphlet, *The Catechism of a Revolutionist*, "For him everything that contributes to the triumph of the revolution is moral, everything that hinders it is immoral and criminal."[3] This meant that all actions—no matter how violent and cruel, including the murder of one's own former comrade—were not only permitted, but necessary and good for the advancement of the revolutionary cause. As the title implied, Nechayev proposed making a religion out of revolution.

To Dostoevsky, Nechayev conformed to biblical and folkloric accounts of someone possessed by the devil, and the young fanatic inspired him to write a novel (published in 1872) titled *The Possessed*, also sometimes translated as *Demons*.[4] The novel tells the story of a young revolutionary named Pyotr Verkhovensky who leads a group of young men to incite chaos and try to seize power in a provincial town. A key character is Ivan

Shatov. Initially a member of the group, he becomes disillusioned with their doctrine and seeks to leave them to embrace orthodox Christianity. Fearing that Shatov will betray them to the authorities, Verkhovensky murders him.

Verkhovensky and his comrades claim their project is for the betterment of humanity, but their professed altruism scarcely veils their self-absorbed, vain, power-seeking, intellectually shallow, and comically ridiculous characters. Given to pretentious talk about abstract "-isms," they have no understanding of the business of administration. Having rejected all time-tested principles of morality and practical politics, they find themselves unable to create anything, and therefore direct all their zeal and energy to destroying everything. Death and destruction are their project, and they exult in it.

As the reader may have sensed, Verkovensky and his comrades portrayed in Dostoevsky's 1872 novel eerily resemble Vladimir Lenin and his comrades who seized power in 1917. One of the revolutionary speakers at a literary gala portrayed in the book even looks and acts like Lenin. Dostoevsky describes the character as around forty years old, balding in the middle, with a greyish beard. While preparing to give his speech, he paces back and forth behind stage, rehearsing his talking points. "At every turn he took, he threw up his right fist, brandished it above his head and suddenly brought it down again as though crushing an antagonist to atoms." His speech is full of sarcasm and cynicism, just like Lenin's real-life speeches that he delivered decades later. *The Possessed* was a prophetic book.

Dostoevsky believed that humans cannot escape their religious nature. Russians who regarded themselves as atheists were disenchanted with Orthodox Christianity and drawn to a materialist worldview. However, these same people then posited a different set of axiomatic claims from which they fashioned their own orthodoxy, and they severely punished anyone who didn't adhere to it. Marxism-Leninism is not a scientific doctrine, but a religion with its own saints (Marx and Lenin) orthodoxy (their writings) and Holy Office of the Inquisition (the Cheka, later the NKVD).

As Dostoevsky saw it, Christianity was superior to the secular doctrines that were transmitting from Europe into Russia in his day. Its superiority is conveyed in Matthew 7:12, in which Jesus states, "In everything, do to others what you would have them do to you." This Golden Rule—a clear moral basis for the life of individuals and society—was the tenet most violated by the revolutionaries, who believed they were justified in killing anyone they so much as suspected of being an impediment to achieving their goals.

For the Bolsheviks, revolution was like a sacred cause. Echoing Nechayev's *Catechism of a Revolutionary*, Lenin proclaimed that morality was subordinate to class struggle. He defined good as everything that destroyed what he characterized as "the old society of exploiters" and helped to build a "new communist society." As he put it:

> We say that our morality is entirely subordinated to the interests of the class struggle of the proletariat. We do not believe in an eternal morality, and we expose the deceit of all the fables about morality. Morality is what serves to destroy the old exploiting society and to unite all the toilers around the proletariat, which is creating a new communist society.[5]

The "old exploiting society" included the Tsar, his family and ministers, the nobility, the Orthodox clergy, the landowning class of peasants called kulaks, the urban bourgeoisie, and even Bolsheviks suspected of being unreliable. Those infected with the Marxist-Leninist mind virus believed that all these people opposed their revolutionary cause and had to be destroyed to usher in a new era of social justice and prosperity. As Joseph Stalin succinctly put it, "Death solves all problems, no man, no problem."

The Russian Civil War (1917–1922) and associated famine and infectious disease outbreaks are estimated to have killed between seven and twelve million people. The Bolsheviks are estimated to have killed approximately two hundred thousand people during the Red Terror (1918–22). In 1929, the Bolsheviks launched their "collectivization and dekulakization" campaign against landholding peasants, murdering hundreds of thousands and causing an estimated six to nine million others to die of starvation by confiscating their grain, seed stocks, and even household food supplies. During the Great Terror (1937–38), Stalin's regime executed approximately seven hundred thousand people and another 2.7 million are estimated to have died from cold, sickness, deprivation, and murder in the Gulag forced labor and prison camps. Altogether, Bolshevik actions are estimated to have resulted in the deaths of over twenty million people in the Soviet Union.[6]

The October Revolution of 1917 did not arise from an organic, grass-roots movement, but from the violently destabilizing events unleashed by the First World War, and the short-sighted decision of Imperial Germany's government to transfer Lenin from his exile in Switzerland to St. Petersburg, and to finance his toppling of the Russian Provisional Government.[7] Their rationale for backing Lenin was his promise to end Russia's participation in World War I against Germany and Austria-Hungary if he succeeded in gaining power. The German schemers got their deal; Lenin succeeded in seizing power and his delegation signed the Treaty of Brest-Litovsk on March 3, 1918. Unfortunately, this arrangement unleashed an even greater threat to all of mankind and did not prevent Germany from losing the war. Marxism-Leninism was the doctrine that destroyed Russia, but it was transmitted to the Russian people by factions of the ruling class in the West. As Winston Churchill put it in a speech to Parliament:

> Lenin was sent into Russia by the Germans in the same way that you might send a phial containing a culture of typhoid or of cholera to be poured into the water supply of a great city, and it worked with amazing accuracy. No sooner did Lenin arrive than he began beckoning a finger here and a finger there to obscure persons in sheltered retreats in New York, in Glasgow, in Bern, and other countries, and he gathered together the leading spirits of a formidable sect, the most formidable sect in the world, of which he was the high priest and chief. With these spirits around him he set to work with demoniacal ability to tear to pieces every institution on which the Russian State and nation depended. Russia was laid low.[8]

The laying low of Russia is a cautionary tale of what can happen to a nation when a virulent mind virus is transmitted to its people. Lenin and his comrades fanatically pursued their sacred cause of revolution without a detailed and practical understanding of how their radical policies would produce a functioning civil society and economy. Their violent actions to overthrow existing institutions and arrangements were guided by poorly defined, ideological concepts such as the "dictatorship of the proletariat" ultimately developing into a "stateless" and "classless" society. In their zeal for creating an ideal future society, they were indifferent to the present needs and suffering of actual human beings, whom they regarded as expendable to the revolutionary cause. Because they didn't count the cost of actual lives and suffering, they had no means of measuring the success of their enterprise apart from seizing power, expanding their state control of property and assets, and increasing industrial quotas.

Lenin proclaimed that his goal was to overthrow the old society of oppressors and exploiters and to put into practice the communist ideals presented in the writings of Karl Marx. These included communal ownership of property, a classless society, a withering away of the state, and maximum individual freedom. Such were his stated intentions, but in practice, the regime he built was far more oppressive than the Tsarist regime it replaced. Far from reducing the size and scope of state power, the Bolsheviks expanded it into an apparatus of totalitarian control. Instead of establishing an egalitarian society, the party bosses obtained special privileges, took up residence in the grand properties they expropriated from the former elite, and reserved the highest quality provisions and restaurants for themselves. Instead of increasing material prosperity and extending it to the entire community, their seizure of productive assets and their collectivization of agriculture lowered the standard of living for many and caused frequent famines. Instead of maximizing individual liberty, they abolished it.

Dostoevsky titled his 1872 novel *Demons* to refer to the way in which ideas have the power to possess people. Mind viruses produce a mental state that may be described as ideological possession. Those who are infected with them see the world in rigidly ideological terms, with a simplified, schematic view of human nature and society. Because they are exclusively focused on achieving their sacred mission, they don't count the costs or perform risk-benefit analyses of their radical policies.

Forty-five years after *Demons* was published, critical observers of the Bolsheviks concluded that many of them seemed possessed. In a 1939 leaflet he wrote while he was exile, Bishop Theophan of Poltava wrote that Russia had become "possessed with devils" during the 1917 civil war. The high-ranking Bolshevik, Yakov Sverdlov, who played a key role in organizing the red terror and murdering the Tsar and his family, was nicknamed the "Black Devil." His friends said he got his nickname from his habit of wearing a black leather jacket. His opponents claimed he really was a devil. They perceived that he and his comrades were determined to achieve their revolutionary goals, no matter how many they had to imprison, starve, or kill to do it.

CHAPTER 1

THE DELUSIONS OF THE RULING CLASS

Throughout history, the ruling class has always grossly overestimated its ability to control, manage, change, and improve things. In Britain during the seventeenth century, members of Parliament and writers such as John Milton articulated this idea in their philosophy that the power of rulers such as their King Charles I should be limited. They regarded King Charles I as deluded in his belief that he possessed a divine right to rule with absolute and unquestionable authority. Most members of Parliament advocated limiting the king's power and subjecting it to the consent of Parliament. Tensions between Parliament and King Charles I resulted in the English Civil War (1642–1651), with Charles I executed in 1649. Following the restoration of the Stewart monarchy, William and Mary deposed James II and were granted the crown by Parliament on the condition that they recognized the legitimacy of the Bill of Rights, which established limited monarchy, and religious toleration provided by the Toleration Act.

Britain's American colonies naturally absorbed this idea of limiting the power of the king during the late seventeenth and early eighteenth centuries. Being situated on the opposite side of the Atlantic and receiving little state support, the colonists developed strong habits of self-reliance. Prime Minister Robert Walpole, who held office from 1721–42, wanted to focus on European affairs, and therefore devoted little attention to regulating the colonies and their trade. It wasn't until around 1760, during the French and Indian War, that King George and his ministers reversed this policy and started enforcing trade regulations and imposing taxes on the colonists.

On March 22, 1775, Edmund Burke addressed Parliament about colonial grievances. He mentioned what he described as the earlier policy of "wise and salutary neglect" as decisive in promoting the commercial success of Britain's North American holdings. Salutary neglect had enabled the colonies to trade with non-British entities, and to spend their wealth on British-made goods, while providing Britain with raw materials. However, as Burke pointed out, because the policy enabled the colonies to operate independently of Britain, it resulted in the colonists forging a new and independent identity.

The framers of the US Constitution, especially James Madison and George Washington, believed that, though government is necessary for regulating human affairs and preventing lawlessness, it was imperative to limit the discretionary power of the governors. A Constitution that expressly limited state power was understood to be an instrument for protecting the people from the arbitrary will and whims of the men who held office. With strict limitations in place, rulers who were deluded or became so after assuming power were limited in how much damage they could inflict on the people they ruled.

Americans have become increasingly susceptible to mind viruses during a time of diminishing interest in the Constitution and understanding of its underlying philosophy. Most Americans now look to the state to solve an array of problems, even though state officials do not possess the competence to do so. On the contrary, many social and economic problems are caused or aggravated by the state. A failure to understand this leaves many people susceptible to mind viruses propagated by the state and its scientific-technological elite.

Where there are zero constitutional protections in place, which typically occurs in the wake of a violent revolution, the people are entirely at the mercy of the revolutionaries who seize power—men like Vladimir Lenin and his right-hand man, Yakov Sverdlov. Prior to becoming chairman of the All-Russian Central Executive Committee with the Bolshevik takeover in 1917, Sverdlov had four years of high school education and no business or administrative experience. His entire life experience consisted of being an underground activist, a prisoner, or an exile. Between becoming

Lenin's right-hand man in 1917 and his death from Spanish Influenza in 1919, he possessed the power of life and death over 170 million Russian people. Like all ranking Bolsheviks, he was inspired by Marx's famous dictum: "The philosophers have hitherto only interpreted the world in various ways; the point, however, is to change it." Though undoubtedly clever and cunning, Yakov and his comrades—equipped with mere slogans—had no idea how to change Russia in a way that was beneficial for most of its people. Indeed, the Bolsheviks didn't even understand how to maintain the elements of Russia that were already well-functioning and productive. They were perfect examples of rulers suffering from the fatal delusion that they possessed the understanding to control and change all of society from the top down.

The way was paved for them to seize power in Russia by the deluded ruling class of Europe that plunged the Continent into the catastrophe of the First World War. In every court and council of war, men of extraordinary hubris made innumerable assumptions about their chances of prevailing in waging total warfare against their opponents. All their assumptions proved false. What caused these men to believe confidently that their side would quickly prevail? Over a hundred thousand books about the First World War have been published, but it remains unclear why exactly the greatest civilization in world history—during the most prosperous time in its history—sent ten million of its young men, including its most educated, to their deaths in the inferno of trench warfare. In Britain, approximately twenty percent of the graduating classes of Oxford and Cambridge in the years 1912–14 were killed in the war.[1] The graduating classes of famous German universities suffered similar casualty rates. On top of the ten million dead, another twenty-three million suffered severe wounds, many of which caused lifelong disabilities. These highly cultivated youths were the flower and the future hope of their respective nations, and they were senselessly flung into artillery and machine gun fire for four years. One searches in vain for a rational motive for this wanton behavior.

In Germany, as the situation became increasingly desperate in the spring of 1917, the top men at court made the decision to send Lenin from his Swiss exile back into Russia to sow chaos and eventually to end to Russia's participation in the war. The German schemers included Erich Ludendorff (First Quartermaster General), Theobald von Bethmann Hollweg (Chancellor), Arthur Zimmermann (Foreign Minister) and Kaiser Wilhelm II. Zimmermann was an exemplar of the technocratic expert who wildly overestimates his understanding and acumen. Having studied law at the prestigious University of Leipzig (where Goethe had studied law), he believed himself to be endowed with profound insight into human affairs. Many of his most crucial decisions affecting the lives of millions were so bad that one wonders if he was drunk when he made them. He was known as a "convivial" man who purportedly drank a large quantity of wine with lunch every day, so maybe he was drunk. He claimed to possess profound insight into American politics and public sentiment based on one transcontinental train tour of the United States.

Zimmermann's support for sending Lenin back to Russia was his second catastrophic mistake in early 1917. His first was sending an encrypted telegram on January 16, 1917, to the German ambassador to Mexico, instructing him to propose a military alliance with Mexico against the United States that would enable Mexico to win back Texas, New Mexico, and Arizona. Zimmermann's telegram was intercepted and decrypted by British intelligence. Even then, he could have controlled the damage by denying the authenticity of the telegram at a time when many Americans thought it was a British forgery to drag the United States into the war. Apparently bent on blundering, Zimmermann publicly admitted on March 3, 1917, that the telegram was authentic, thereby greatly boosting support in the US for going to war against Germany. Just one month later, Zimmerman strongly endorsed sending Lenin back into Russia.

That Kaiser Wilhelm II approved of the incredibly perfidious and short-sighted decision to send Lenin back to Russia seems even more insane when one considers that he and Tsar Nicholas II were third cousins who had long expressed affection for each other prior to the war, despite their competing national interests. When the Kaiser received the news that the Tsar and his entire family had been murdered by Lenin's henchmen, he was overcome with horror, perhaps only then grasping the terrible mistake he and his ministers had made.

The delusions of the ruling class are by far the most destructive when they animate the rulers to wage war, and they use propaganda to animate the masses to go to war. Through propaganda, the delusions of the ruling class are transmitted to the people. As a tribal, warmaking animal, humans are easily excited and frightened by the prospect of being attacked or invaded by hostile foreigners. As James Madison pointed out, this has, going back to ancient Rome, enabled states to maintain large armies, even though doing so places an enormous burden on the taxpaying citizen and frequently threatens his liberty. In a June 29, 1787, debate at the US Constitutional Convention, Madison remarked:

> In time of actual war, great discretionary powers are constantly given to the Executive Magistrate. Constant apprehension of war has the same tendency to render the head too large for the body. A standing military force, with an overgrown Executive will not long be safe companions to liberty. The means of defence against foreign danger have been always the instruments of tyranny at home.[2]

Picking up this theme 174 years later, President Eisenhower warned Americans in his January 17, 1961, Farewell Address:

> We must guard against the acquisition of unwarranted influence, whether sought or unsought, by the military-industrial complex. The potential for the disastrous rise of misplaced power exists and will persist. We must never let the weight of this combination endanger our liberties or democratic processes.[3]

As the reader will see in the following chapters, the declaration that we must wage war against an enemy—real, perceived, exaggerated or fabricated—is the essential psychological drama out of which all mind viruses emerge, while fear of the enemy is the primary emotional driver. Responsible and prudent rulers avoid saying and doing things that cause fear and loathing to spread in the populace. A tragic feature of the human condition is the strong and persistent tendency of rulers to incite fear to manipulate the people to wage war. The enemy could be framed as any class, ethnic group, religious sect, nation, political party, or even natural phenomena such as "climate change" or an infectious disease pathogen such as SARS-CoV-2, the causative agent of COVID-19. Incited and amplified by propaganda, fear may spread through a population, compelling the people to participate in highly irrational and destructive collective actions. Rulers can either take action to dampen fear, or they can fan the flames because they believe that doing so serves their interests.

CHAPTER 2

WITCH HUNTS AND SCAPEGOATS

During the fifteenth and sixteenth centuries, the German-speaking lands of Europe were struck by a perfect storm of natural, cultural, and spiritual destabilization. A major contributing factor was the so-called Little Ice Age (LIA)—a period of cooling, primarily in the North Atlantic, that lasted roughly from 1300 to 1850.[1] During this period, the primarily agrarian lands of Germany and Switzerland experienced markedly colder winters and cooler summers, probably caused by volcanic eruptions and lower solar activity. Short, cool summers and long, cold winters resulted in lower crop yields and even crop failures. Resulting undernourishment increased the incidence of infectious diseases and caused major social and economic hardship. Pieter Bruegel the Elder captured the hardship of winter during this period with his famous painting, "Hunters in the Snow," dated 1565. The Flemish landscape appears completely frozen, and the exhausted looking hunters have little to show for their effort. During these hard years, many wondered if a curse had fallen on Flemish, German, and Swiss lands.

Since around AD 900, Canon Law had defined witchcraft as the highly punishable practice of those who had been seduced by the Devil. However, rooting out and punishing alleged witches only became a historically noteworthy practice during the latter half of the fifteenth century. A major figure in the genesis of witch trials was a Catholic monk named Heinrich Kramer (a.k.a. Henricus Institor). Born in Alsace, after entering the Dominican Order, he became an industrious and enthusiastic Inquisitor—a Church officer charged with investigating and prosecuting heresy. In 1484, after achieving prominence as the right-hand man of the Archbishop of Salzburg, he wrote letter to Pope Innocent VIII, requesting papal authorization to root out and punish witches. The Pope responded with the Papal Bull *Summis desiderantes affectibus* (Latin: "desiring with supreme ardor"). With this authorization, Kramer moved to Innsbruck to detect and punish witches.

In Innsbruck, he came into conflict with an outspoken woman named Helene Scheuberin, the wife of a prominent Burgher. Apparently, after attending some of his sermons in which he spoke about the danger of witches in their midst, Helena concluded that Kramer was a dangerous crank, and she spoke out against him in public. One day, she encountered him in the street, spat at his feet, and said something along the lines of "to hell with you, you evil monk." Shortly thereafter, she and six other women were accused of witchcraft, with Kramer serving as an expert for the prosecution. The defendants' lawyer, Johann Merwart, raised procedural objections that Judge Christian Turner, representing the Bishop of Brixen, Georg Golser, upheld.[2] Helena and her co-defendants were acquitted, which badly damaged Kramer's intellectual prestige. Bishop Golser found Kramer's methods and his accusations of sexual misconduct distasteful and ordered the Inquisitor to leave his diocese. Apparently feeling humiliated, Kramer returned to Cologne and got to work writing his guidebook on how to detect, investigate, interrogate, and convict witches.

Malleus Maleficarum is a remarkably malevolent, sadistic, and prurient book, and an expression of the most pathological virtue-signaling.[3] Today's reader will quickly conclude that Helene Scheuberin was correct in her perception that Kramer was an evil and twisted monk, and that Bishop Golser was justified in telling him to beat it. At the time the book was published in 1486–87, it was highly controversial, with many admirers and detractors. Top theologians of the Inquisition on the Faculty of Cologne University condemned it as recommending illegal procedures and presenting ideas inconsistent with Catholic doctrine pertaining to heresy. The book only really caught on and became an authoritative text after 1517, when the Augustinian friar, Martin Luther, published his

Ninety-Five Theses. This led to an intense conflict between the Protestant Reformation and Catholic Counter-Reformation. In German lands that remained Catholic, Luther's *Theses* were deemed heresy. The prominent German educator, theologian, and polemicist, Johannes Cochlaeus, proclaimed that Luther was the offspring of a demon who copulated with his mother, Margarethe, and that those who followed him were therefore followers of the devil. The notion that the devil and his followers were afoot amplified the stress of crop failures, infectious diseases and infertility, with many wondering if the natural disasters were caused by the malevolence of heretics.

In the years 1581–1593, an intense fear of witches spread through the diocese of Trier, Germany. As Johann Linden, canon of the Cathedral of Trier, wrote of the hysteria:

> In as much as it was popularly believed that the continued sterility of many years was caused by witches through the malice of the Devil, the whole country rose to exterminate the witches. This movement was promoted by many in office, who hoped for wealth from the persecution. And so, from court to court throughout the towns and villages of all the diocese, scurried special accusers, inquisitors, notaries, jurors, judges, constables, dragging to trial and torture human beings of both sexes and burning them in great numbers. Scarcely any of those who were accused escaped punishment or were there spared even the leading men in the city of Trier. For the Judge, two Burgomasters, several Councilors and Associate Judges, canons of sundry collegiate churches, parish priests, rural deans, were swept away in this ruin. So far, at length, did the madness of the furious populace and of the courts go in this thirst for blood and booty that there was scarcely anybody who was not smirched some suspicion of this crime.[4]

Archbishop-Elector Johann von Schönenberg, the ruler of Trier during this time, did not so much incite the witch hysteria as harness it to purge Protestants, Jews, and anyone else he deemed a nonconformist. Though he seems to have sincerely believed in witchcraft, he also perceived the trials to be an expedient way to consolidate his power in the diocese. Thus, we see how rulers and the people they rule engage in an irrational, destructive, and corrupt enterprise that proves to be ruinous for all involved.

Though German dioceses like Trier engaged in the greatest total number of witch trials, the disaster visited upon Switzerland was far greater on a per capita basis. With so much of the country lying within the high elevation of the Alps, the Little Ice Age struck even harder, producing even shorter growing seasons and longer and harsher winters. Divided into multiple cantons and situated on the fault line of the Reformation and Counter-Reformation, the country was rife with political rivals who used secular courts as instruments for asserting their authority, seizing property, and settling scores. At the height of the witch hysteria in Switzerland during the early seventeenth century, the incidence of witch trials was approximately 980 per one hundred thousand people.[5] Older, motherless women were viewed as the primary suspects, and in some towns virtually all of them were accused, tortured, and burned.

During the 1930s, while observing events in Germany with the rise to power of the National Socialist Party, the psychiatrist, Carl Jung, reflected on the witch trials that had happened in his native Switzerland three hundred years earlier. Within the country afflicted with religious conflict, economic hardship, and political instability, the archetypal image of the witch became an object of fear and loathing onto which all fears and frustrations could be projected. The private projections of individuals were then validated by inquisitors and magistrates. Confessions extracted under torture generated frightening stories that were circulated in the community, thereby fueling the hysteria. Jung called this kind of collective participation in a communal, irrational, and destructive action a "psychic epidemic" because of the way in which irrational thoughts and feelings spread like a contagion.[6]

The apparent cure for contagion was to burn those accused of witchcraft. Burning the alleged witch was conceived not only a symbolic ritual, but also as a means of destroying the alleged cause of the collective distress. A commonly used term for this social mechanism is scapegoating. This focusing of negative emotions has the effect of reducing overall conflict in the community by uniting the majority against the minority on which the blame is heaped. Ritualized violence against the feared and loathed minority has a cathartic effect that seemingly resolves the crisis.

The French author and Stanford professor, René Girard, argued that the story of the life and crucifixion of Jesus bore enormous moral significance because it revealed the innocence of the victim, thereby teaching humanity about its capacity for unjust collective violence.

The witch hysteria climaxed around 1625 and then precipitously declined, with a big leg down around the time of the Treaty of Westphalia in 1648 that ended the Thirty Years War between Catholics and Protestants. Historians often credit the Scientific Revolution in European thought as a major contributing factor to outlawing the trials, but the influence of this factor is overstated. Sir Isaac Newton, who published his *Principia Mathematica* in 1687—probably the most influential book in the history of scientific thought—also believed in supernatural spirits, including witches.

During the late seventeenth century, the most influential intellectual in the British American colonies was Cotton Mather. Along with his father Increase Mather, he was co-pastor of the Congregationalist Old North Meeting House in Boston, where he continued to preach the Puritan theology of his forefathers. A child prodigy, he attended Harvard at age eleven and remains the youngest student in the college's history. Like Newton, Mather perceived the world to be comprised of two realms—the supernatural and the natural—and he saw no contradiction between these worlds. On the one hand, he was a strong supporter of empirical, experimental science and became a member of the Royal Society in 1713. On the other hand, he believed in the existence of devils and witches who could exert their power in the world and do evil. During the Salem Witch Trials, he served as a consultant to the presiding judges and defended his view of the matter in his 1693 book *Wonders of the Invisible World.*

The trials were unique in the history of American jurisprudence because the court admitted so-called "spectral evidence"—that is, testimony of a witness who claimed that the accused appeared to her and harmed her in a dream or a vision. The proceedings got especially spooky when some witnesses cried out as though they were being tormented while the accused were questioned. When asked for his opinion of spectral evidence, Mather pointed out that it could be proper evidence, but he cautioned that the Devil could also assume the image of an innocent person.[7]

During the witch trials, witnesses seemed to be suffering from invisible causes, and they claimed they were being tormented by apparitions that only they could see. Were the witnesses pretending, suffering from intoxication or illness, or really being tormented by witches doing the Devil's work? The judges concluded that, of the two hundred accused, twenty had indeed practiced witchcraft on the witnesses. They drew this conclusion with no reliable means of knowing whether it was indeed the cause.

During the 1930s and early '40s, Carl Jung perceived events in Germany to resemble the witch hysteria of sixteenth- and seventeenth-century Europe. As he saw it, Germany was in the grip of a national, psychic epidemic, with the great insecurity, anxiety, and divisions of the Weimar Republic causing a prevalence of highly negative emotions that made it increasingly difficult to maintain a constitutional republic in which the state was restrained by reason and law. As Jung put it:

> Rational argument can be conducted with some prospect of success only so long as the emotionality of a given situation does not exceed a certain critical degree. If the affective temperature rises above this level, the possibility of reason having any effect ceases, and its place is taken by slogans and chimerical wish fantasies. A sort of collective possession results, which rapidly develops into a psychic epidemic.[8]

Within this atmosphere of stress, insecurity, and high emotionality, individuals suffering from deep-seated mental abnormalities could rise to the top, harnessing and channeling the collective negative emotions. Again, to quote Carl Jung:

> In this state, all those elements whose existence is merely tolerated as asocial under the rule of reason, come to the top. Such individuals are by no means rare curiosities to be met only in prisons and lunatic asylums or every manifest case of insanity, there are, in my estimation, at least 10 latent cases who seldom get to the point of breaking out openly, but whose views and behavior, for all their appearance of normality, are influenced by unconsciously morbid and perverse factors. . . . Their mental state is that of a collectively excited group ruled by affective judgments and wish fantasies. . . . Their chimerical ideas, spawned by fanatical resentment, appeal

> to the collective irrationality and find fruitful soil there, for they express all those motives and resentments which lurk in more normal people under the cloak of reason and insight.[9]

This observation recalls the warning of George Messersmith, US Consul General to Germany in a 1933 dispatch to the State Department:

> With few exceptions, the men who are running the government are of a mentality that you and I cannot understand. Some of them are psychopathic cases and would ordinarily be receiving treatment somewhere.[10]

Nazi Germany was an especially shocking example of a country in the grip of a psychic epidemic that emerged in the wake of the terrible trauma of World War I and the severe penalties imposed on the nation by the Treaty of Versailles, which forced the German people to accept full responsibility for the war and to pay massive reparations. These caused severe economic distress and humiliation that gave rise to widespread feelings of resentment and dread. Hitler was able to harness these feelings while invoking the specter of enemies at home and abroad. By proclaiming that these enemies sought to destroy the German people, he psychologically prepared the nation for another war.

CHAPTER 3

WAR, THE FATHER OF ALL MIND VIRUSES

On February 23, 1942, a submarine of the Imperial Japanese Navy, commanded by Kozo Nishino, fired its 14-cm deck gun at an oil field on the coast of Ellwood, California near Santa Barbara. The crew fired around twenty shells, destroying an oil derrick and pump house. Commander Nishino believed that, despite doing almost no damage to the oil field, he accomplished his mission—namely, to spread fear of a Japanese attack among the residents of California. Nishino was aware that the residents and military personnel in Southern California were already suffering from highly inflamed "war nerves" after the Japanese bombing of Pearl Harbor on December 7, 1941, and his objective was to throw fuel on the fire. For as Nishino correctly understood, fear causes people to do extremely foolish things.

Fear is a critically important emotion for rapidly detecting and reacting to mortal dangers and avoiding them in the future. Fear keenly sharpens one's focus on a threat and prepares the body to fight it or flee from it. Within the hostile natural environment in which humans evolved, fear kept people alive. Without it, the human species would not have survived. However, as the conditions of modern life have become more secure and complex, fear may greatly impair the ability of individuals and societies to respond to events in a rational manner that serves their best interests. Unless fear is checked by strong mental habits, it can quickly take over the brain and suppress critical reasoning and perspective. A mind gripped by fear sees the world in categorical, black and white terms and may interpret ambiguous, neutral, and even good-intentioned signals as threatening. Fearful people find it difficult to grasp complexity and nuance, and they may grossly overreact to a perceived threat in destructive and dangerous ways.

Japanese Commander Nishino's ineffectual shelling of the Ellwood oil field was reported on the radio, which caused the civilian population and military personnel in Southern California to enter a mental state of extreme hypervigilance. A hypervigilant person is so sensitive to all conceivable signs of danger that he becomes highly error-prone in distinguishing true signs of it from harmless phenomena. Hypervigilant people may feel themselves to be in grave and immediate danger even when their environment is perfectly safe.

About thirty hours after Commander Nishino shelled the Ellwood oilfield, at 2:25 a.m. on February 25, 1942, an errant weather balloon over Los Angeles triggered an air raid alert and blackout. This, in turn, triggered a massive anti-aircraft barrage of approximately 1,400 shells fired into the sky over Los Angeles at perceived enemy aircraft, even though none was clearly detected and identified.[1] Five people died during the incident from stress-related heart attacks and traffic accidents caused by the panic. Later, the Army declared the incident to have been the result of "war nerves and imagination."

The Battle of Los Angeles is an example of how intense and widespread fear can trigger an extreme reaction to a perceived threat that doesn't exist. The Imperial Japanese Navy never sent more than a few submarines to the California coast. At no point during the war were the residents of California in danger of attack or invasion from the Japanese Pacific fleet. Nevertheless, because war nerves were so inflamed in early 1942, Lieutenant General John L. DeWitt, Commander of the Western Defense Command, argued for the mass removal of approximately 120,000 Japanese Americans—two-thirds of whom were US citizens—from their homes in California, and transferring them to internment camps. DeWitt claimed they were potential saboteurs and spies, and that it was impossible to determine if they were loyal to the United States. California's Attorney General, Earl Warren, agreed, as did Governor Culbert Olson and the renowned Hearst newspaper columnist Walter Lippmann.

On February 19, 1942, President Franklin D. Roosevelt signed Executive Order 9066, authorizing the forced removal and incarceration of Japanese Americans from the West Coast without charges or trial, and no presentation of evidence of disloyalty.[2] This caused them enormous distress and the loss of their homes and businesses, many through forced sales at fire-sale prices. Other properties were looted, defaced, or seized for unpaid taxes. Standing up to this outrage, a twenty-three-year-old Japanese American man named Fred Korematsu refused to leave the newly declared "exclusion zone" and challenged the order on the grounds that it violated the Fifth Amendment. His case eventually went to the Supreme Court.

In *Korematsu v. United States* in 1944, the Court upheld Executive Order 9066, stating it wasn't based on racial prejudice but military necessity to neutralize "the grave imminent danger" posed by Japanese Americans residing on the Pacific coast, where they could allegedly serve as spies or saboteurs for Imperial Japan and assist an invasion fleet. Associate Justice Hugo Black wrote the majority opinion. In a remarkable concurring opinion, Justice Felix Frankfurter—renowned for his fine grasp of jurisprudence—stated that the US government's pressing need to wage war effectively superseded Constitutional protections for individual citizens such as Fred Korematsu.[3] Frankfurter's sentiment in this case reminds one of James Madison's warning about the grave threat that war poses to liberty.

> Of all the evils to public liberty, war is perhaps the most to be dreaded, because it comprises and develops every other. War is the patent of armies; from these proceed debts and taxes. And armies, and debts, and taxes, are the known instruments for bringing the many under the dominion of the few. In war, too, the discretionary power of the executive is extended; its influence in dealing out offices, honors, and emoluments is multiplied; and all the means of seducing the minds are added to those of subduing the force of the people! No nation could preserve its freedom in the midst of continual warfare.[4]

Here it is important to note that not all nine Justices upheld Order 9066. Three vehemently dissented, and as Justice Frank Murphy wrote in his dissenting opinion.

> [Racial discrimination] is unattractive in any setting, but it is utterly revolting among a free people who have embraced the principles set forth in the Constitution of the United States. All residents of this nation are kin in some way by blood or culture to a foreign land. Yet they are primarily and necessarily a part of the new and distinct civilization of the United States. They must, accordingly, be treated at all times as the heirs of the American experiment, and as entitled to all the rights and freedoms guaranteed by the Constitution.[5]

Looking back at *Korematsu v. United States*, many legal scholars have found it unfathomable that six justices found Order 9066 to be constitutional. The case seems to be an example of how even the most intellectually agile men, capable of the highest level of reasoning, may still fall into something like a trance when they are under the influence of war nerves.

In 1943—one year before the Supreme Court heard the case of *Korematsu v. United States*—the Lutheran pastor, Dietrich Bonhoeffer, was arrested and incarcerated in Tegel Prison for his participation in a plot to assassinate Hitler. There, he pondered the question of why the German people—despite their education, culture, and intellectual achievements—had fallen so far from reason and morality. He concluded that they had been afflicted with collective stupidity (German: *Dummheit*). He was not being flippant or sarcastic, and he made it clear that stupidity is not the opposite of native intellect. On the contrary, the events in Germany between 1933 and 1943 had shown him that perfectly intelligent people were, under the pressure of fear and propaganda, rendered stupid—that is, incapable of critical reasoning. As he put it:

> There are people who are intellectually agile who are stupid, while intellectually inept people may be anything but stupid. We discover this to our surprise in certain situations. One gets the impression that stupidity is often not an innate defect, but one that emerges under certain circumstances in which people are made stupid. . . . A closer look reveals that the strong exertion of external power, be it political or religious, strikes a large part of the people with stupidity. Yes, it seems as if this is a sociological-psychological law. The power of some requires the stupidity of others. Under this influence,

> human abilities suddenly wither or fail, robbing people of their inner independence, which they—more or less unconsciously—renounce to adapt their behavior to the prevailing situation.
>
> The fact that stupid people are often stubborn should not hide the fact that they are not independent. When talking to him, one feels that one is not dealing with him personally, but with catch-phrases and slogans that have taken possession of him. He is under a spell; he is blinded; he is abused in his own being. Having become an instrument without an independent will, the fool will also be capable of all evil, and at the same time, unable to recognize it as evil. Here lies the danger of diabolical abuse. Through this, a people can be ruined forever.
>
> But it is also quite clear here that it is not an act of instruction, but only an act of liberation that can overcome stupidity. In doing so, one will have to accept the fact that, in most cases, real inner liberation is only possible after outer liberation has taken place. . . . The Bible states that the fear of God is the beginning of wisdom. Thus, the inner liberation of man begins by living responsibly before God.[6]

How can one explain the decision of six Supreme Court justices to uphold the US government's right to force American citizens (of Japanese ancestry) into internment camps, or Dietrich Bonhoeffer's observation that so many of his countrymen had been seized by stupidity? The obvious answer is that their feelings and thoughts had been hideously deformed by war, the father of all mind viruses.

For about 95–99 percent of our species' history (from the emergence of Homo sapiens about 300,000 years ago until the development of large-scale agriculture about 10,000 years ago), humans likely lived in small hunter-gatherer bands of 20–150 people. Survival depended on close, tribal cooperation for hunting and defense from competing tribes. Natural selection favored psychological traits that promoted "coalitional" psychology—that is, fierce loyalty to "us" and hostility toward "them," adherence to group norms, and allegiance to shared symbols, ideas, and gods.[7] These are not quirks of culture. Evidence that we have inherited these characteristics from our pre-historic ancestors is expressed in brain imaging that reveals strong amygdala activation when one is shown the faces of people who are identified as members of the "out-group."[8] Psychologists have performed countless experiments that show our strong favoritism for what we perceive as our "in-group" and derogation of people we perceive as belonging to an "out group."[9]

Within our own tribe (now modern nation) we maintain the ancient practice of glorifying great warriors. For tens of thousands of years, apex male warriors played a decisive role not only in defending the tribe, but augmenting its status, wealth, territory, and access to women. Indeed, the so-called Rape of the Sabine Women is a foundational myth of ancient Rome that tells of first-generation Roman men, under Romulus, abducting young women from neighboring Sabine families to take as wives. In this context, the word "rape" derives from the Latin *raptio*, meaning mass kidnapping or abduction. The myth has been depicted in multiple Old Master paintings.

Recent genetic studies have shown that Icelandic women are largely descended from Gaelic (Irish/Scottish) ancestors on their maternal side, and Norse Vikings on their paternal side.[10] This suggests that the island nation was settled by a band of Viking men who abducted the women from Ireland. This anecdote seems to support the theory that a given tribe may eventually have to contend with the problem of apex warrior males taking all the attractive females for themselves, thereby obliging other males in the tribe to go out and abduct women from other tribes.

Since World War I, government propaganda agencies have figured out how to manipulate these atavistic instincts. Propagandists portray the enemy as subhuman, barbaric, or existential threats. This activates our tribal circuitry to suppress our inhibitions about killing people. Propaganda is a "tribal call to arms," accentuating the "us vs. them" drama to promote tribal cohesion and prepare the tribe to destroy the enemy. Militarism binds us together through shared symbols (flags, anthems, and slogans), and produces excitement and elation with imagery and reports of destroying the enemy. The same process expunges empathy for innocent civilians who are destroyed as "collateral damage." In other words, war propaganda works like magic because it hijacks survival circuitry that evolved when the destruction of one's tribe meant certain death for everyone in it.

The Nazi propagandist, Joseph Goebbels understood that endlessly repeating a claim ultimately results in it being widely perceived as the entire truth of the matter, even if there is little evidence to support it. A statement heard frequently feels familiar and normal, thereby creating a strong cognitive bias to believe it. Psychologists call this the illusory truth effect. Wartime environments amplify this through relentless messaging via television and social media. Emotional appeals bypass the need for proof. Propaganda targets primal fears, hatred, pride, and the desire for security and belonging. The enemy is dehumanized by portraying its soldiers and civilians as depraved monsters. Outrage is stoked with stories of the enemy's alleged atrocities, often with fragmentary, fabricated, or exaggerated evidence. This triggers feelings of horror and repugnance.

Propaganda systematically conceals the factual record of how one's own tribe has contributed to the conflict. For example, in America's current war with Iran, we constantly hear about the atrocities of the Iranian regime and its proxies, but nothing about how the CIA overthrew the Iranian government in 1953 and replaced it with a military dictator elevated to nobility who enforced his will with secret police who frequently used torture. We also hear nothing about how the US government armed the Iraqi dictator Saddam Hussein with every nasty weapon under the sun, including chemical and biological weapons such as anthrax and bubonic plague, and encouraged him to attack Iran for eight years between 1980 and 1989.

Within a tribe that feels threatened, dissenters face social ostracism and other severe penalties, including death. It's likely that Socrates would not have been put to death for his heterodox ideas if the ruling class of Athens had not felt highly stressed by setbacks in their war against Sparta. Likewise, it's unlikely that Pontius Pilate would have agreed to put Jesus to death if he hadn't been under great pressure from Rome to prevent insurrections in Judea. The threatening atmosphere of war (or civil war) motivates people to take actions that they wouldn't consider taking during times of peace. Fear and anger short-circuit critical thinking, causing people to demand action with little or no concern for verification. This is the mental state that Lord Salisbury, British Prime Minister from 1885–1902 complained about when he remarked that governing during an outbreak of bellicose, jingoistic sentiment was "like having a huge lunatic asylum on one's back."

Most people express their allegiance to the propagandist's narrative because everyone around them appears to accept it. As we saw during the COVID-19 pandemic, members of a tribe that felt threatened were relentlessly called upon to demonstrate their tribal cohesion by adhering to mask mandates and lining up to receive the experimental gene therapy shots. Members of a frightened tribe must also contend with limited information (imposed by censors) about what is happening and search for an explanation. Simple narratives—stripped of all complexity and nuance—placate the anxiety of uncertainty. Dramatic accusations of the enemy's depravity, and celebration of one's own moral righteousness offer clarity and purpose. When barraged with propaganda, few people feel any motivation to verify it, which requires time, effort, and a great deal of education and research skill. It's far easier to accept the unifying narrative.

Man's atavistic, tribal, warlike nature would not pose an existential threat to humanity if it weren't for the fact that our weapons have become so immensely destructive. This was the theme of Stanley Kubrick's film, *Dr. Strangelove*, which he was inspired to produce from his study of the Cuban Missile Crisis in which humanity came to the brink of annihilation.

CHAPTER 4

RESPONSIBILITY VERSUS ACQUIESCENCE

From their study of history, the US Founding Fathers believed that—human nature being what it is—rulers would inevitably seek, by whatever means possible, to expand their power at the expense of public liberty. It was imperative for a people to understand this, to keep a watchful eye on their rulers, and to be acutely aware of the various pretexts through which rulers will attempt to augment their power and curtail the rights of the people. The most common pretext is invoking emergency power to counter a danger to public safety. The danger may be real—that is, "clear and present," as Supreme Court Justice Oliver Wendell Holmes put it in a 1919 opinion—or it may be exaggerated, fabricated, or arise as the result of the rulers' reckless and incompetent actions.

To develop an awareness and the ability to recognize the deceptions of the powerful, a people must constantly strive to acquire knowledge and stay informed about what their government is doing. The Founding Fathers believed that only an educated citizenry could remain free and ensure the republic's survival. Conversely, an ignorant populace could be easily manipulated. As Madison put it:

> A popular Government, without popular information, or the means of acquiring it, is but a Prologue to a Farce or a Tragedy; or, perhaps both. Knowledge will forever govern ignorance: And a

> people who mean to be their own Governors, must arm themselves with the power which knowledge gives.[1]

As Thomas Jefferson put it:

> If a nation expects to be ignorant and free, in a state of civilization, it expects what never was and never will be.[2]

The Founding Fathers further believed that only a reasonable and moral people could maintain true representative government. It was therefore imperative for most adult citizens to possess the cardinal virtues of prudence, justice, fortitude, and temperance. As John Adams put it:

> Because We have no Government armed with Power capable of contending with human Passions unbridled by morality and Religion. Avarice, Ambition, Revenge or Gallantry, would break the strongest Cords of our Constitution as a Whale goes through a Net. Our Constitution was made only for a moral and religious people. It is wholly inadequate to the government of any other.[3]

In other words, a free people must assume responsibility for maintaining the integrity of their constitutional republic instead of blindly trusting their rulers to do so. Keeping tyranny at bay requires that all citizens pay attention to what their rulers are doing and have the courage to speak up if the rulers become abusive or adopt destructive policies that imperil the freedom and constitutional protections of the people.

Aleksandr Solzhenitsyn was born in 1918 into a family that embraced the Russian Orthodox Faith and rejected Bolshevik ideology. However, as a young man, he became an atheist and ardent believer in Marxist-Leninist doctrine. In February 1945, while serving as a captain in the Red Army, he was charged with "anti-Soviet propaganda" after his private letter criticizing Joseph Stalin was opened and read by censors. He was then convicted under Article 58 of the Soviet criminal code and sentenced to eight years in labor camps. The Bolsheviks claimed they would liberate Russian society from Tsarist tyranny, but, as the reader will recall, Dostoevsky only got a six-year prison camp sentence for distributing a letter criticizing the Tsar. Solzhenitsyn got eight years for criticizing Stalin in a private letter.

In the gulag, while enduring terrible brutality and degradation, he experienced a spiritual awakening. As he saw it, he and his fellow Russians bore responsibility for allowing the tyranny of the Soviet regime to come into existence. As he famously put it in *The Gulag Archipelago*, "the line dividing good and evil cuts through the heart of every human being." In other words, the monstrous regime of Joseph Stalin had been enabled and tolerated by millions who abdicated their responsibility to oppose it. By acquiescing to the tyranny, they became complicit in it. From his harrowing experience in the gulag, Solzhenitsyn came to believe in the same truth that John Adams expressed in his 1798 letter—namely, that only a people possessing moral and intellectual virtue can remain free. When millions of individuals abdicate their responsibility to cultivate these virtues and to oppose tyranny in its nascent phase, they become complicit with their own enslavement and destruction.

James Madison understood that one of the greatest challenges confronting a free people is learning to recognize when their minds are being seduced and manipulated by the ruling class. Historically, the ruling class has frequently used war as a pretext for distracting the people from domestic problems and diverting their attention to the purported threat of attack by foreign tribes or pirates or domestic gangs or terrorists. As he put it, "Among the Romans it was a standing maxim to excite a war, whenever a revolt [in the homeland] was apprehended."[4]

In Madison's day, pamphlets and newspapers were the primary media for shaping public sentiment. In the 1840s, many American newspapers supported the Mexican–American War in an aggressive, jingoistic fashion, claiming it was an expression of America's "Manifest Destiny." A notable critic of the war—and the propaganda published to justify it—was Henry David Thoreau, who correctly believed that the US government declared war on Mexico due to the influence of a relatively small group of powerful southern men who used the government and military as their instrument to gain new territory for slave states. In his 1849 essay, "Civil Disobedience," Thoreau argued that when people acquiesce to immoral government actions, they become complicit.

In the 1880s, William Randolph Hearst and Joseph Pulitzer used their newspapers to generate popular sentiment in favor of the Spanish-American War in 1898, proclaiming that the USS Maine armored cruiser sank in Havana Harbor after it struck a Spanish mine. Their newspaper reporting omitted to mention the suspicion expressed by some US Navy officers that the explosion was more likely caused by a spontaneous fire in the ship's coal bunker.[5]

During World War I, the US government—specifically its Committee on Public Information—tapped the burgeoning field of psychology to develop more sophisticated methods of manipulating the public mind. A key figure on the Committee was the Austro-American Edward Bernays, often called the father of public relations. The nephew of Sigmund Freud, he made a careful study of how masses of people can be influenced by the power of suggestion and association. After the war he worked as an advertising executive. His most famous PR campaign was for the American Tobacco Company to promote cigarette smoking among women, for whom smoking had historically been stigmatized. Bernays's first move was to promote smoking as a substitute for eating to appeal to women's desire to be thin. Newspaper and magazine ads displayed photos of beautiful slender ladies smoking cigarettes, along with messages from medical authorities about the benefit of smoking instead of eating sweets.

Far more ambitious was Bernays's 1929 "Torches of Freedom" PR campaign for which he hired scores of women to march in that year's New York City Easter Parade while conspicuously smoking cigarettes. He hired photographers to capture high-quality images of these subjects, which he published all over the world. The imagery of women proudly smoking at a major public event—defying the traditional taboo—proved to be highly effective. Rates of female smoking immediately and sharply increased.

As Bernays understood, the most effective propaganda creates desirable associations for what is being promoted, and negative associations with those who oppose it. The association of smoking with women's liberation was positive. Those who opposed it, such as the Anti-Cigarette League of America, were negatively characterized as wanting to keep women oppressed and cloistered at home. As Bernays proved with his PR campaigns and proclaimed in his 1929 book *Propaganda*, the art of propaganda is highly effective at shaping public perceptions. Even when people are vaguely aware of its role in public affairs, this awareness doesn't diminish propaganda's potency. As he famously noted in his book:

> The conscious and intelligent manipulation of the organized habits and opinions of the masses is an important element in democratic society. Those who manipulate this unseen mechanism of society constitute an invisible government which is the true ruling power of our country.[6]

In the late 1920s, Joseph Goebbels studied Bernays's writings and endeavored to put them to use as minister of propaganda for the Third Reich. In 1933, Bernays was shocked to learn this from a foreign correspondent for Hearst newspapers. As he later recounted in his autobiography:

> They were using my books as the basis for a destructive campaign against the Jews of Germany. This shocked me, but I knew any human activity can be used for social purposes or misused for antisocial ones.[7]

In a 1932 article in the *American Mercury*, Columbia University professor of journalism, Henry Pringle, wrote that "Eddie is a stern realist who operates on the demonstrable theory that men in a democracy are sheep waiting to be led to slaughter." During World War II, Bernays sought a position in the Roosevelt administration. Upon learning of this, Supreme Court Justice Felix Frankfurter advised the president that Bernays and his fellow propagandist Ivy Lee are "professional poisoners of the public mind, exploiters of foolishness, fanaticism and self-interest."[8]

During the late 1920s, as Joseph Stalin was consolidating his power in Russia and his regime was establishing the network of prison camps that Aleksandr Solzhenitsyn later called the "Gulag Archipelago" (the title of his 1973 book), the *New York Times* published favorable and highly sanitized reports about Stalin's regime. The newspaper's pro-Stalin slant was partly for ideological reasons, but also in support of US financial and industrial interests who were keen to supply the Bolshevik's enormous ambition to industrialize Russia as quickly as possible. The Amtorg Trading Company, founded in 1924 and headquartered in New York, facilitated US investments in Russia under the new Bolshevik regime. During the 1920s and 30s, American industrial firms such as Arthur G. McKee & Co. and Albert Kahn Inc. designed hundreds of Soviet factories. During World War II, American firms designed massive Soviet factories and American engineers helped to build them, while the Lend-Lease program provided military trucks, aircraft, fueling, and railway equipment, ultimately amounting to around $11 billion in aid (roughly $290 billion in buying power today).[9]

In the United States, the dominant narrative of the new Bolshevik regime in Russia in the 1920s and 30s was that propagated by Walter Duranty, who became the *New York Times* Moscow bureau chief in 1922. Duranty became a key propagandist for Stalin, and for his mendacious reporting he won the Pulitzer Prize in 1932.[10] The Pulitzer Board cited his "dispassionate interpretive reporting" on Russia, especially for his 1931 articles on the USSR's Five-Year Plan. The Board further praised Duranty for his "profound and intimate comprehension of conditions in Russia."

Duranty was instrumental in shaping American sentiment in favor of formally recognizing the Soviet Union in 1933. He was a guest of honor at a lavish dinner at the Waldorf-Astoria Hotel in New York City on November 24, 1933, to celebrate the establishment of diplomatic relations. The gala happened about six months after Duranty whitewashed one of the worst crimes in European history, committed by Stalin's regime in the winter of 1932–33. The Holodomor (Ukrainian "famine extermination") was caused by Stalin's forced collectivization of agriculture, confiscating the farms of prosperous landowning peasants, as well as his insistence on the delivery of unattainable grain quotas from the especially fertile farmland of Ukraine. An estimated 5 million died of starvation.[11]

In his reporting for the *New York Times*, Walter Duranty did not mention the Holodomor apart from denying the veracity of reports by Malcolm Muggeridge, the only western journalist who covered the atrocity. Malcolm Muggeridge lived in Moscow in 1933, working for the *Manchester Guardian*. Though attracted to communism in his youth, his experience of being in Stalin's Russia and observing what was going on in the country caused him to become disillusioned. He was especially disturbed by his realization that Stalin's army and police were—as part of their collectivization program—starving millions of people.

When Muggeridge's reports were published in 1933, many of his fellow writers—including George Bernard Shaw, Aldous Huxley, Jean-Paul Sartre, Upton Sinclair, Theodore Dreiser, and Sidney and Beatrice Webb—refused to believe them and passionately asserted that he was spreading falsehoods about Stalin's regime. On March 2, 1933, Shaw and twenty other writers and intellectuals published an open letter in *Manchester Guardian* that dismissed Muggeridge's reports of famine as malicious lie. In the final analysis, Duranty and his fellow propagandists prevailed in presenting Stalin as a great leader, worthy of full US support. The legacy of his *New York Times* reporting in the twenties and thirties is still evident today in the simple fact that most Americans have never heard of the Holodomor or Malcolm Muggeridge.

With the advent of radio in the 1920s, television in the 1950s, twenty-four-hour cable network news in the 1980s, and the internet in the 1990s, mass media for shaping and manipulating public sentiment became ever more powerful. During the 1950s, the CIA initiated Operation Mockingbird in which it recruited hundreds of journalists to write propaganda.[12] The operation purportedly ended in the 1970s following Church Committee investigations. Even if this is true, many journalists covering government affairs must still contend with losing access to information if they do not report the narratives fed to them by official sources. During World War I, US government offices formed deep ties with the Hollywood motion picture industry to produce pro-war propaganda, and both the Department of Defense and the CIA have maintained this relationship ever since.

Amplifying this trend was the consolidation of print and broadcast media companies into a few corporate behemoths whose chief officers and board members developed ever closer ties with the US government. An especially dubious undertaking was the British Broadcasting Corporation's "Trusted News Initiative" whose very name is suggestive of its Orwellian "Newspeak" character. Though the internet was initially developed by the Department of Defense, the first generation of internet search engine and media companies and social media companies proclaimed that the internet would effectively democratize information, creating a far richer "marketplace of ideas" than what existed in the United States when information was disseminated by traditional print and broadcast media companies.

With the internet becoming ever more developed, and humanity spending ever more of its waking hours online, the vast propaganda potential of the internet became frighteningly clear. Internet search engines and social media sites track the online behavior of users. This created an entirely new relationship between the media consumer and provider, because now the provider can "watch" the consumer, who is constantly signaling to the provider what resonates with him and appeals to his sensibilities. Instead of populating his social media feed with content that challenges his worldview and his biases, social media sites show him content that confirms his worldview and reinforce his biases. The result is that this vast, online marketplace of ideas has become ever more divided into opposing political and ideological camps of people who look across the abyss at each other with mutual incomprehension and hostility.

During the COVID-19 pandemic, the US Executive Branch established direct communication with internet and social media executives at Google, Twitter, and Facebook and applied considerable pressure on them to censor internet content that the federal government deemed inimical to its pandemic policies.[13] In other words, instead of directly abridging the First Amendment, the Executive effectively outsourced this task to social media companies, as was revealed in the discovery process of *Missouri v. Biden.*[14] As the reader will see in the chapter on the COVID-19 mind virus, the federal government's pandemic response was the closest it came to naked tyranny since President Roosevelt's Executive Order 9066.

CHAPTER 5

THE SCIENTIFIC-TECHNOLOGICAL ELITE

In his 1961 Farewell Address, President Eisenhower warned the American people not only about the "military-industrial complex," but also about what he called a "scientific-technological elite." As he put it:

> Akin to, and largely responsible for the sweeping changes in our industrial-military posture, has been the technological revolution during recent decades. In this revolution, research has become central; it also becomes more formalized, complex, and costly. A steadily increasing share is conducted for, by, or at the direction of, the Federal government. Today, the solitary inventor, tinkering in his shop, has been overshadowed by task forces of scientists in laboratories and testing fields. In the same fashion, the free university, historically the fountainhead of free ideas and scientific discovery, has experienced a revolution in the conduct of research. Partly because of the huge costs involved, a government contract becomes virtually a substitute for intellectual curiosity. For every old blackboard there are now hundreds of new electronic computers. The prospect of domination of the nation's scholars by Federal employment, project allocations, and the power of money is ever present and is gravely to be regarded. Yet, in holding scientific research and discovery in respect, as we should, we must also be alert to the equal and opposite danger

> that public policy could itself become the captive of a scientific-technological elite.[1]

In a nutshell, what troubled Eisenhower was the way in which most of the nation's top scientists had started working in a close-knit, organized fashioned with the military-industrial complex. Prior to World War I, most scientific research was conducted primarily by exceptionally curious and talented individuals who shared their discoveries in papers and learned societies. With enormous expansion of the central state and the advent of total warfare in the twentieth century, scientists—even those who held academic university positions—became ever more co-opted by state and industrial interests. Because they were being integrated into the state and augmenting its power, they were amassing a disproportionate amount of influence over public policy, with elected representatives increasingly deferring to them for their purported expertise. Thus, in matters of critical importance, eminent scientists could invoke their special authority to make policy decisions that profoundly affected the lives of millions.

The scientific-technological elite that President Eisenhower warned about became fully fledged during World War II, but it was incubated and hatched during World War I. In their war planning and prosecution, the belligerent powers sought advice from an array of technical experts about financing, railroad capacity, munitions production, new weapons development, trench construction, medicine and pharmaceuticals, and agriculture. In Germany, a tragic member of the scientific-technological elite was the great chemist, Fritz Haber.

In 1909, Haber—founding director of the Kaiser Wilhelm Institute for Physical Chemistry and Electrochemistry in Berlin-Dahlem—developed the Haber–Bosch process of synthesizing ammonia from nitrogen gas and hydrogen gas, which enabled the industrial-scale synthesis of fertilizers and explosives. About one-third of annual global food production uses ammonia from the Haber–Bosch process, supporting nearly half of the world's population. For this achievement, he richly deserved the 1918 Nobel Prize for Chemistry.

However, during World War I, he became known as "the father of chemical warfare." A fierce German nationalist, he applied his genius to developing and weaponizing chlorine and other poisonous gases for the German military during World War I. His work directly resulted in the widespread practice of chlorine gas attacks. His wife, Clara Immerwahr, was so horrified by reports of the Second Battle of Ypres, where chlorine gas resulted in thousands of casualties, that it may have contributed to her decision to commit suicide with her husband's service revolver.[2] How could her husband, a distinguished German professor, possibly justify burning out the eyes and lungs of young men? What, she wondered, had possessed him?

Professor Haber always defended his work on chlorine gas weapons. It's an infernal irony of history that he was one of the founders of Degesch (Deutsche Gesellschaft für Schädlingsbekämpfung mbH) which developed Zyklon B under the direction of his personal assistant, Bruno Tesch, who became the director of Degesch in 1920. Zyklon B, a hydrogen cyanide pesticide, was later used for the mass murder of Jewish concentration camp inmates during the Nazi era. Haber was born into a prominent Jewish family in the Prussian city of Breslau. He had no way of foreseeing the terrible future application of the compound he was instrumental in developing, but therein lies the great risk of developing dangerous chemicals that can be used by powerful state actors to kill millions of purported enemies. World War I conferred great power and prestige on scientific experts, but the net result was mass death, maiming, and destruction.[3]

During World War II, the scientific-technological elite was tasked with developing ever more destructive weapons for killing not only soldiers on the battlefield, but also civilians in cities. Advances in aircraft design, radio (FM and LORAN), radar and microwave, computing and cryptology, jet and rocket engines were made during the war to increase the ability to bomb people. In 1942, Louis F. Fieser, a Harvard organic chemistry professor, led his team to develop a chemical compound made of aluminum soap, naphthenate, and palmitate ("napalm") to thicken gasoline for incendiary bombs. On March 10, 1945, a US squadron of 279 Boeing B-29 Superfortress bombers dropped 1,665 tons of incendiary cluster bombs composed largely of napalm on Tokyo, intentionally causing a firestorm that killed approximately 100,000 civilians in a single night.[4]

Perhaps the most famous (or infamous) collaboration of the scientific-technical elite in history was the Manhattan Project to build the first atomic bomb, which officially ran from August 1942 to December 1946. The key experts who worked on the project were director Robert Oppenheimer, military director General Leslie Groves, plus the scientists Hans Bethe, Enrico Fermi, Richard Feynman, John von Neumann, Glenn Seaborg, and Leo Szilard. Their great and ingenious labor culminated with the detonation of the world's first nuclear device, code-named Trinity, on July 16, 1945, in the New Mexico desert. This successful test led directly to the bombings of Hiroshima and Nagasaki in August 1945, which killed over two hundred thousand civilians.

One of the strangest historical developments to emerge from the Manhattan Project was John von Neumann's proposal—while serving as a consultant for the RAND corporation in the early 1950s—to launch a preemptive nuclear strike against the Soviet Union. Von Neumann's thinking emerged from his work on game theory, particularly zero-sum games in which one player's gain is another's loss. As he saw it in the early fifties, the United States should exploit its nuclear advantage before the Soviets became nuclear peers. He believed that once the Soviets acquired comparable nuclear capabilities, the likely result would be a catastrophic war in which both the Russian and American people would be destroyed instead of only the Russians. And so, to prevent the Americans from eventually being destroyed, von Neumann proposed getting on with nuking the Russians sooner rather than later. As he pithily put it, "If you say why not bomb them tomorrow, I say why not today?"[5]

Von Neumann's strategic advice to the RAND Corporation was not adopted as US policy. Many of his contemporaries found it disturbing how his scientific mind, pondering abstract game theory, could advocate incinerating millions of people on the grounds that doing so was the most rational choice. Von Neumann's rationale for preemptively destroying Russia also eerily resembled Hitler's rationale for launching Operation Barbarossa in 1941. As Hitler saw it, war between Germany and the Soviet Union was inevitable, so Germany might as well get on with it while it had an apparent military and industrial advantage.[6]

Hitler almost certainly would have succeeded if Stalin had not been able to build his war machine with the indispensable help of American industrial capital and engineering, and the US Lend-Lease program. Moreover, the Soviet atomic bomb program was accelerated when British citizen Klaus Fuchs and US citizens Julius and Ethel Rosenberg passed classified information about the US nuclear weapons program to the Soviets. In other words, after the US scientific-technological elite armed the monstrous tyrant Stalin, the most intelligent and prominent member of this elite in 1950 proposed preemptively destroying the Russian people who had been enslaved by the tyrant.

The film director Stanley Kubrick satirized the terrifying moral imbecility of the scientific-technological elite in his 1964 film *Dr. Strangelove*—perhaps the grandest depiction of human intelligence unmoored from common sense and empathy and unable to resist our most archaic impulses. Dr. Strangelove (original German surname Dr. Merkwürdigliebe) was apparently inspired by John von Neumann and Wernher von Braun, who had worked on Nazi Germany's V-2 rocket program and was brought to the United States, along with about 1,600 other German scientists and engineers as part of the CIA's Operation Paperclip.

While the scientific-technological elite made enormous advances in developing methods for killing people during World War Two, their development of knowledge and technology for helping people was less successful. A wondrous exception was the development of penicillin as a safe and effective pharmaceutical product that could be manufactured at a large scale. One of the greatest scientific achievements in history for the relief of suffering and death (in humans and in animals), it is a story worth telling in detail.

Alexander Fleming is credited with discovering penicillin in 1928, but it took an array of dedicated scientists, clinicians, and industrial manufacturers to turn Fleming's lab discovery into a safe and effective antibiotic agent that could be mass manufactured and administered. Fleming, a bacteriologist at St Mary's Hospital in London, observed that a mold on one of his culture plates seemed to kill *Staphylococcus* bacteria that came into contact with it. He characterized the substance produced by the mold (*Penicillium notatum*) as "penicillin," but he was unable to develop the substance into a medicine. As a result, penicillin's potential remained undeveloped until the late 1930s, when an Oxford research team, led by Howard Florey, Norman Heatley, and Ernst Boris Chain developed a method to isolate and concentrate it. They then conducted animal and early human trials that demonstrated its ability to treat severe infections with relatively low toxicity.

During the Second World War, a major push was made to develop a technique for manufacturing it on a large scale to treat wounded soldiers. British and American scientists collaborated with pharmaceutical companies to achieve this objective. Norman Heatley traveled to the United States to work with Andrew J. Moyer to improve production yields with more efficient fermentation techniques. Pfizer engineers Jasper Kane and John McKeen developed industrial fermentation methods—originally used in food and chemical industries—to mass manufacture penicillin. The first large shipments of pharmaceutical penicillin were sent to Europe in early 1944 to prepare for the D-Day invasion of Normandy. One year later, the antibiotic became widely available to the public. Quickly it showed great efficacy in treating diseases that had long caused enormous suffering and death, such as bacterial septicemia (blood poisoning), bacterial pneumonia, streptococcal meningitis, and syphilis.

The scientific-technological elite consists of men of exceptional intelligence who have made great advances in our understanding of nature and our ability to manipulate it. Many of these advances have been for the purpose of killing humans as efficiently as possible while others have been for preserving life. Intellectual prowess applied to the business of destroying and creating has resulted in many members of this elite suffering from hubris that compels them to intervene in complex systems of which they possess limited understanding. As the reader will see, this elite has played a decisive role in developing and transmitting mind viruses to the public.

CHAPTER 6

THE END OF THE COLD WAR AND ITS DISCONTENTS

With the fall of the Berlin Wall on November 9, 1989, it became clear that the Soviet Union was in the final stage of losing the Cold War and was in a state of retreat, perhaps all the way back to its 1918 borders established by the Treaty of Brest-Litovsk, signed by the Bolshevik government and the Central Powers in World War I. On July 1, 1991, the Warsaw Pact dissolved, and a few months later, on December 26, 1991, the Soviet Union officially dissolved. While the great majority of Americans rejoiced that the United States won the Cold War, the victory left the US military-industrial complex in a very difficult position. Without a titanic Soviet adversary left to menace the free world, how was the vast US national security state going to justify its ongoing existence?

Of immediate concern was how to justify the bloated defense budget, which was around $300 billion in the years 1990, 1991, and 1992. Inflation-adjusted, this came to around $750 billion in 2025 US dollars. Quickly the military-industrial-complex and its friends in the US foreign policy establishment concluded that one way to maintain their interests was to expand NATO, thereby creating new markets for its defense-related products and services. In the years 1993 and 1994, the Clinton administration decided to go forward with the policy. Following the 1994 NATO summit, the administration announced the Partnership for Peace (PfP) initiative, setting the stage for inviting Poland, Hungary, and the Czech Republic to join.

This action broke the solemn promise that US Secretary of State James Baker made to Mikhail Gorbachev on February 9, 1990, that if the Soviet leader would cooperate with the dissolution of the German Democratic Republic (a.k.a. East Germany) and German unification, NATO would not expand "one inch eastward."[1] As the reader will see in the chapter on the anti-Russia mind virus, this broken promise set in motion a long and predicted chain of events that culminated in the current US proxy war against Russia in Ukraine.

Right as the Cold War was ending, the Washington foreign policy establishment identified the Middle East as another key strategic area for maintaining a strong and aggressive US military presence. Operation Desert Storm in Iraq, between August 1990 to January 1991, gave the Department of Defense a temporary reprieve from having to worry about budget downsizing. Moreover, in August 1990, Secretary of Defense Dick Cheney persuaded Saudi Arabian King Fahd to allow US military personnel to be stationed in Saudi Arabia—an arrangement that held until September 2003, when American forces in Saudia Arabia were withdrawn to Qatar. Though few if any mainstream media pundits mentioned it, the presence of US military personnel in Saudi Arabia was Osama bin Laden's primary grievance against the United States.[2]

Though the United States left Saddam Hussein in power, it nevertheless, in coordination with the UN, imposed sweeping sanctions on Iraq, thereby crippling its economy, infrastructure, and basic civil services. By 1996, UNICEF and other humanitarian organizations published estimates that hundreds of thousands of Iraqi children died during this period due to malnutrition and preventable illnesses. This resulted in international criticism of US and UN policy. During a May 12, 1996, interview on CBS's *60 Minutes*, then-UN Ambassador Madeleine Albright was asked if the death of half a million Iraqi children because of US-led sanctions was a price worth paying, she replied, "I think this is a very hard choice, but the price—we think the price is worth it."[3]

Apparently recognizing the untenability of Iraqi sanctions, US foreign policy wonks such as Paul Wolfowitz, Raymond Tanter, Douglas Feith, and Richard Perle, argued that the United States should get rid of Saddam

Hussein altogether and apply military power to reshape the Middle East, transforming it from a fragmented places of tribal and religious conflict into an American-style liberal democracy. A study group led by Richard Perle memorialized this grand scheme in an essay titled, "A Clean Break: A New Strategy for Securing the Realm," which was published in June 1996 by the Institute for Advanced Strategic and Political Studies (IASPS), an Israeli-based think tank.[4] Perle et al. prepared their study for incoming Israeli Prime Minister Benjamin Netanyahu. As Raymond Tanter and Paul Wolfowitz were apparently fond of saying, "the road to Damascus leads through Baghdad"—meaning that getting rid of Saddam Hussein was the first step to getting rid of the Assad regime in Syria, thereby eliminating Israel's troubles with its two of its most bloody-minded rivals.

In November 1996, Osama bin Laden wrote a long essay that was published by the London-based Arabic newspaper, *Al-Quds al-Arabi*, in which he articulated specific grievances against the US government. His three primary grievances were the US military presence in Saudi Arabia, US support for Israel, and US actions against Iraq that had resulted in the deaths of half a million Iraqi children.[5] On February 23, 1998, Osama published a follow-up essay titled "Declaration of the World Islamic Front for Jihad against the Jews and the Crusaders" in the same newspaper. Though the US foreign policy establishment took little note of the essays, Bernard Lewis, a professor emeritus at Princeton University, reported the essay in the November 1, 1998, issue of *Foreign Affairs*. Professor Lewis wrote that he'd stumbled across Osama's essay in September 1998 and felt compelled to write about it because he found it a "very interesting text" that made a clear declaration of war against the United States.[6]

CHAPTER 7

ISLAMIC TERROR

Mind Virus: Fear and loathing of Muslim terrorists who were allegedly determined to keep striking US targets after the September 11, 2001, terrorist attacks because "they hate us for our freedoms."

Proposed Remedy: Vastly increasing the size and power of the US national security state and its federal funding and waging interminable wars abroad that achieve no constructive political objective or benefit for the American people.

In September 2001, I visited an old friend in Manhattan to attend New York Fashion Week. On the evening of September 10, I went to an event in SoHo, and around 1:30 a.m., I left the venue and caught a cab home. Just before I got into the taxi, my eyes were drawn upwards to the World Trade Center, looming above, and I thought the Twin Towers were conspicuously out of proportion with the rest of downtown. There was, I thought, something crazy about how huge and high they were.

That night I slept at my friend's apartment on Central Park West and was awakened by the phone ringing. It was my friend's sister, frantically saying a plane had flown into the World Trade Center. I looked out the window of the apartment building, south, down Central Park West, and saw a massive plume of smoke over downtown. After some fumbling with the television remote control, I managed to turn on the TV shortly before the second plane flew into the other tower. Thus began a traumatic and deeply disturbing period of American public affairs that struck me as a total rupture from what I had known my whole life until that moment.

How could this possibly be happening in the greatest city of the most powerful nation in history?

Even with my perceptions distorted by shock, I still thought it was strange how quickly federal law enforcement identified and seemed to know everything about the young men who were mostly from Saudi Arabia. Wasn't Saudi Arabia a close ally and trading partner of the United States? This marked the beginning of my belated journey (at the age of thirty-one) to realizing that the US government lies to its citizens all the time.

Shortly after the attacks, the Senate Select Committee on Intelligence and the US Permanent Select Committee on Intelligence, launched a *Joint Inquiry into Intelligence Community Activities Before and After the Terrorist Attacks of September 11, 2001*. In its capacity of representing "We the People," Congress wanted to know what US intelligence and federal law enforcement agencies knew about the hijackers before and after the attacks. Who exactly were these guys, who were they connected with, and who directed and supported them while they were in the United States?

In December 2002, members of Congress received a classified version of the Joint Inquiry's findings. On July 24, 2003, a redacted, unclassified version was publicly released. At first glance, this seemed an admirable example of our legislative branch doing its job for the American people. However, concerned citizens who read it—especially the relatives of those who died in the attacks—noticed that an entire section of the report titled "Finding, Discussion, and Narrative Regarding Certain Sensitive National Security Matters" had been redacted. Many citizens reckoned the whole point of the inquiry was to ascertain why our intelligence and law enforcement agencies had so catastrophically failed to protect our national security, so redacting an entire section because it pertained "to sensitive national security matters" seemed ridiculous. This raised the suspicion that Congress was protecting influential "friends" and "allies" from embarrassment.

Relatives of people who had died in the terrorist attacks filed a Freedom of Information Act (FOIA) request for the redacted pages. After a fourteen-year legal contest, Congress was finally ordered to publish the document, which it did on Friday, July 15, 2016. For years, the redacted section had been referenced as "the twenty-eight redacted pages," but the total number turned out to be twenty-nine. The key finding of the redacted section is as follows:

> While in the United States, some of these September 11 hijackers were in contact with, and received support or assistance from individuals who may be connected to the Saudi government. There is information, primarily from FBI sources, that at least two of those individuals were alleged by some to be Saudi intelligence officers. . . .
>
> Omar al-Bayoumi: The FBI has received numerous reports from individuals in the Muslim community dating back to 1999 alleging that al-Bayoumi may be a Saudi intelligence officer. FBI files suggest that al-Bayoumi provided substantial assistance to hijacker Khalid al-Mihdar, Nawaf al-Hazmi after they arrived in San Diego in February 2000.[1]

Another suspected Saudi intelligence officer was Osama Bassnan, who lived across the street from two of the hijackers when they resided in San Diego and was in close contact with many of their associates, including suspected Saudi intelligence agent, Omar al-Bayoumi. According to the report:

> Bassnan has many ties to the Saudi government, including past employment by the Saudi Arabian education mission. The FBI also received reports from individuals in the Muslim community alleging that Bessan might be a Saudi intelligence officer. According to a CIA memo, Bassnan has reportedly received funding, and possibly a fake passport, from Saudi government officials. He and his wife have received financial support from the Saudi ambassador to the United States and his wife.
>
> On at least one occasion, Bassnan received a check directly from Prince Bandar's account. According to the FBI, on May 14, 1998, Bassnan cashed the check from Bandar in the amount of $15,000. Bassnan's wife also received at least one check directly from Bandar. She also received one additional check from Bandar's wife which she cashed on January 8, 1998 for $10,000.[2]

While such statements might pique someone's curiosity to learn more about this connection between President George W. Bush's friend, Prince Bandar bin Sultan, and suspected Saudi intelligence agents providing support for hijackers in San Diego, Congress apparently wasn't interested. As the Committees stated in their report:

> It should be clear that this joint inquiry has made no final determinations as to the reliability or sufficiency of the information regarding these issues that we found contained in FBI and CIA documents.[3]

US mainstream media coverage of the release was minimal, and it downplayed the significance of what was contained in the document. A CNN report quoted Senators Richard Burr and Dianne Feinstein.

> Sens. Richard Burr and Dianne Feinstein, the chair and top Democrat of the Senate Intelligence Committee, issued a statement that they agreed with the decision to declassify the report. But they cautioned, "These pages include unconfirmed allegations and raw reporting and have been the subject of conspiracy theories for years."[4]

The FBI gave Congress what it asked for, but Congress didn't like what it saw, so it did not order a follow-up investigation into the activities of the Saudi state actors referenced in the report, including Bandar bin Sultan Al Saud. Instead, Congress redacted the twenty-nine pages from its report and moved on to what it considered more important business—that is, working with the Bush Administration to prepare for the invasion of Iraq the following spring.

What were the American people to make of the astonishing fact that nineteen young men—fifteen from Saudi Arabia, two from the United Arab Emirates, one from Egypt, and one from Lebanon—managed to hijack four commercial airliners, murder three thousand Americans, destroy the largest office towers in New York, and make a direct hit on the Pentagon? At least three of the hijackers—Khalid al-Mihdar, Nawaf al-Hazmi, and Salem al-Hazmi—were known to the CIA as al-Qaeda terrorists.[5] And what were we to make of the fact that many of the hijackers had invalid or expired visas at the time of the attacks? Five had overstayed their authorized periods of admission. All the hijacker pilots violated their tourist visas by immediately taking flight training; another never attended the school for which his student visa was issued.

On August 28, 2025, US District Judge George B. Daniels in Manhattan denied Saudi Arabia's motion to dismiss a long-running lawsuit, allowing 9/11 victims' families to proceed to trial for their complaint that the Kingdom aided the terrorists. Judge Daniels found that Saudi Arabia failed to prove that the lawsuit is not covered by the Justice Against Sponsors of Terrorism Act (JASTA).[6] Passed in 2016, it provides US nationals with a legal avenue to sue foreign states and entities for aiding, abetting, or conspiring to commit acts of international terrorism that injure Americans. Judge Daniels found that the body of undisputed facts is sufficient for the court to retain jurisdiction, and the plaintiffs may proceed to trial.

A couple of months after Judge Daniels's ruling, Tucker Carlson released a five-part documentary film titled *The 9/11 Files,* presenting witness testimony from CIA officers and analysts, FBI agents from the Bin Laden Unit, and family members of the victims. The totality of circumstances indicates that the Saudi General Intelligence Directorate aided and abetted Khalid al-Mihdar and Nawaf al-Hazmi, that the CIA knew about the operation, failed to alert the FBI to stop it, and then—after the attacks were carried out—concealed its knowledge.[7] Following the release of a major tranche of US Department of Justice (DOJ) "Epstein Files" on January 30, 2026, it was discovered that Jeffrey Epstein potentially acted as a go-between or representative for Saudi Arabia to block or stall 9/11-related lawsuits.[8]

Additional evidence suggests that Israeli Mossad had foreknowledge of the attacks. Especially suspicious were five Israeli nationals who worked for a moving company in New Jersey. Shortly after the planes flew into the Twin Towers, they were observed on the roof of a white moving van, parked in a lot near Liberty State Park in Jersey City, directly across the river from the burning buildings. According to the eyewitness, "They seemed to be taking a movie. They were like happy, you know . . . they didn't look shocked to me. I thought it was strange."[9]

The woman noted the license plate number and gave it to the local police, which stopped the van near Giants Stadium about four hours after the attacks. Searching the van, the officers found $4,700 in cash hidden in a sock, two foreign passports, and box cutters. While some US intelligence officials believed the moving company was a front for a surveillance operation, the FBI eventually concluded (for reasons it never elucidated) that the men had no foreknowledge of the 9/11 attacks. After being detained for seventy-one days, they were deported to Israel on immigration violations. Back in Israel, three of them—Oded Ellner, Omer Marmari, and Yaron Shmuel—went on the news program *LaHadashot* to discuss their adventures. Oded Ellner stated they were at the site to "document the event."[10]

At the very least, the terrorist attacks should have been regarded as a colossal failure of the Bush administration to protect the American homeland. The proper and lawful response to the crime—a response that respected the American people and the US Constitution—was to get to the bottom of how exactly the attacks had come about, who knew about the operational planning, and who failed to intervene to stop them. Instead of doing this—and at least firing the officials responsible for the massive intelligence failure—the Bush administration launched a vast and sweeping expansion of the US national security state. Instead of resolving to detain dubious foreign nationals on terrorist watch lists or in the country with expired visas, the administration declared a "War on Terror" and pushed the passage of the USA PATRIOT Act in October 2001, vastly expanding the government's surveillance, intelligence-gathering, and law-enforcement powers.

In 2002, the administration created the Department of Homeland Security. Though the hijackers had apparently waltzed right through airport security, the new airport security regimen imposed after 9/11 including frisking American octogenarians. In December 2001, Richard Reid—a British national with a long criminal record and history of traveling to Afghanistan, who'd already drawn scrutiny from airport security the day before—was allowed to get on an American Airlines flight from Paris to Miami in December 2001 and almost detonated his explosive-packed shoe. Following this incident, ordinary American citizens were obliged to take off their shoes to run them through airport X-ray machines for decades to come.

Prior to September 11, 2001, few Americans had even heard of Osama bin Laden. I happen to have been a subscriber to *Foreign Affairs* in 1998 and saw Bernard Lewis's piece on Osama's essays in the London Arabic newspaper. Even Lewis, a great authority on the Middle East, had known little about him prior to stumbling across his essays in a London Arabic newspaper. The Clinton administration had apparently devoted little attention to Al-Qaeda, despite the 1993 World Trade Center bombing, 1998 embassy bombings, and the USS Cole attack.

The August 6, 2001, Presidential Daily Brief (PDB) titled "Bin Ladin Determined to Strike in U.S." was delivered to President George W. Bush at his ranch in Crawford, Texas. The classified memo warned that al-Qaida wanted to perform attacks in the United States, including potential hijackings and explosives. Still, "We the People" heard nothing about this threat until the planes flew into the World Trade Center. Thenceforth, Osama bin Ladin and Al-Qaeda were all we heard about. After years of being a niche concern of intelligence agencies, now it seemed that Al-Qaeda was on the march everywhere, and the world was a veritable hive of terror cells that posed an existential threat to our civilization. Like Churchill taking on the Nazis, President Bush proclaimed on September 20 that "We will not tire, we will not falter, and we will not fail" to defeat this great menace that most of us had scarcely heard of two weeks earlier.

Instead of holding Saudi Arabia accountable for the actions of the fifteen Saudi hijackers and their Saudi supporters in the United States, the Bush administration launched massive wars against Afghanistan and Iraq, even though none of the hijackers were from either of these countries. These attacks were framed as expressions of the Bush Doctrine, which declared that the US would take preemptive military action against perceived threats. This vast expansion of the domestic and foreign security state was accompanied by equally vast increases of federal spending. Between fiscal years 2001 and 2003, security state funding increased by $145–$160 billion above previous inflation-adjusted projections. The new wars abroad were supported with emergency, supplemental funding of $748 billion to $803 billion for "Overseas Contingency Operations" (OCO). Discretionary funding for homeland security tripled. In 2018,

Brown University's Watson Institute concluded that the US government had spent an additional $5.9 trillion on post-911 wars.[11]

The same foreign policy wonks who advocated getting rid of Saddam Hussein in their 1996 paper, "A Clean Break: A New Strategy for Securing the Realm," happened to hold either official or advisory positions in the Bush administration, and they immediately set about lobbying for the Iraq invasion. As the reader will recall, the paper was written for then Israeli Prime Minister, Benjamin Netanyahu. The day after the September 11 attacks, Netanyahu was asked what the terrorist strikes meant for US-Israeli relations, to which he replied, "It's very good." He then corrected himself by saying, "Well, it's not good, but it will generate immediate sympathy for Israel from Americans."[12]

For about two years between early 2003 and 2005, Tom Ridge served as the first Secretary of Homeland Security, where he maintained the "Homeland Security Advisory System," introduced shortly after 9/11 attacks. The system used a color-coded scale—ranging from green (low risk) to red (severe risk)—to display the terror threat level. In frequent press conferences, he announced rising and falling levels, with his scale shifting to yellow (elevated) and orange (high) in accordance with intelligence reports about what the bad guys were scheming to do to us.

What was the point of these threat level advisories, apart from putting citizens into a stressful state of hypervigilance? What were we ordinary citizens supposed to do about it? A few months after September 11, after I'd returned to Vienna, Austria, where I was living at the time, I saw a notice that Al-Qaeda might try to hit American targets abroad. That night I went to my favorite cocktail bar in Vienna—the Loos American Bar—whose façade is adorned with a stained-glass mosaic of an American flag. While sipping a Manhattan at a table with friends, I noticed a man walk into the bar and place a briefcase under his stool. A few minutes later he walked out without his briefcase. I panicked and gesticulated to the head barkeeper, loudly saying what I'd just seen as though the briefcase might explode at any second.

"He's a friend of mine and he just stepped out to get cigarettes," the bartender shot back. "Why don't you try to relax. You're not in the States." The interior of the Loos Bar is very small, and everyone there witnessed this embarrassing exchange.

"I'm sorry," I said. "I was in New York on September 11, and I guess I'm still a bit nervous."

"Like I said, you're not there now."

With each passing year, my perception grew stronger that the entire War on Terror was a sham for expanding the power of the US government at home and abroad. The charade wasn't about protecting American citizens but controlling us and our money while enriching and aggrandizing the military-industrial complex, the intelligence agencies, and the US government's corrupt "allies" in the Middle East. The wars were a terrible waste, and by the time the Financial Crisis of 2008 struck, most Americans were sick of hearing about them. A study published in the *Lancet* medical journal in 2006 estimated that, during the first three years of the Iraq war, over 650,000 Iraqis were killed.[13] A 2021 study conducted by Brown University researchers estimated that about 200,000 Afghanis were killed during the twenty-year war. Ultimately, the campaigns in Afghanistan and Iraq killed about 7,000 and, according to official accounts, wounded about 50,000 US servicemen.[14]

A bizarre feature of early epidemiological studies of the Iraq and Afghanistan wars is that they enormously undercounted, underreported, or simply didn't document Traumatic Brain Injuries (TBIs). A decade after September 11, 2001, I became friends with a psychiatrist who worked at VA hospitals in Palo Alto and Menlo Park, California. On a few occasions I accompanied him when he visited his patients. By far the most common injury I saw was a Traumatic Brain Injury (TBI). These were typically caused by explosive blasts, especially from roadside bombs, and are considered a "signature injury" of post-9/11 conflicts.

The majority of TBIs are considered mild, but a "mild" diagnosis is cold comfort for those suffering from the syndrome and their family members. "Mild" symptoms include headaches, dizziness, nausea and vomiting, fatigue, sensitivity to light and noise, blurred or double vision, balance problems, confusion and difficulty concentrating, memory loss or problems with recall, difficulty with attention or problem-solving, and slowed thinking or processing speed, irritability or mood swings, anxiety or depression, difficulty sleeping, and changes in appetite. The young men I saw in VA hospitals were suffering from debilitating TBIs, and they would never again be self-sufficient. Many were married with small children. According to a recently published study, from 2000 to 2021, an estimated 449,026 active-duty US service members experienced a TBI.[15]

In December 2009, when the War on Terror seemed to be winding down, I transferred through Amsterdam on my way to the United States. At the Schiphol airport, I was subjected to a surprisingly aggressive interrogation about who I am and why I was traveling. I figured the Dutch had received intelligence that a bad guy was going to try to board a plane in Amsterdam to fly to the States. A couple of days later, I saw in the news that Umar Farouk Abdulmutallab had succeeded in boarding a plane in Amsterdam wearing "explosive underwear" for a flight to Detroit. On board, he detonated his explosive device, which caused a fire that was rapidly extinguished. Unlike me, Abdulmutallab had purchased a one-way ticket, had no checked baggage, and was the subject of several desperate attempts from his father (in Nigeria) to warn authorities of his son's intentions. Seeing this news, I thought of the extraordinary rigor of my own interaction with Dutch airport authorities compared to the laxity of their handling of Abdulmutallab. I wondered how it was possible that he was allowed to board the plane, and if the incident had been a form of theater to keep the War on Terror going.

In the final analysis, the only winners of the Iraq War were the foreign policy gurus who advocated getting rid of Saddam Hussein and Bashar al Assad. I was reminded of these Neocon policy wonks when I saw the news that Assad's regime had officially collapsed on December 8, 2024. The writing had been on the wall for a while. About a month earlier, Assad's de facto (later official) US-recognized replacement, Ahmed al-Sharaa, visited the White House for an audience with President Trump. The date, November 10, happened to be the official birthday of the US Marine Corps and National Forget-Me-Not Day (commemorating the sacrifices returning soldiers have made of body, blood, and limb).

Ahmed Al-Sharaa began his career with the Islamic State of Iraq (ISIL), joining the group in Iraq after the 2003 invasion. For those that don't remember ISIL: the group was formed in 2004 by Abu Musab al-Zarqawi, who pledged allegiance to Osama bin Laden, and was known as Al-Qaeda in Iraq (AQI). US Marine Corps veterans remember Abu Musab al-Zarqawi as a key leader in the insurgency that fought the Marines during the two battles of Fallujah in 2004, which included some of the hottest house to house fighting in US Marine Corps history. Indeed, the fighting got so fierce during the first battle in March 2004 that President Bush decided to pause it—ordering the Marines to pull back from the city and give up their initial gains—because it was creating political blowback in the US, and Bush was afraid it could hurt his reelection prospects. Two days after he was reelected in November, he sent the Marines back into the Fallujah meat grinder.

Al-Sharaa was detained by American troops in 2006 when he was caught in the act of planting an Improvised Explosive Device (IED) along a road near Mosul in northern Iraq and imprisoned for five years. Though no evidence linking him to previous IED attacks on US service personnel was detected, he was suspected of having fought with Al-Qaeda Iraq (AQI) for some time, so it's a logical inference that it wasn't the first time he planted a roadside bomb. Following his release from American custody in 2011, he moved to Syria. In 2012, he founded the Syrian group, Jabhat al-Nusra, and worked closely with ISIS and al-Qaeda in Syria until purportedly splitting from the former in 2013 and the latter in 2016. His activities in Syria coincided with the CIA's Timber Sycamore program to train and arm "moderate" Syrian rebels.[16]

Ahmed Al-Sharaa remained on the US Wanted List with a $10 million bounty on his head until November 7, 2025—three days before his White House visit.[17] The US government apparently perceived that he had experienced a "damascene moment," referring to Saul of Tarsus on the road to Damascus. During Al-Sharaa's White House visit, President Trump emphasized the idea of letting bygones be bygones.

"He's a very strong leader. He comes from a very tough place, and he's a tough guy. I liked him. I get along with him," Trump told reporters.

"We'll do everything we can to make Syria successful, because that's part of the Middle East. We have peace now in the Middle East."

Trump acknowledged that al-Sharaa has a "rough past," and then said, "We've all had rough pasts."[18]

Al-Sharaa's "damascene moment" apparently occurred when he played a decisive role in overthrowing Syrian President Bashar al-Assad. For over twenty years, the longstanding secular politician and former medical doctor who received his training in ophthalmology in London had consistently stated his opposition to Israel for its treatment of Palestinians and its occupation of the Golan Heights (forty miles southwest of Damascus) since 1967.

CHAPTER 8

BIOTERRORISM

Mind Virus: Extreme fear of infectious disease pathogens that could be used as weapons to attack the American people.
Proposed Remedy: Transfer of billions of public funds to biosecurity labs (working on dangerous pathogens), pandemic planning organizations, and manufacturers of infectious disease "countermeasures" such as vaccines. Pass legislation to grant liability immunity to all companies participating in the enterprise.

As was noted in the preface, the declaration that we must wage war against an enemy—real, perceived, exaggerated, or fabricated—is the essential psychological drama out of which all mind viruses emerge, while fear of the enemy is the primary emotional driver. For most of prehistory and history, tribes (and later nation states) were haunted by the specter of an invasion by armed men. In the United States in 2001, the military-industrial complex recognized the implausibility of armed soldiers attacking the American homeland. Flanked by oceans patrolled by a vast fleet of US Navy vessels equipped with enough firepower to destroy entire cities, the continental United States is virtually impregnable to foreign armies.

On September 18, 2001, the American people were presented with what appeared to be a new threat to the homeland—not invading soldiers that one can see and kill, but invisible pathogens that spread silently and insidiously, making everyone sick. On that day, letters containing anthrax spores arrived at news media offices and at the offices of senators Tom Daschle and Patrick Leahy. These attacks killed five people and infected seventeen others. The attacks resuscitated the military's anthrax vaccine program, which had been heavily restricted to a few select personnel on June 5, 2001.[1] A year later, on June 28, 2002, all military personnel were again required to receive the shot.

Though the anthrax attacks were staged to appear to be the work of either Iraqi agents or Islamic terrorists, the FBI suspected that the perpetrator was someone working within the American biodefense industry. Suspicion ultimately fell on Bruce Edwards Ivins, a scientist working at Fort Detrick's biodefense lab. As author Scott R. Decker described the suspect in the book *Recounting the Anthrax Attacks:*

> Ivins was a senior member of the US Army's Bacteriology Division at USAMRIID and had been instrumental in anthrax vaccine development and production. Until recently, the army had viewed his vaccine work as critical. In December 1997, Secretary of Defense William S. Cohen went so far as to mandate that all US soldiers, sailors, and airmen receive the inoculation. However, claims of the vaccine being connected to Gulf War Syndrome . . . made Cohen's directive controversial. . . . Also in year 2000, Ivins had coauthored a patent application for a new generation of vaccine developed through genetic engineering, which Ivins clearly hoped would replace the decades-old, controversial BioPort product.[2]

According to Decker, Ivins feared that his life's work was imperiled, and therefore decided to show the US government and media just how much the country needed his anthrax vaccine by attacking both establishments with anthrax spores. Even though the FBI quickly concluded the attacks were not the action of a hostile foreign agent, Ivins's gambit initially worked as he intended. In June 2002, the DoD reinstated the anthrax vaccine mandate for US service personnel and Congress passed the *Public Health Security and Bioterrorism Preparedness and Response Act* with additional funds allocated for vaccine development.[3]

However, due to ongoing safety concerns, the anthrax vaccine mandate for US soldiers was again challenged in court, and protracted litigation ensued that lasted until 2008, when a federal judge upheld an earlier ruling that it was "a violation of federal law for military personnel to be subjected to involuntary AVA inoculation because the vaccine was neither the subject of a presidential waiver nor licensed for use against inhalation anthrax."[4]

Ivins was a person of interest for six years, but the investigation of him intensified only *after* the DoD lost the legal battle in March 2008. On July 29, 2008, he purportedly committed suicide by overdosing on acetaminophen after he learned that he was probably going to be arrested. On August 6, 2008, federal prosecutors declared Ivins the sole perpetrator.[5] In other words, according to the FBI, the anthrax bioterrorism attack of 2001 that seemingly justified the DoD's controversial anthrax vaccine mandate for US service personnel was committed by a senior DoD scientist.

Some of his Ivins's colleagues and others in the field who knew him are not convinced he was the culprit. Suspicions have also arisen that the true culprit was someone who wanted to pin the attacks on Iraq to justify US military action to overthrow Saddam Hussein. The FBI never found evidence that Iraqi agents or Islamic terrorists mailed the anthrax contaminated letters. If it wasn't Bruce Ivins, it was likely someone else within the US or Israeli national security state. Reviewing the record of US biodefense blunders over the last twenty-five years, one may reasonably conclude that the biggest threat to the American people is *not* hostile foreign actors or emerging infectious diseases, but the US bio-pharmaceutical complex and its laboratories stocked with dangerous infectious agents and its obsession with creating experimental vaccines against them.

On March 19, 2003, the United State military launched its war against Iraq with the stated mission of disarming Saddam Hussein, whom the US government claimed to be in possession of illegal weapons of mass destruction, including anthrax. Rarely mentioned in the press was the fact that US firms, with CDC approval, that had shipped anthrax spores to the Iraqi government agencies in the 1980s for purportedly legitimate medical research. In fact, the shipments were part of the US policy of supporting Iraq during the Iran-Iraq War and were approved under "dual-use" export licenses by the Commerce Department.[6]

Critical observers noted that if there was ever a time for Hussein to use these purported weapons that he'd received from the United States twenty years earlier, it was against the invading US military. The salient fact that he didn't, and the equally salient fact that no weapons of mass destruction were found, did not diminish the US government's zeal for further expanding the power of the national security state, especially the bio-security apparatus in which the alleged anthrax serial killer Bruce Ivins had worked.

In 2004, Congress passed the *BioShield Act* "to accelerate the research, development, purchase, and availability of effective medical countermeasures against CBRN [chemical, biological, radiological, and nuclear] threats."[7] The following year, Congress passed the *Public Readiness and Emergency Preparedness* (PREP) Act, which granted liability protection for "countermeasures" such as new vaccines against biological threats. While Ted Kennedy from Massachusetts grumbled about the PREP Act being a gigantic liability protection giveaway to Big Pharma, not a single Senator voted against it (though seven abstained from voting).[8]

The American people were told that biodefense scientists could, with vast funding, counter the threat of bioterrorism. In the event of a public health emergency—declared by the Secretary of Health and Human Services—these scientists and their associates in the pharmaceutical industry would create countermeasures such as vaccines to protect every man, woman, and child in the country from the invisible menace. All that was required of the citizenry was to trust this high priesthood of biotechnicians, and to accept that they could not be held liable if their products injured or killed people.

Though anthrax had long been a staple of biological weapons development going back to Imperial Japan's notorious Unit 731 in Manchuria during World War II, the spores must be physically delivered and dispersed by military or intelligence agency personnel. US bioweapons researchers were further restricted from playing with anthrax in 1969, when President Richard Nixon declared that the United States would destroy its biological weapons and limit its research program to defensive measures such as vaccines.

This was the first time in history that a major power had unilaterally banned an entire armament category, and it paved the way for the 1972 Biological and Toxin Weapons Convention (BWC). However, the provision for maintaining a "defensive" biological research program created a loophole that later came to be known as *dual-use research of concern* (DURC)—that is, researching and even enhancing potential bioweapons for the declared purpose of creating vaccines against them.

Here it is important to understand that a highly transmissible respiratory virus can spread without military equipment and munitions. Because of this, biodefense researchers in the nations that signed the 1972 convention turned their attention to influenza and (about a decade later) to coronavirus as potential bioweapons. The objective was to find and possibly modify influenza and coronaviruses with pandemic potential that could severely disrupt and impair a foreign adversary's military personnel and civilian populations. The same researchers who discovered, isolated, and possibly modified respiratory viruses of pandemic potential could also participate in developing vaccines against them, which could have immense strategic and commercial value.

In early 1976, US Army and CDC personnel believed they discovered an influenza strain of pandemic potential in a respiratory tract sample taken from a deceased soldier at the Fort Dix army base in New Jersey. Pharmaceutical companies seized on this to persuade Congress to prepurchase millions of doses of a hastily developed influenza vaccine before a predicted outbreak in the fall of 1976.[9] Congress not only agreed to the bulk purchases, but also provided the pharmaceutical companies with guaranteed profits and full liability protection in the event the rapidly developed vaccine for the theoretical flu caused injuries or deaths. With the onset of flu season that fall, the predicted new strain of flu never emerged, though hundreds of people who received the vaccine—aggressively promoted by the Ford administration—were afflicted with Guillain-Barré syndrome. The pharmaceutical companies booked enormous profits, and the US federal government and taxpayers were left holding the bag for the enormous lawsuits that followed.[10] The "Swine Flu Fiasco," as it was called by the *New York Times* and *60-Minutes*, taught the nation about the hazards of listening to CDC "experts" and pharmaceutical companies.[11] However, by the time of the September 11, 2001, terrorist attacks, this lesson had been largely forgotten.

For the predicted Swine Flu of 1976, Congress granted pharmaceutical companies liability protection for *only* the vaccine they produced for the predicted pandemic flu strain that fall. This starkly contrasted with the PREP Act of 2005, which granted biodefense researchers and pharmaceutical companies blanket liability protection for all "medical countermeasures"—diagnostic tests, Personal Protective Equipment (PPE), anti-viral medical, and vaccines—anytime the Secretary of Health and Human Services declared a public health emergency. When the PREP Act was passed, everyone working in biodefense understood that, in the event of such a declaration, the US government would open the floodgates of money to purchase whatever countermeasures were on offer—a liability free bonanza of epic proportions.

Shortly after the PREP Act was passed, the biodefense industry stepped up its planning and preparation for the next pandemic. They reasoned that it was only a matter of time before another influenza pandemic as devastating as the Spanish Flu of 1918 emerged. The industry enjoyed a booming year of business in 2009 with the emergence of what was characterized as a novel swine flu with pandemic potential. After President Barack Obama's HHS Secretary Kathleen Sebelius declared a public health emergency, the US, UK, and EU governments also spent hundreds of millions stockpiling vaccines and anti-viral drugs that were never used because the so-called "pandemic flu strain" proved less virulent than that year's seasonal flu strain.[12]

The 2009 Swine Flu was profitable, but it was doubtful that the influenza industry could keep the gravy train rolling without the emergence of a truly virulent strain. And so, because nature hadn't yielded one since 1918, the virologists Yoshihiro Kawaoka and Ron Fouchier decided to create one. Far more terrifying than the swine flu virus of the phony 2009 pandemic is avian influenza, especially H5N1, which has been shown to have a high mortality rate (60 percent of reported human cases in which the patient sought urgent medical care) but has never achieved human-to-human transmission. By 2011, both Kawaoka (University of Wisconsin–Madison) and Fouchier (Erasmus Medical Center, Netherlands) independently conducted Gain-of-Function (GoF) experiments to make H5N1 transmissible between ferrets, whose respiratory tract physiology closely resembles that of human. Both research teams succeeded and documented their work in papers they submitted in 2011, Fouchier's to *Science*[13] and Kawaoka's to *Nature*,[14] which sparked widespread alarm in the scientific community. The US National Science Advisory Board for Biosecurity (NSABB) recommended redacting key methodological details due to bioterrorism and biosafety concerns. Ultimately, both papers were published, Kawaoka's in May 2012 and Fouchier's in June. The episode ignited an ongoing global debate over the ethics and safety of creating highly pathogenic agents that could, accidentally or deliberately, be released from a lab.

Fouchier and Kawaoka claimed their research enables mankind to stay ahead of the natural evolution of influenza viruses to prepare for their eventual emergence. Equipped with these pathogens, researchers could, they claimed, develop vaccines and antiviral medications to counter them if viruses like them should ever strike. The trouble with this reasoning is that such dangerous pathogens are far more likely to escape from a lab than to evolve naturally—a purely theoretical prospect that may never happen in millions of years. In 2020, humanity would learn the hard way how dangerous it is to engineer pathogenic and highly transmissible agents in a lab. However, the genie that got out of bottle in 2019 was not an influenza virus, but a coronavirus.

And so, we see how the US government's meddling and dysfunctional Middle East policy and intelligence failure begat the problem of Islamic terror. Exaggerated fear of Islamic terror begat the irrational fear of bioterrorism, which begat the twenty-first-century biodefense industry, which begat SARS Coronavirus 2 (SARS-CoV-2), the causative agent of COVID-19, which begat global mass hysteria.

CHAPTER 9

CRISIS AND BAILOUT CAPITALISM

Mind Virus: Extreme fear of global financial collapse set in motion by the reckless conduct and fraudulent financial instruments of Wall Street bankers.

Proposed Remedy: Massive Treasury Department and Federal Reserve bailouts of the Wall Street bankers who generated the crisis.

In his 2002 Berkshire Hathaway letter, Warren Buffet characterized derivatives such as mortgage-backed securities (MBS) as "financial weapons of mass destruction" or "time bombs" bearing enormous though obscure risks. He proclaimed that Wall Street's proliferation of unregulated and interconnected derivative positions was likely generating catastrophic systemic risk. Six years later, the disaster about which Buffet warned struck and caused the financial crisis of 2008.

On September 15, 2008, Lehman Brothers declared bankruptcy—the largest in US history—which caused a major panic in the financial markets. Ten days later, Treasury Secretary Hank Paulson kneeled before House Speaker Nancy Pelosi and begged her and other lawmakers to pass the $700 billion Troubled Asset Relief Program (TARP). Thus began the massive, organized grifting that has become endemic to American public life since 2008, when the Treasury Department and Federal Reserve bailed out the world's biggest banks, thereby enriching the very people whose reckless and fraudulent behavior caused the financial crisis.

The lynchpin of the racket was the bond rating agencies that were captured by the big investment banks. Bank executives incentivized bond raters to give top, investment grade ratings to large tranches of mortgage-backed securities whose underlying mortgages were, in fact, unsound. As the reader will see in the chapter on COVID-19, major pharmaceutical companies have similarly captured FDA regulators and incentivized them to bestow the "safe and effective" stamp of approval on a new generation of mRNA gene therapy shots that were neither.

After causing a global financial crisis that imperiled the economic well-being of humanity, Wall Street executives deftly engineered their own gigantic enrichment from federal funds. The most remarkable evidence of this may be found in a series of emails from Citibank managing director, Michael Froman, to then presidential candidate Barack Obama's advisory team. Froman closely advised John Podesta and others in crafting Obama's financial and economic policies. The Citibank executive's emails included names for cabinet and sub-cabinet positions, purportedly driven by "diversity" considerations, and many of the individuals he recommended got the positions.[1]

Froman assumed a leadership role in the 2008–09 transition before becoming a top aide in the White House. At the time he was serving as a key advisor, his company, Citibank, was imploding from its enormous portfolio of fraudulently rated mortgage-backed securities. On October 28, 2008, Citigroup received a $25 billion TARP capital injection, followed by another $20 billion injection and a $301 billion asset guarantee in November.[2] The Treasury bailouts were just the beginning. In November, the Federal Reserve began its program of "Quantitative Easing"—an abstract Orwellian name for bailing out Wall Street banks by purchasing their dubious bond portfolios for which there was no actual market. Citibank topped the list of Federal Reserve bailout funds, with cumulative Fed lending ultimately reaching over $2.5 trillion.[3] The anatomy of this spectacular act of legalized corruption was revealed by the former Federal Reserve official Andrew Huszar in his 2013 *Wall Street Journal* piece, "Confessions of a Quantitative Easer."[4] Not only did Wall Street banks receive trillions of bailout funds in response to the Financial Crisis that they created, not a single Wall Street executive was prosecuted for fraud, despite an abundance of evidence. This isn't surprising, given that President Obama's Attorney General, Eric Holder, was recommended for the job by the Citibank executive, Michael Froman.

Froman's email correspondence with the Obama Transition Team in the autumn of 2008 was published by Wikileaks on October 10, 2016, less than a month before the presidential election between candidates Donald Trump and Hillary Clinton. Given the stupendous corruption revealed by the emails, it was no wonder that the Clinton campaign and DNC launched a media blitzkrieg to peddle the narrative that Russian agents had hacked the DNC server. Their gambit was obvious—namely, to change the subject from the emails' contents to the "Russian threat" to American democracy. As the reader will see in the following chapter on the anti-Russia mind virus, the endless bloviating about the wickedness of Russian President Vladimir Putin since 2016 has been a handy pretext for distracting attention away from the corruption and ineptitude of the American political establishment on both sides of the aisle.

The lesson from the 2008 Financial Crisis and subsequent US government bailouts was clear to those who were paying attention. With every fresh crisis, Uncle Sam will come to the rescue with checkbook in hand, ready, able, and willing to send vast sums of money to whatever industry or interest group is apparently able to respond to the crisis. Uncle Sam's infinite largesse has been enabled because Congress no longer even pretends to place limits of federal indebtedness. Since 2013, it has suspended the debt ceiling eight times, allowing for continued borrowing without a specific dollar limit for set periods.[5] This being the case, it's no surprise that all the mind viruses documented in this book became especially virulent and epidemic after the 2008 Financial Crisis and the pernicious lessons that were learned from it.

CHAPTER 10

RACISM

Mind Virus: The destructive and debilitating belief—reinforced by constant messaging—that American society and institutions are infused with "systemic racism."

Proposed Remedy: Donating hundreds of millions of dollars to activists and organizations such as Black Lives Matter. Transferring hundreds of billions of taxpayer dollars to Diversity, Equity, and Inclusion (DEI) programs across federal, academic, and corporate sectors.

The election of Barack Obama in 2008 was initially celebrated as a historic milestone in American racial progress. Throughout the United States and the world, many perceived the first Black president of the United States to be living proof that the nation had moved beyond the racial discrimination of the past. And yet, shortly after Obama was sworn into office—which coincided with Wall Street bank bailouts—media reporting and public discourse became increasingly preoccupied, even obsessed with the proposition that the American people and institutions remained deeply racist.

Between the years 2011 and 2019, the frequency of the terms "racism" and "racist" increased 700 percent in the *New York Times* and nearly 1,000 percent in the *Washington Post*.[1] At the same time, many commentators and pundits increasingly spoke about the "systemic" or "structural" racism that is allegedly so woven into the fabric of law, institutions, and culture that most people are unaware of how it operates for maintaining white supremacy. Such "systemic racism" is alleged to be far more insidious than the overt segregation of American life before the passage of the Civil Rights Act in 1964.

A benign interpretation of America's irrational obsession with race after 2009 is that it was animated by the same psychology that Alexis de Tocqueville perceived to have animated the French revolutionaries. As he pointed out, hatred for the French Old Regime fanned into revolutionary fanaticism *after* the Old Regime began giving up its privileges and making concessions to the burgeoning urban middle class. As Tocqueville remarked, the trouble wasn't lack of favorable change, but that change didn't happen fast enough to meet growing expectations.[2]

The shortcoming of this interpretation is that enormous progress had already been made in rectifying racial injustice in the United States since 1938, when the blues musician Lead Belly recorded the song "Scottsboro Boys," with its exhortation to "stay woke" about the dangers faced by Black Americans in the Jim Crow South. I was born in Dallas in 1970 and grew up in an affluent White community, and I witnessed a total rejection of the racial sentiments I occasionally heard expressed among people of my grandparents' generation. By the time I graduated university in 1993, no one in my social circle, which extended to residents of cities all over the country, expressed racist sentiments or treated Black individuals as social inferiors. Most college-educated Americans of my generation therefore believed that we had come a long way to achieving Martin Luther King Jr.'s dream of living in a colorblind country.

Even though I studied philosophy at Boston University, I didn't know about of a new school of academic thought called critical race theory (CRT) that was taking shape during my college years. Only later did I learn about a 1991 paper by Neil Gotanda—professor of law at Western State College of Law in Fullerton, California—titled "A Critique of 'Our Constitution Is Color-Blind,'" in which he rejected King's dream of a "colorblind" society.[3] Gotanda argued that colorblind racial ideology is a sophisticated mechanism for preserving white supremacy. As he saw it, the insistence that race is irrelevant in law and policy conceals the reality of race, thereby securing for Whites the economic and political advantages that they accumulated in the overtly racist past. At the heart of this theory is Karl Marx's concept of "false consciousness"—that is, the way in which the exploited working class (the proletariat) internalizes the ideology of the ruling class (the bourgeoisie). This false consciousness renders the proletariat unable to grasp that it is being dominated and exploited.

Marx's critical theory for interpreting economic and social arrangements is useful for describing the way in which subordinate people in a hierarchical society can be abused. Such abuses *should* be criticized and corrected. However, the fatal flaw of Marxism and the critical race theory that it spawned (by way of the neo-Marxist Frankfurt School) lies in the fact that human society—like the social life of all living creatures—is inescapably hierarchical. This hard reality is evident in the fact that every Marxist-inspired revolution of the twentieth century established a new hierarchy that was more abusive than the hierarchy it replaced.

During Obama's presidency (January 2009–January 2016) tenets of critical race theory were increasingly adopted by mainstream commentators and pundits. However, because it was extremely difficult to find concrete and compelling examples of systemic racism, media reporting focused on dramatic incidents of police brutality directed at Black men. America's obsession with race in the post-2009 era emerged as a full-blown mind virus in 2013 with the acquittal of George Zimmerman, who had been charged for murdering a Black teenager named Travyon Martin.

On February 26, 2012, Zimmerman—a man of half Hispanic ancestry—was serving as a neighborhood watchman in a gated community in Sanford, Florida when he got into a fight with Martin. Their violent struggle culminated with Zimmerman shooting Martin. Zimmerman claimed he shot in self-defense while Martin was on top of him and punching his face. His broken nose, two black eyes, and two lacerations to the back of his head—injuries that the medical examiner later described as "very insignificant"—seemed to support his contention. Nevertheless, he was charged with second-degree murder on the grounds that he had profiled, followed, and confronted the unarmed teenager, thereby initiating the violent conflict that culminated in Zimmerman shooting Martin.

The defense argued that Zimmerman's community had recently experienced multiple burglaries committed by Black males, which justified his decision to confront Martin. Zimmerman's injuries, plus witness testimony that he was indeed on the ground and being badly beaten by Martin when he drew his pistol and fired, persuaded the jury to acquit him. News of his acquittal sparked protests in Los Angeles and other American cities, and it inspired California residents Alicia Garza and Patrisse Cullors to found Black Lives Matter.

The passionate reaction to Zimmerman's acquittal arose from the assumption that racial animus had motivated him to confront Martin. Media reporting cited his initial phone call to the Sanford police—which he made from his cell phone while sitting in his car—to report the "suspicious guy." However, the call transcript does not support the claim that Zimmerman acted out of racial animus.

Zimmerman: Hey, we've had some break-ins in my neighborhood, and there's a real suspicious guy. . . . This guy looks like he's up to no good, or he's on drugs or something. It's raining and he's just walking around, looking about.
Sanford PD Dispatcher (Sean Noffke): Okay, and this guy is he White, Black, or Hispanic?
Zimmerman: He looks Black.
Dispatcher: Did you see what he was wearing?
Zimmerman: Yeah. A dark hoodie, like a grey hoodie, and either jeans or sweatpants and white tennis shoes. He's [unintelligible] he was just staring . . .
Dispatcher: Okay, he's just walking around the area . . .
Zimmerman: . . . looking at all the houses.
Dispatcher: Okay.
Zimmerman: Now he's just staring at me. . . . Yeah, now he's coming towards me.
Dispatcher: Okay.
Zimmerman: He's got his hand in his waistband. And he's a Black male.
Dispatcher: How old would you say he looks?
Zimmerman: . . . late teens.
Dispatcher: Late teens, ok.
Zimmerman: Something's wrong with him. Yup, he's coming to check me out, he's got something in his hands, I don't know what his deal is.
Dispatcher: Just let me know if he does anything, okay?
Zimmerman: How long until you get an officer over here?

Dispatcher: Yeah, we've got someone on the way . . .
Zimmerman: Okay. These assholes, they always get away. . . . Shit, he's running.
Dispatcher: He's running? Which way is he running?
Zimmerman: Down towards the other entrance to the neighborhood.
Dispatcher: Which entrance is that that he's heading towards?
Zimmerman: The back entrance. . . . Fucking punks. These assholes, they always get away.
Dispatcher: Are you following him?
Zimmerman: Yeah.
Dispatcher: Okay, we don't need you to do that.
Zimmerman: Okay.[4]

After the incident, Zimmerman told the police that he had ceased pursuing Martin, and that Martin had turned around and confronted him, asking "What the fuck's your problem, homey?" and then punching him. Witness Rachel Jeantel testified that she was on the phone with Martin and heard him say, "Why are you following me for?" followed by a man's voice saying, "What are you doing here?"[5]

Even if Jeantel's version of how the conflict started was more truthful than Zimmerman's, it was still not evidence that Zimmerman was motivated by racial animus. He only drew his pistol and fired while Martin was punching him, and the jury had no reason to believe he would have acted differently if his assailant had been White.

The same drama played out the following year in Ferguson, Missouri, when police officer Dorian Wilson shot Michael Brown. An investigation conducted by Attorney General Eric Holder's Department of Justice concluded that Brown had reached into the vehicle, punched Officer Brown, and attempted to grab his service weapon.[6] Forensic evidence, including Brown's DNA on Wilson's collar and gun, and a gunshot wound to Brown's hand, supported Wilson's account of a close-quarters struggle inside the car. Once again, zero evidence was presented that any of Officer Wilson's actions had been motivated by racial animus. The officer's interaction with Brown began when he saw the young man and his companion walking down the middle of the street and blocking vehicle traffic. Nevertheless, the shooting provided a pretext for Black Lives Matter to organize several events and a protest, which elevated the organization's profile and funding, enabling it to expand its presence with chapters in eighteen cities.

The apotheosis of Black Lives Matter status and influence occurred in the aftermath of the death of George Floyd on May 25, 2020. Floyd died while Minneapolis police officer Derek Chauvin knelt on his neck and upper back for nine minutes and twenty-nine seconds. Floyd was loaded into an ambulance and pronounced dead at Hennepin County Medical Center at 9:25 p.m. The Hennepin County Medical Examiner, Dr. Andrew Baker, performed the autopsy. His final report stated the cause of death as "cardiopulmonary arrest complicating law enforcement subdual, restraint, and neck compression," and the manner of death homicide. Floyd was suffering from severe arteriosclerotic and hypertensive heart disease with cardiomegaly (enlarged heart weighing 540 grams). Toxicology results revealed blood concentrations of fentanyl at 11 ng/mL.[7] This was a significant finding, given that concentrations exceeding 3 ng/mL are frequently associated with severe respiratory depression, which can lead to respiratory failure and subsequent cardiac arrest. A level of 11 ng/mL significantly exceeds these common toxicity thresholds.

Floyd's blood also tested positive for methamphetamine at 19 ng/mL, and a positive postmortem nasal swab for SARS-CoV-2. Dr. Baker noted these as "other significant conditions" but testified that the police subdual, restraint, and neck compression remained the precipitating cause. The medical examiner's ruling was further complicated by the fact that he did not find that the neck restraint had caused asphyxiation or brain death from compression of Floyd's carotid arteries.[8]

The positive SARS-CoV-2 was a notable detail of the report. During a time when hospital doctors and medical examiners were widely noting COVID-19 as the cause of death, even if the patient was suffering from grave comorbidities and other injuries, the positive test in Floyd's case wasn't listed as the cause. The ensuing nationwide protests occurred during COVID-19 lockdowns, imposed on the grounds that the highly contagious viral illness posed such a risk to public health—including that of young people—that it was necessary for everyone to stay at home. The lockdowns imposed enormous financial costs on small to midsize business owners, as well as economic, educational, and social disruptions for the entire country. However, shortly after Floyd's death, infectious disease experts at the University of Washington proclaimed that the protests of police brutality were a necessary "vital public health" imperative that outweighed the risks of COVID-19 transmission. They therefore made exceptions to COVID-19 lockdown restrictions for the protestors. The letter was signed by more than 1,200 public health professionals, physicians, epidemiologists.[9] All of these public health experts had previously endorsed strict stay-at-home orders.

Interpretations of Officer Chauvin's decision to continue kneeling on Floyd, even after the restrained man ceased struggling, were debated at Chauvin's murder trial. Video recordings of the incident convey the strong impression that Chauvin applied excessive and unnecessary force, especially after Floyd fell completely silent. At trial he was found guilty of "unintentional second-degree murder"—that is, a "depraved heart" killing characterized by reckless actions with disregard for life but no specific intent to kill.

Though Officer Chauvin may have a "depraved heart," his actions contained no proof of being motivated by racial animus. During his nineteen-year career, Chauvin had been the subject of eighteen excessive force complaints, including using the same restraint technique against Julian Hernandez (a White man with a Spanish surname) and his shooting Wayne Reyes, a White man.[10] If Chauvin's professional service record displayed signs of racial animus—as distinct from a general tendency to use excessive force—one wonders why his ultimate superior, Minneapolis Chief of Police, Medaria Arradondo, a Black man, did not subject him to greater discipline.

The question of whether Officer Chauvin was indeed motivated by racial animus against George Floyd wasn't examined, but generally presumed to be the case. There were no rational grounds for this presumption, as there have been tens of thousands of documented cases in the United State of police brutality against White men. In 2005, I was threatened by an off-duty Dallas Police officer who was working as a night watchman in an upscale Dallas apartment complex. The officer objected to me and my girlfriend sitting in the complex's community hot tub after midnight. For no reason, he told me he suspected me of raping my girlfriend (with whom I was merely sitting in the hot tub) and he declared he would be justified in shooting me with his service pistol to stop the assault. He said this while holding his right hand near his holster, and he only backed off when my girlfriend assured him that his suspicion was completely unwarranted. Race had nothing to do with this incident, as all involved were White. The officer was suffering from some kind of mental health or personality disorder.

In 2019, again in my native Dallas, police bodycam footage was published (in connection with a lawsuit) that documented the case of Tony Timpa, a thirty-two-year-old White man who struggled with schizophrenia. In 2016, while off his medication, he called 911 and asked for help. He was already handcuffed by security guards when Dallas police officers arrived. The bodycam footage shows them holding Timpa facedown, with one officer kneeling on his upper back and neck area for over fourteen minutes while Timpa repeatedly pleaded for help and said he couldn't breathe.[11] He became unresponsive, but even then, paramedics were reportedly told not to intervene. Timpa was pronounced dead at the scene. The autopsy listed the cause as homicide due to "sudden cardiac death during physical restraint" with contributing factors including cocaine and methamphetamine. The publication of the bodycam footage did not result in any protests in Dallas or anywhere else.

Even it was proven that racial animus had motivated Derek Chauvin to use excessive force on George Floyd, this would not have proved the existence of systemic racism in US law enforcement. Moreover, given that Officer Chauvin was arrested on May 29, it's not clear what was being protested in the thousands of demonstrations that took place after his arrest. These occurred in more than two thousand cities and towns across all fifty states and Washington, DC. According to Armed Conflict Location & Event Data (ACLED), Black Lives Matter played a key role in organizing over 7,750 demonstrations in 2,440 locations from late May through August 22, 2020.[12] An estimated fifteen to twenty-six million Americans participated, making these the largest protests in US history. The wave of protests also extended to sixty foreign countries. Demonstrations prompted curfews in at least two hundred cities and activation of over ninety-six thousand National Guard and other military personnel—the largest domestic military mobilization outside of war in American history.

Media coverage of these demonstrations characterized them as peaceful or mostly peaceful. Nevertheless, twenty-five people were killed in connection with the protests. More than two thousand officers were injured by assaults, projectiles, and vehicle incidents. Arson, vandalism, and looting between May 26 and June 8 generated $1–2 billion in insurance claims—the highest figure for civil disorder in US history. In cities tracked by the Major Cities Chiefs Association, authorities logged 2,385 looting incidents and 624 arsons, including ninety-seven police vehicles burned.[13] In Minneapolis and St. Paul, hundreds of buildings were damaged or destroyed, with estimates exceeding $500 million in property damage. The destruction resulted in lasting economic burdens on businesses and communities. In Washington, DC, a fire was set in the basement of St. John's Episcopal Church, while the Lincoln Memorial and the World War II Memorials were vandalized.

A few months after the George Floyd demonstrations, Patrisse Cullors, co-founder of Black Lives Matter, purchased a home in Studio City, Los Angeles, for nearly $6 million of the $90 million in donations her organization received that year.[14] The value of the property grossly exceeded her compensation for directing a 501(c)(3) nonprofit organization. In December 2025, Tashella Dickerson, the executive director of Black Lives Matter Oklahoma City, was indicted on federal charges of wire fraud and money laundering. She is accused of embezzling over $3.15 million in donor funds intended for bail assistance and using them for personal expenses, including luxury travel, shopping, and real estate.[15]

I believe it is no coincidence that the incessant talk of racism in the American public forum after 2009 began at the same time America's financial class began receiving trillions of Treasury and Federal Reserve dollars to bail it out of the financial crisis of 2008. The great bankers who caused the crisis became the chief beneficiaries of it, while the working and middle classes were left to struggle with a shrinking real economy and steadily rising costs. There is a large academic literature about the marked tendency of banking crises—especially those perceived to have been caused by excessive greed and recklessness—to generate resentment and fertile ground for populist movements against the financial class. Thus, talking about police brutality and the purported menace of rising white supremacy in the United States was an effective means of changing the subject.

The true systemic or structural injustice in the United States after 2009 was the de facto immunity from criminal prosecution granted to financial industry executives. Despite an abundance of documentary evidence that many defrauded their clients and created systemic risk in the global financial system, not a single senior executive of a major Wall Street bank was prosecuted by Obama's Attorney General, Eric Holder.

For many years, the Black economist, Thomas Sowell, has argued that racial discrimination is no longer a major barrier to Black social and economic advancement in the United States. He believes the breakdown of the Black nuclear family—the increasing number of fatherless households—has played a much greater role in causing social problems such as poverty and crime.[16] Sowell contends that welfare policies undermined personal responsibility and enabled many Black men to abandon the home after fathering children.

Sowell has also argued that many Black leaders, activists, and organizations have incentives to maintain the belief that systemic racism remains a dominant force in American life. By emphasizing that racial injustice is still pervasive and proclaiming that they are fighting it, they may obtain influence, political support, funding, and status. The bogeyman of systemic racism has also served as a pretext for channeling hundreds of billions of taxpayer dollars into federal diversity, equity, and inclusion (DEI) programs. A 2025 study conducted by the Functional Government Initiative and the Center for Renewing America, identified 460 programs across twenty-four government agencies in the Biden administration in which approximately $1 trillion dollars was invested for DEI initiatives.[17]

The documentary filmmaker, Chad O. Jackson, contends that constant messaging about systemic racism does nothing to advance Black people. On the contrary, telling young Blacks that they are victims of systemic racism is itself a form of oppression because it causes them to feel helpless and demoralized. Jackson suffered profound cognitive dissonance while attending a Texas public high school in the years 2004–2008. He often heard that Black boys like him were oppressed by racial discrimination, but he searched in vain for evidence of this in his lived experience. His White teachers and peers were always friendly and welcoming. Because he was a good student and player on his high school football team, he was treated with respect and admiration. Where, he wondered, was the discrimination? Ultimately, he concluded that, by fostering a negative and self-defeating mindset, the incessant talk of racism hinders many young Black people from advancing.

Even if one disagrees with the viewpoint articulated by Sowell and Jackson, one will still be hard pressed to explain how the public discourse about racism in recent years has helped Black people to advance. Since 2009, the "racist" label has been applied to innumerable features of the human condition that were previously understood to have nothing to do with race. Especially bizarre has been the application of the racist label to cultural traits long associated with flourishing and success.

In 2020, the Smithsonian's National Museum of African American History and Culture posted a chart of "Whiteness" traits that included hard work, self-reliance, the nuclear family, objective rational thinking, and delayed gratification.[18] In recent years, universities and even medical schools have characterized rational thinking and merit-based advancement as artifacts of an oppressive era that should be "dismantled." This bizarre declaration overlooks the obvious fact that all these traits associated with "whiteness" correlate with socioeconomic mobility in every group that adopts them, from Asian immigrants to West African entrepreneurs.[19]

In 2021, Seattle Public Schools and California's "Equitable Math" educational initiative described "getting the right answer" as perpetuating white supremacy.[20] Standardized tests such as the SAT are now frequently called racist for revealing achievement gaps that persist after controlling for socioeconomic status. As everyone who has studied math knows, math is not racially contingent. Its axioms function identically in every region of the world. Thus, changing the curriculum to favor "lived experience" over "getting the right answer" is manifestly insane.

The irrational obsession with racism since 2009 has also found expression in the realms of symbols, monuments, and even in the natural world. In 2018, the City of Palm Springs cut down a beautiful and dense row of tamarisk trees along the parameter of the Tahquitz Creek Golf Course following complaints that the trees were planted in the 1960s to segregate the predominantly Black neighborhood from the municipal golf course, which is open to the public and charges a modest green's fee.[21]

On May 31, 2020, the Robert Gould Shaw and the 54th Regiment Memorial on Boston Common—commemorating the valiant service of the Black Union Army regiment—was vandalized with graffiti. On June 19, 2020, in San Francisco, the monumental bust of Ulysses Grant — the Union general who defeated the Confederacy—was toppled on the grounds that he'd briefly owned a slave before the Civil War.

In the realm of politics, voter-ID requirements are commonly branded as racist because it purportedly makes voting harder for Blacks and is therefore assumed to be motivated by racial animus rather than preventing fraud. The proposition ignores the obvious fact that IDs are required for boarding planes, buying alcohol, and cashing checks.

All the above fosters resentment by claiming that minority advancement requires dismantling universal standards rather than cultivating them. Instead of judging people by the "content of their character instead of the color of their skin," the mind virus of racial doctrine since 2009 strips people of their individual qualities and assigns them a racial identity. Instead of bringing the American people together in the spirit of good will and cooperation, the pernicious racial doctrine that became prevalent after 2009 tears us apart by sowing fear, resentment, and distrust.

CHAPTER 11

RUSSIA

Mind Virus: Fear and loathing of Russia, especially President Vladimir Putin.
Proposed Remedy: Scapegoating Putin for America's political divisions and dysfunctions. Maintaining high US national security state expenditures to counter Russia's alleged meddling, seeking to expand American influence in Ukraine and Georgia, sabotaging Europe's purchase of natural gas from Russia.

On June 12, 2016, in an interview with ITV's *Peston on Sunday*, Julian Assange announced that WikiLeaks had "upcoming leaks in relation to Hillary Clinton" and that documents were "pending publication." Two days later, on June 14, the final Democratic primary election was held in the District of Columbia. Hillary Clinton won the primary against Bernie Sanders. On the same day, the *Washington Post* first reported that Russian government hackers had breached the Democratic National Committee (DNC) and stolen opposition research for the benefit of Donald Trump.[1]

On July 10—twelve days before Wikileaks published the embarrassing emails—a young DNC staffer named Seth Rich was murdered at approximately 4:20 a.m. while walking home in the Bloomingdale neighborhood of Washington, DC. At the southwest corner of Flagler Place and W Street Northwest, about a block from his apartment, he was shot twice in the back. The Metropolitan Police quickly announced—before they'd had time to investigate—that Rich had been shot because of a "botched" armed robbery.[2] At the time he was found, his valuable watch, wallet, and cell phone where still on him, indicating the assailant had shot him twice in the back and then fled without taking anything. Other armed muggings in the area had involved the assailant holding the victim at gunpoint and demanding his valuables, *not* shooting him in the back and fleeing.

In the year 2016, there were 135 homicides in the District of Columbia, which has a resident population of 672,000.[3] This comes to approximately one murder per 5,000 residents—a dramatic decline from the city's murder rate in the early nineties. The Metropolitan Police has published an analysis of homicides in 1998–2000. During this period, homicides were not equally distributed throughout the city but were concentrated in specific neighborhoods. Ninety-two percent of the victims were Black, 3.2 percent were Hispanic, and 3.2 percent were White.[4] Though one must consider the possibility that homicide trends in DC have changed since 2000 (apart from merely decreasing in numbers) it's notable that, of the currently unsolved homicides in Washington, DC in the year 2016, Seth Rich was the only White victim in a city that is forty-four percent White.[5]

Though the Metropolitan Police never identified a suspect, the agency dismissed the theory of a political motive. Nevertheless, the murder quickly became a matter of widespread speculation in connection with the DNC emails that were pending publication by Wikileaks. Speculation centered on a conflict between Democratic primary candidates Hillary Clinton and Bernie Sanders. In December 2015, Sanders sued the DNC for denying his campaign access to a crucial voter database. When the DNC emails were leaked shortly after Rich's murder, they revealed many staffers mocking Sanders and discussing ways to thwart his campaign, despite the organization's insistence it was neutral.[6]

Was Seth Rich (like many others) appalled by the DNC's unfair and undemocratic treatment of Sanders and felt compelled to expose it?

Just over a year after Rich was murdered, on November 2, 2017, former interim DNC chair Donna Brazile revealed that in August 2015, the DNC had signed a "Joint Fundraising Agreement" with the Clinton campaign, granting it control of the party's finances, staffing, and strategy in exchange for funding the debt-burdened organization.[7] Though knowledge of the shady agreement was purportedly limited to senior staff, independent investigators of the Seth Rich murder wondered if he had learned about it.

Julian Assange insisted the DNC emails were leaked and not hacked. Former NSA technical director, William Binney, also rejected the claim that Russian agents hacked the DNC server. Along with his fellow Veteran Intelligence Professionals for Sanity (VIPS), he argued that the data was downloaded from the server onto a storage device. Binney insisted the download speed was consistent with a local transfer, not a remote hack. Moreover, had the data been hacked, it would have been easy for the NSA to trace the hack quickly and precisely.[8]

Regarding motive, a good investigator would consider the hypothesis that Seth Rich was murdered not in retaliation, but to eliminate him as a witness that the DNC emails were leaked by an insider, and not hacked by Russians. As the reader will recall, immediately after Julian Assange announced that Wikileaks had DNC emails and would soon publish them, the *Washington Post* asserted the emails had been hacked by Russian agents. As soon as the emails were published, the DNC and its allies in the media changed the subject from their embarrassing content to the sensational story of evil Russians interfering in America's sacrosanct democratic elections.

The intriguing and still unsolved murder of Seth Rich—and the great controversy it ignited in the American public forum—happened within the context of deep social and political divisions in American society, widespread loss of faith in our institutions and democratic processes, and highly polarizing political candidates. Most of Trump's first term was encumbered by allegations that Russian agents had used US social media platforms to manipulate the American electorate to vote for him instead of Hillary Clinton. This made it virtually impossible for him to work in a constructive fashion with Russian President Vladimir Putin to improve US-Russian relations.

Even more damaging were allegations that members of Trump's campaign had colluded with Russian agents to obtain compromising information about Hillary Clinton. This charge struck many as the pot calling the kettle black after it was revealed (in 2017) that, in April 2016, the DNC and Hillary Clinton campaign hired—through their attorney Marc Elias—the Washington, DC–based firm Fusion GPS to perform "opposition research" against Donald Trump. Fusion GPS hired former British intelligence officer Christopher Steele to conduct the research. Steele used his network of contacts in Russia to gather dirt on Donald Trump, including unsubstantiated claims that Russia possessed compromising material on him and that he had engaged in activities while in Russia that could be used to blackmail him.[9]

Students of the Swiss psychiatrist, Carl Jung, may perceive in the sordid melodrama of the 2016 US presidential election a massive amount of psychological projection—that is, the way in which people attribute their own designs and motives onto others. Jung proposed that, within the context of a large social group or polity, projection is a key driver of scapegoating, in which social pathologies are cast onto an external target. Amid all the division, dysfunction, impropriety, rapacity, ruthlessness, and rivalry within America's political class, both major parties have often found it expedient to invoke the specter of the perfidious Russians and their president, Vladimir Putin, who is frequently characterized as a "ruthless thug."

After allegations of "Russian interference" in the 2016 elections emerged, it was common to hear expressions of outrage. "How dare the Russians try to manipulate our elections!" was a common refrain. This was a conspicuous example of our "American exceptionalism"—that is, the idea that we are, as a nation, exceptional, and the standards normally applied to other nations do not necessarily apply to us. By the year 2016, most Americans had forgotten the July 17, 1996, *Time* magazine cover story titled "Yanks to the Rescue: The Secret Story of How American Advisors Helped Yeltsin Win." The report boasted and celebrated how American political operatives, some directly connected with the Clinton White House, had deeply meddled in the 1996 Russian presidential election that Yeltsin was destined to lose until they came to his rescue. This election was an illustrative example of how, since the end of the Cold War, powerful US interests have repeatedly revealed their ambition to subjugate Russia and access its vast markets and natural resources on the most favorable terms for themselves.

On December 12, 2017, the National Security Archive at George Washington University declassified US, Soviet, German, British, and French documents about this momentous occasion. As the National Security Archive reported at this time:

> The documents show that multiple national leaders were considering and rejecting Central and Eastern European membership

> in NATO as of early 1990 and through 1991, that discussions of NATO in the context of German unification negotiations in 1990 were not at all narrowly limited to the status of East German territory, and that subsequent Soviet and Russian complaints about being misled about NATO expansion were founded in written contemporaneous memcons and telcons at the highest levels.[10]

The documents reinforce former CIA Director Robert Gates's criticism of "pressing ahead with expansion of NATO eastward [in the 1990s], when Gorbachev and others were led to believe that wouldn't happen." The key phrase, buttressed by the documents, is "led to believe." The US decision to press ahead with NATO expansion was announced at the end of 1996. On February 5, 1997, George Kennan, who led the US effort to contain the Soviet Union during the Cold War, published an essay in the *New York Times* in which he characterized the decision as "A Fateful Error" that would likely cause precisely the instability and conflict in Eastern Europe that it was purportedly conceived to prevent. As Kennan put it:

> The view, bluntly stated, is that expanding NATO would be the most fateful error of American policy in the entire post-cold-war era. Such a decision may be expected to inflame the nationalistic, anti-Western and militaristic tendencies in Russian opinion; to have an adverse effect on the development of Russian democracy; to restore the atmosphere of the cold war to East-West relations, and to impel Russian foreign policy in directions decidedly not to our liking. And, last but not least, it might make it much more difficult, if not impossible, to secure the Russian Duma's ratification of the Start II agreement and to achieve further reductions of nuclear weaponry. . . . Russians are little impressed with American assurances that it reflects no hostile intentions. They would see their prestige (always uppermost in the Russian mind) and their security interests as adversely affected. They would, of course, have no choice but to accept expansion as a military fait accompli. But they would continue to regard it as a rebuff by the West and would likely look elsewhere for guarantees of a secure and hopeful future for themselves.[11]

Kennan understood Russia's long and fraught relationship with the West, and the deep traumas to the Russian psyche that were inflicted by Napoleon's invasion in 1812 (through Lithuania) and especially by Hitler's Operation Barbarossa (through Ukraine) in 1941. These Western military offenses resulted in tens of millions of Russian casualties and catastrophic suffering for the civilian population. Kennan understood that, for good reason, the Russians are therefore afraid of Western military powers getting too close to Russia's borders.

Conversely, Kennan understood how nervous it made the US government when Russia placed missiles in Cuba. On October 27, 1962, he gave a lecture in Belgrade in which he defended the US "quarantine" of Cuba, arguing that the Soviets had no right to place missiles in the American sphere of influence. The distance from Cuba to Washington, DC is about 1,300 miles, which Kennan regarded as close enough to give the Russians a first strike advantage. He also understood President John F. Kennedy's rationale for negotiating a deal with Soviet Premier Nikita Khruschev in October 1962 for Russia to remove its missiles from Cuba in exchange for the US removing its Jupiter missiles from Turkey. This deal was finalized on October 28, 1962, via back-channel discussions between by Robert F. Kennedy and Soviet Ambassador Anatoly Dobrynin.

For Kennan's generation of Cold warriors, the Cuban Missile Crisis was an example of how close mankind can come to total annihilation unless cooler heads prevail with rational negotiations instead of hotheaded brinkmanship of the sort that Airforce General Curtis LeMay proposed. Just as the United States insists on maintaining a large sphere of influence around its territory in the Western Hemisphere—a doctrine inaugurated by President James Monroe in 1823—Russia has legitimate security interests in the nations on its western border, especially Ukraine, whose northwest border lies less than five-hundred miles from Moscow.

Before his death in 2005, George Kennan was repeatedly shocked by the US government's brazen provocations of Russia. They included:

- 1999: Poland, Hungary, and Czech Republic join NATO
- 1999: United States leads NATO in bombing Serbia.

- 2001: United States unilaterally withdrawals from the US-Soviet Anti-Ballistic Missile Treaty of 1972, a key component of European security architecture.
- 2005: US Department of Defense invests $200 million in forty-six Ukrainian biolabs containing pathogenic agents suitable for biowarfare.[12]

After Kennan's death, the US government continued its extremely provocative actions against Russia. These included:

- 2008: United States announces plan for Ukraine and Georgia to join NATO.
- 2014: US National Endowment for Democracy (NED)—long suspected of being a CIA front organization—provides substantial funding for Euromaidan protests that oust Ukrainian President Victor Yanukovich, who rejected an EU Association Agreement for Ukraine.[13] The Agreement required that Ukraine borrow a large sum from International Monetary Fund (IMF) with onerous terms, including the elimination of natural gas subsidies for Ukrainian households.
- Substantial forensic evidence emerges that the Maidan Massacre of February 20, 2014, which galvanized the movement to overthrow President Yanukovich, was perpetrated from snipers firing from surrounding buildings controlled by Maidan protestors. This raises the suspicion it was a false flag attack.[14]
- 2014: Assistant Secretary of State Victoria Nuland and US Ambassador to Ukraine Geoffrey Pyatt have phone call (intercepted by Russian intelligence) revealing their covert engineering of Ukrainian political leadership and meddling in Ukraine's sovereignty.[15]
- 2014: Baltic countries join NATO.
- 2015–2022: CIA establishes as many as twelve secret "forward operating bases" along Ukraine's border with Russia and training elite Ukrainian commando units (Unit 2245) to capture Russian drones and decrypt communications.[16]

- 2015 and 2021: United States provides over $2.7 billion in security assistance to train and equip the Ukrainian military.[17]
- 2021, Russian intelligence informs President Putin that the CIA and British intelligence (MI6) are essentially controlling Ukrainian intelligence and turning it into a "springboard for operations against Moscow."
- December 2021: United States and NATO reject Russian neutrality proposal for Ukraine.
- February 2022: Vice President Kamala Harris attends Munich Security Conference and reiterates US intention for Ukraine to join NATO.

I started following US, Ukrainian, and Russian affairs while I was living in Vienna in the years 2000–2011. On dreary winter weekends, I sometimes went to the Burg Cinema, where the *The Third Man*, a 1949 film noir masterpiece, still played on the big screen every Sunday. Shot on location in Vienna during the Four Powers Occupation of 1945–1955, the film and its deeply intriguing back story never ceased to fascinate me.

The Four Power occupation began in the spring of 1945 when the Soviet army entered Austria from the east and the American army entered from the west and converged on the capital of Vienna. By then it was already evident that as soon as Nazi Germany was defeated, the wartime alliance of the United States and Soviet Union would give way to a fierce rivalry over the fate of Europe. Austria lay in the middle of this conflict. To prevent each other from gaining the upper hand, the US military (along with those of Britain and France) occupied parts of Austria while the Soviet military occupied others. By 1947, US Department of Defense became convinced that withdrawing Western troops would leave the country open to complete Soviet occupation.

After Stalin died in 1953, Soviet Foreign Minister Vyacheslav Molotov told Austrian Chancellor Julius Raab that he was willing to entertain Austrian independence. In April 1955, Raab travelled to Moscow to discuss the matter. Despite his reputation for icy formality, Molotov quickly warmed up to Raab. Ten years after their armies had engaged in the most brutal warfare in history, the two men became conspicuously amiable over a state dinner of conviviality and frequent toasts, and they ironed out the terms of an Austrian neutrality deal. Raab agreed to pay for the "German assets" and oil fields left by the Soviets. Molotov also promised the release and repatriation of Austrian POWs still languishing in Russia.[18]

The Western powers were amazed by the deal, with British diplomat, Geoffrey Wallinger reporting to London that it "was far too good to be true." Nevertheless, it proceeded as planned and was signed by the representatives of all Four Occupying Powers on May 15, 1955, and came into force on July 27. By October 25, all occupying soldiers had withdrawn from the country, and the next day, Austria's parliament enacted a Declaration of Neutrality that Austria would never join a military alliance such as NATO or the Warsaw Pact or allow foreign troops to be based in the country. Russia and the United States have honored Austrian neutrality ever since.

Upon his return from Moscow, Chancellor Raab addressed a crowd assembled outside the chancery. His voice breaking with emotion, he said, "I must thank the Lord God that we have been able to experience this hour for Austria." And indeed, Austrian neutrality has been a great blessing for the nation and its people, and it enabled Vienna to become one of the most open, laid-back, and cosmopolitan capitals in Europe. I believe a similar neutrality arrangement for Ukraine would have served its people equally well. On December 15, 2021, Russian President Vladimir Putin submitted a security proposal to the US government, with Ukrainian neutrality a key provision, but the Biden administration rejected it out of hand.[19]

CHAPTER 12

THE GREAT PIPELINE OPERA ENDS WITH A BANG

Fear and loathing of a purported enemy render many unable to comprehend and protest the fantastically wanton actions of the ruling class, done in the name of combatting the purported enemy. A spectacular example of this was the destruction of the Nord Stream pipeline on September 26, 2022. Deliberately destroying civilian infrastructure was not only a war crime against Russia, but also a crime against the German, Dutch, and French shareholders who owned 49 percent of the pipeline, as well as all the peoples of Europe who received affordable natural gas from it. Destroying the pipeline sabotaged a beneficial and cooperative partnership between Russia and Europe that promoted peace and prosperity for everyone concerned.

Around the year 2005, I started following what was referred to in the press as the "Pipeline Opera"—that is, the competition between two major projects for increasing Europe's natural gas supply. In 2002, a consortium of European natural gas companies, led by Austria's partly state-owned OMV, conceived the Nabucco Pipeline to bring gas directly into Europe from the Caspian Sea. The project's announcement was met with strong approval from the EU and US governments, who wanted Europe to reduce its dependency on Russian natural gas. However, due to political and financing complications, the project was abandoned in 2013.

To the great chagrin of the US government, in September 2005, President Putin and German Chancellor Gerhard Schroeder signed a deal for the Nord Stream pipeline. The $5.7 billion project was conceived to transport gas directly from Russia to Germany under the Baltic Sea. Nord Stream One—consisting of two parallel pipelines—was built in the years 2010 to 2012. The two pipelines started delivering gas in November 2011 and October 2012. Nord Stream Two—also consisting of two parallel pipelines—was completed in September 2021 but never entered service due to the Russo-Ukrainian War.

I became so intrigued by the Pipeline Opera that I wrote the first draft of a detective novel, set in Vienna, with this geopolitical drama part of the plot. My story opens with the murder of an opera singer in the Hotel Sacher. The suspects included a Russian agent and a Ukrainian agent, the latter being far more sympathetic. At the time I submitted the first draft to my agent, he told me it would be hard to get Americans to care about the Ukrainian female character, given that "most Americans couldn't locate Ukraine on a map." One can therefore imagine my surprise when, seven years later, millions of American citizens suddenly perceived the Donbas region of Eastern Ukraine to be something akin to sacred territory, worth fighting over at the expense of hundreds of thousands of dead and wounded and elevating the risk of nuclear war with Russia.

While Nord Stream One was operating, it mutually benefitted Russia and Germany and gave both nations a powerful incentive to maintain friendly relations. The project was the fruit of the close friendship that developed between Putin and Schroeder in the early 2000s.[1] At the height of its service, Nord Stream One supplied about six billion cubic feet of natural gas per day to German industry and homes. The US government's reaction to this arrangement was extremely hostile. This raises the suspicion that Washington's greatest fear is not a resurgent Russia, but a confident and independent Germany forming closer ties with Russia and using cheap Russian gas to make its manufacturing economy ever more dominant while the US manufacturing economy languishes.

In what was surely one of the strangest and most disturbing incidents in twenty-first-century history, on September 26, 2022, saboteurs blew up both lines of Nord Stream One and one (Line B) of the Nord Stream Two, which was fully built but had not yet entered service. The pipelines were the joint property of Russia and Germany—even though Germany was not at war with Russia and could not benefit from destroying its own pipelines even if it were at war. The rupturing of the pipelines released approximately 778 million standard cubic meters of natural gas, composed largely of methane, a potent greenhouse case.[2] This was by far the largest single incident of human-caused methane pollution in history—five times larger than the 2015 Aliso Canyon leak in the United States. Unlike previous major incidents of methane pollution, the Nord Stream disaster was no accident, but the result of deliberate sabotage.[3]

At a press conference on February 7, 2022, with German Chancellor Olaf Scholz standing next to him and displaying total humility and deference, President Biden stated, "If Russia invades, that means tanks or troops crossing the border of Ukraine again—then there will be no longer a Nord Stream Two. We will bring an end to it." A reporter asked how he would bring an end to the pipeline, given that it was under German control. Biden replied, "I promise you; we will be able to do it." This statement indicates that US government agents, possibly of Ukrainian nationality, bombed the pipelines. Especially stunning was the fact that the deliberate destruction of this extremely valuable and critical German infrastructure was met with scarcely a peep of protest from the German government.

Since 2022, with its previously excellent relationship with Russia destroyed along with its gas pipeline, Germany has greatly increased its imports of Liquefied Natural Gas from the United States, shipped across the Atlantic on huge LNG tankers burning 100 to 130+ metric tons of LNG per voyage to propel the enormous vessels. At the height of the European energy crisis of 2022, following the destruction of the Nord Stream pipeline, Germany paid up to six times more for natural gas than it did before the Russo-Ukrainian War began.[4] Germany now pays US LNG suppliers more than twice as much as it paid for Russian gas piped through the Nord Stream pipeline that it jointly owned with Russia. Rarely in history has a purportedly sovereign nation submitted to such a humiliating economic arrangement that is fitting for an abject vassal. It reminds one of the old saying, attributed to Lord Hastings Ismay, the first Secretary General of NATO, that the purpose of NATO is "to keep the Russians out, the Americans in, and the Germans down."

CHAPTER 13

CLIMATE CHANGE

Mind Virus: Extreme fear that an increasing amount of carbon dioxide in Earth's atmosphere, caused by humans burning fossil fuels, is causing the planet's surface temperature to rise to a dangerous level, change the climate, and do terrible things to nature and civilization.
Proposed Remedy: Enormous increase of government regulation and investment to switch from fossil fuels to "clean energies."

In 1824, the French physicist, Joseph Fourier postulated that the earth's atmosphere acts like a blanket, holding surface heat instead of allowing it to radiate immediately back into space. In 1856, Eunice Newton Foote, an American experimental scientist and women's rights campaigner, conducted experiments using cylinders containing different gases, and found that moist air and carbon dioxide (CO_2) trapped more heat than dry air. In 1859, John Tyndall, an Irish physicist and Alpine explorer, conducted lab experiments with different gases to determine if some absorb heat more than others. Using a custom ratio spectrophotometer, he showed that infrared radiation is absorbed or trapped by water vapor, carbon dioxide and methane, and passes through nitrogen and oxygen. In 1896, Swedish chemist Svante Arrhenius made the first quantitative prediction of warming from increased CO2. In 1901, the Swedish meteorologist Nils Gustaf Ekholm coined the term "greenhouse effect."

In 1955, a few years after John von Neumann proposed a preemptive nuclear strike on Russia, he wrote an essay for *Fortune* magazine titled "Can We Survive Technology?" in which he argued that man's technological and industrial prowess had reached such a large scale that it was unleashing forces that could disrupt the earth's natural equilibrium, and that this would likely cause a major crisis between 1955 and 1980. "When or how it will end—or to what state of affairs it will yield—nobody can say," he declared.

After acknowledging the risk of nuclear war that he'd helped to usher in, he proceeds to outline the risk of man-made climate change in what was probably the first time a major scientist issued this warning in a popular publication. His reflections on the possibility of human caused climate change are worth quoting in full, as they set forth the basic elements of a theory that ultimately became a widespread obsession and a major driver of public policy in the United States, Great Britain, and Europe.

> All major weather phenomena, as well as climate as such, are ultimately controlled by the solar energy that falls on the earth. To modify the amount of solar energy, is, of course, beyond human power. But what really matters is not the amount that hits the earth, but the fraction retained by the earth, since that reflected back into space is no more useful than if it had never arrived. Now, the amount absorbed by the solid earth, the sea, or the atmosphere seems to be subject to delicate influences. True, none of these has so far been substantially controlled by human will, but there are strong indications of control possibilities.
>
> The carbon dioxide released into the atmosphere by industry's burning of coal and oil—more than half of it during the last generation—may have changed the atmosphere's composition sufficiently to account for a general warming of the world by about one degree Fahrenheit. The volcano Krakatao erupted in 1883 and released an amount of energy by no means exorbitant. Had the dust of the eruption stayed in the stratosphere for fifteen years, reflecting sunlight away from the earth, it might have sufficed to lower the world's temperature by six degrees (in fact, it stayed for about three years, and five such eruptions would probably have achieved the result mentioned). This would have been a substantial cooling; the last Ice Age, when half of North America and all of northern and western Europe were under an ice cap like that of Greenland or

> Antarctica, was only fifteen degrees colder than the present age. On the other hand, another fifteen degrees of warming would probably melt the ice of Greenland and Antarctica and produce world-wide tropical to semi-tropical climate.

Following these opening reflections, von Neumann proceeds to make a series of vague assertions and wild speculations about how humans could, in theory, take measures to alter the climate to make it either cooler or warmer. The trouble, he claims, is making the determination about which alteration is more desirable. As he put it:

> What could be done, of course, is no index to what should be done; to make a new ice age in order to annoy others, or a new tropical, "interglacial" age in order to please everybody, is not necessarily a rational program. In fact, to evaluate the ultimate consequences of either a general cooling or a general heating would be a complex matter. Changes would affect the level of the seas, and hence the habitability of the continental coastal shelves; the evaporation of the seas, and hence general precipitation and glaciation levels; and so on. What would be harmful and what beneficial—and to which regions of the earth—is not immediately obvious. But there is little doubt that one could carry out analyses needed to predict results, intervene on any desired scale, and ultimately achieve rather fantastic effects.[1]

Von Neumann's assertion that "to evaluate the ultimate consequences of either general cooling or general heating would be a complex matter" is the crux of his reflections. The earth's climate is an extremely complex system composed of many interacting parts. Interactions among its various components may produce emergent and unpredictable results. Defining features of any complex system includes nonlinear relationships, feedback loops, adaptive responses, varied components, and multiple scales of time and space. Notable examples include the human body, ecosystems, economies, and the earth's climate. As in all complex systems, it is extremely difficult if not impossible to predict the consequences of a major human intervention in the system. Any human intervention therefore carries a high risk of unintended consequences.

Von Neumann understood this, but he nevertheless proffered the wild claim that one could "intervene on any desired scale and ultimately achieve rather fantastic results." As one says in German (the language of von Neumann's formal education) *er spinnt*. The expression literally means "he spins" (a yarn); metaphorically it means "he's talking crazy." It's possible that von Neumann believed his essay would be interpreted as low-resolution musings about theoretical possibilities that needed far more investigation and refinement before they could be considered scientific propositions. As it turned out, his vague musings have remained the basic tenets of "climate change" doctrine ever since. These include the following assertions:

- Human activity, primarily the burning of fossil fuels, is rapidly releasing a quantity of carbon dioxide (CO2) into the atmosphere that is trapping surface heat, causing the earth's surface to warm at an unnatural rate that will change its climate in a way that will be terrible for civilization and the natural world.
- Changes would affect the level of the seas, and hence the habitability of the continental coastal shelves; the evaporation of the seas, and hence general precipitation and glaciation levels; and so on.
- There is little doubt that one could carry out analyses needed to predict results, intervene on any desired scale, and ultimately achieve rather fantastic effects.

Of these assertions, the final remains totally unsupported by *any* evidence. Seventy-one years after von Neumann's essay was published, and forty-six years after he predicted the climate "crisis" would occur by 1980, no analyst has successfully predicted "what would be harmful and what beneficial—and to which regions of the earth"—about human-induced climate change. The entire notion remains as nebulous and ill-defined as it was in 1955. To von Neumann's credit, he entertained the possibility that human-induced climate change could be *beneficial*. He expressly mentions "a new tropical" or "interglacial" age, referring to the conspicuous fact that humans are currently enjoying the immeasurable benefit of living during a warm period in the earth's history, with no glaciers covering much of what is now the United States.

When thinking about climate change, it is critical to understand that the earth's climate has dramatically changed over geologic time, with significant mean surface temperature fluctuations. We are currently living in what geologists call the Holocene (from Greek: "entirely new") Epoch—that is, the last 11,700 years since the end of the last major ice age. Our epoch is defined by a relatively warm, stable climate that allowed for the development of human civilization, agriculture, and recorded history. The Holocene Epoch has been a brief warm spell within the context of the Quaternary Period that began 2.58 million years ago.[2] The Quaternary has been defined by a series of glaciations (ice ages), the evolution and dominance of modern humans, and the extinction of large mammals. The period is divided into two epochs: the Pleistocene and the Holocene. The Quaternary is the most recent period within the much longer time span of the Cenozoic Era that began 66 million years ago. The Cenozoic, sometimes called the "Age of Mammals," began after the Cretaceous-Paleogene extinction event wiped out non-avian dinosaurs, allowing mammals, birds, and flowering plants to diversify. The Cenozoic is the most recent era of the Phanerozoic Eon that began 538 million years ago. Known as the "visible life" eon, it is defined by the rapid diversification of complex organisms, the emergence of plants and animals, the colonization of land, and five major mass extinction events.

Prior to the Quaternary Period that began 2.58 million years ago, the earth was much warmer that it is today. In 2022, Professor Eske Willerslev and his team at the University of Cambridge and University of Copenhagen published in the journal *Nature* a study of two-million-year-old DNA from northern Greenland, revealing that the region was once home to mastodons, lemmings, and geese.[3] A report in the *Guardian* succinctly summarized the paper's key findings.

> The breakthrough in ancient DNA analysis pushes back the DNA record by one million years to a time when the Arctic region was 11–19C warmer than the present day. The analysis reveals that the northern peninsula of Greenland, now a polar desert, once featured boreal forests of poplar and birch trees teeming with wildlife.[4]

To reiterate, this extremely warm period ended with the advent of the Quaternary Glaciation period within which we are currently enjoying our Holocene respite. During the last ice age 20,000 years ago, tribes of humans managed to survive in North America and Europe, hunting bison and caribou, but they could not develop agriculture and civilization until the glaciers receded. During the last so-called "Glacial Maximum" that occurred about 20,000–25,000 years ago, North American glaciers are estimated to have pushed as far south as roughly 38° N latitude, extending into northern Missouri, Kansas, Illinois, Indiana, and Ohio.

In the Pacific Northwest, a massive ice sheet known as the Puget Lobe of the Cordilleran Ice Sheet covered what is now the Seattle area to a depth of approximately 3,000 to 3,300 feet.[5] While some readers might find it satisfying to contemplate the idea of Bill Gates's "Xanadu 2" 66,000-square-foot mansion near Seattle under 3,000 feet of ice, such a situation would have catastrophic consequences for human civilization in North America and Europe.

Many climatologists claim that current summer insolation in the Northern Hemisphere (specifically at high latitudes, around 65°N) is relatively low, near its minimum in the current glacial cycle.[6] Thus, based on Milankovitch cycles, North America should currently be headed for a new ice age. Milankovitch cycles are the collective, long-term variations in Earth's orbit and tilt that significantly influence the planet's climate over tens to hundreds of thousands of years. Named after Serbian astrophysicist Milutin Milanković, these cycles of eccentricity, obliquity, and precession determine the amount of solar radiation (insolation) reaching the earth, acting as the primary driver of ice ages and warmer interglacial periods. In other words, according to mainstream climatologists, current high greenhouse gas concentrations may be enabling our civilization to *continue* enjoying a relatively warm and glacier-free existence for far longer than the Milankovitch cycle would normally dictate.

The last ice age is thought to have ended about eleven thousand years ago primarily because of the Milankovitch cycle that resulted in more summer sunlight in the Northern Hemisphere.[7] Obviously, the glaciers didn't rapidly melt because of human carbon emissions, given that the entire human population on Earth at the time is estimated to have been just a few million hunter gatherers. Bearing this is mind, consider the following misleading statement in a 2022 article published by on the US Climate.gov website (a division of the National Atmospheric and Oceanic Administration).

> The increase [of carbon dioxide] between the year 1800 and today is 70 percent larger than the increase that occurred when Earth climbed out of the last ice age between 17,500 and 11,500 years ago, and it occurred 100–200 times faster.[8]

The article implies it was increasing carbon dioxide, and not the Milankovitch cycle, that caused the last ice age to end. While large amounts of carbon dioxide were released from the melting ice, this wasn't the primary driver, and much of this carbon dioxide was reabsorbed by the rapid growth of forests following the glaciers' retreat.

That the sun is the key determinant of air temperature at any location on Earth is obvious to anyone who has visited Canada during the summer and winter months. Saskatoon, Canada experienced a record high temperature on 105.1 degrees Fahrenheit on June 6, 1988, and a record low of minus 58.0 degrees Fahrenheit on February 1, 1893. Saskatoon is cold in the winter when the earth's 23.5-degree axial tilt causes the northern hemisphere to lean away from the sun, resulting in lower-angle, less intense solar radiation. It is hot in the summer because the same axial tilt causes it to lean toward the sun, resulting in more direct and intense solar radiation. While other factors play a role, its position relative to the sun is by far the dominant factor.

Carbon dioxide makes up approximately 0.04 percent of the earth's atmosphere. Over the course of geologic time, the amount of carbon dioxide in the earth's atmosphere is estimated to have significantly fluctuated. During the early Paleozoic Era, particularly the Cambrian period (about 500 million years ago) carbon dioxide levels are estimated to have been fifteen times higher than they are today, primarily from the era's intense volcanic activity combined with a scarcity of terrestrial plants and trees to draw the gas from the atmosphere and sequester it.[9] Our current Holocene era is marked by far less volcanic activity and much of the earth is now covered with plants and trees.

Seventy-one years after von Neumann's warning in *Fortune,* scientists are no closer to being able to "predict results, intervene on any desired scale, and ultimately achieve rather fantastic effects" than they were in 1955. No one can measure or predict how aggressive measures taken to reduce greenhouse gas emissions by any nation or federal state will alter the magnitude and rate of climate change, or how such an alteration will produce negative or positive effects on human civilization, or when any of these effects will occur in a measurable way. Additionally, no one can measure how much *their* reduction of human emissions will contribute to mitigating climate change compared to fluctuations of natural emission sources such as volcanoes and forest fires.

For example, according to a 2022 study conducted by researchers at UCLA and the University of Chicago, a nearly two-decade effort by Californians to cut their emissions of planet-warming carbon dioxide may have been erased by the 2020 California wildfire season.[10] If this study's estimate is accurate, it indicates that the most rational intervention that could be taken by California officials is to do a better job of forestry management, which would reduce carbon emissions far more than, for example, phasing out useful and efficient natural gas stoves to replace them with electric stoves, fueled by electricity largely produced by natural gas–fired power plants.

Even if a nation could measure and predict the effects of its contribution to greenhouse gas reduction, this could only yield a rational policy if all large nations made a proportional reduction. This is especially true of nations such as India and China that have enormous human populations that aspire to develop their economies to achieve the same living standards as Western industrialized nations. While the governments of India and China have acknowledged the need to reduce greenhouse gas emissions, neither nation has adhered to uniform emissions standards of an international climate protocol. Instead, they have agreed to the framework of Common but Differentiated Responsibilities (CBDR)—a euphemistic way of saying that they can continue to emit far more CO_2 than developed nations such as Germany due to their status as developing nations. Anyone who has studied the conduct of nation states understands that there are no realistic mechanisms for ensuring that all nations strictly adhere to making major financial and economic sacrifices for the greater good of humanity.

Within the same nation state, political and economic priorities may dramatically shift over time due to periodic economic downturns, financial problems, and with each new government that comes into office. Within the developed nations of the West, the costs of legally mandated measures to reduce greenhouse gas emissions are disproportionately borne by the working and middle classes, for whom increases in food and energy costs are burdensome. For example, servicemen who work in construction and infrastructure maintenance must drive utility vehicles such as pickup trucks that necessarily consume more fuel to accelerate larger masses.

In other words, the notion that humanity must wage war on climate change is based on fantastically wild speculations that cannot be evaluated by the scientific method. This method requires that a theory be testable and falsifiable, and that its purported effects be measurable, reproducible, and predictable. Not a single claim made about human induced climate change can be proven, falsified, measured, or predicted. A nation or a federal state within a nation may make enormous sacrifices and investments in carbon reduction, but the results of their contribution to combatting "climate change" cannot be measured. If the climate remains stable, the people who made the effort can congratulate themselves for their contribution. If they continue to be afflicted with unusually hot summers and other apparent climate disturbances, they will be told that their efforts weren't enough.

Most climatologists agree that Earth's current global mean surface temperature of 59 degrees Fahrenheit is cooler than most of the Phanerozoic Eon (last 485 million years), in which temperatures often exceeded 71.6 degrees Fahrenheit.[11] However, many climatologists hasten to assert that the current rate of warming—hypothesized to be caused by human activity—is faster than any other time in our current Cenozoic Era.

And so, the people of the world's 195 nations are told that if humanity does not take immediate and aggressive action to reduce carbon and other greenhouse gas emissions, a broad range of ill-defined but apparently terrible things will happen to the earth and all its inhabitants in the near (though unspecified) future. As former Vice President Al Gore put it in his 2006 documentary film, *An Inconvenient Truth,* the world is facing "a rising, imminent danger" of climate change, and the planet is facing a "fever."

Given that "the future" is an infinite span of time while a human life is short one, it is impossible for any generation to comprehend how this "imminent danger" is likely to affect their lives or even the lives of their children and grandchildren. In 2006, Al Gore predicted a sea-level rise of up to 20 feet, increased hurricane intensity, and widespread climate-driven refugee crises. As of this writing in 2026, none of these specific predictions that pertain to human civilization have happened, just as von Neumann's 1955 prediction of a crisis by the year 1980 didn't happen.

CHAPTER 14

THE CLIMATE-INDUSTRIAL COMPLEX

For the last twenty years, Al Gore has been a key figure in what Danish political scientist Bjørn Lomborg calls the "climate-industrial complex"—that is, an alliance between governments, corporations, lobbyists, and non-governmental organizations (NGOs) that profit and gain power from policies and investments in combatting "climate change." Corporations in the renewable energy, carbon trading, and insurance sectors benefit from subsidies, new regulations, and disaster recovery contracts. Politicians and lobbyists use climate change to justify increased regulation, taxation, and government spending. NGOs, academics, and researchers obtain vast climate-related funding and therefore have a vested financial interest in maintaining fear of climate change to keep donations and grants flowing.

In a May 22, 2009, opinion piece in the *Wall Street Journal* titled "The Climate-Industrial Complex," Lomborg wrote:

> We are told that very expensive carbon regulations are the only way to respond to global warming, despite ample evidence that this approach does not pass a basic cost-benefit test. We must ask whether a "climate-industrial complex" is emerging, pressing taxpayers to fork over money to please those who stand to gain. This phenomenon will be on display at the World Business Summit on Climate Change in Copenhagen this weekend. . . . The opening keynote address is to be delivered by Al Gore, who actually

> represents all three groups: He is a politician, a campaigner and the chair of a green private-equity firm invested in products that a climate-scared world would buy. Naturally, many CEOs are genuinely concerned about global warming. But many of the most vocal stand to profit from carbon regulations. The term used by economists for their behavior is "rent-seeking." The world's largest wind-turbine manufacturer, Copenhagen Climate Council member Vestas, urges governments to invest heavily in the wind market. It sponsors CNN's "Climate in Peril" segment, increasing support for policies that would increase Vestas's earnings. A fellow council member, Mr. Gore's green investment firm Generation Investment Management, warns of a significant risk to the U.S. economy unless a price is quickly placed on carbon.[1]

Even more absurd than all the wild claims about human-induced climate change have been the ridiculous, counterproductive, wasteful, environmentally destructive, and fraudulent measures that have been taken to mitigate it. Consider the electric car craze and the hundreds of billions of tax incentives, subsidies, and investments that have been poured into it. In the United States, instead of major incentives to drive smaller and more fuel-efficient cars such as sedans and station wagons instead of heavy SUVs, we were told that electric vehicles such as the Tesla Model X were the way forward for reducing greenhouse gas emissions.

And yet, a 2017 study conducted by the Swedish Environmental Research Institute found that producing a large EV battery emitted 150–200 kilograms of carbon dioxide equivalent per kilowatt-hour. This production cost was estimated to be comparable to the emissions produced by driving an F-150 pickup truck for five years or 250,000 kilometers.[2] The study was criticized for overstating these inefficiencies, with counterclaims made that manufacturing and power generation processes were rapidly becoming more efficient.

Nevertheless, there is no getting around that fact that it requires vast amounts of energy to extract lithium, cobalt, nickel, manganese, graphite, and copper, refine them, ship them to North America, and turn them into an EV battery, ranging in size from 1,000 to 2,000 pounds of finished material. It wasn't so long ago that metal mining was widely regarded as one of man's most environmentally devastating activities. Copper, cobalt, and lithium results in massive toxic waste, high water usage in arid regions, and significant carbon emissions. Smelting and processing releases heavy metals, sulfur dioxide, and creates slag waste, which leads to acid rain and air pollution.

In California, which has enacted plans to phase out the sale of new internal combustion engine (ICE) passenger vehicles by 2035, forty to fifty percent of the state's electrical power is generated by natural gas-fired power plants, and it will require far more electrical power—possibly up to eight five percent more—to convert the state's car fleet from ICE to EV. Considering all the above, California's Advanced Clean Cars II regulation that characterizes EVs as "zero-emission" is completely misleading.

Gasoline and diesel are extremely energy dense fuels that are easy to ship and store in large quantities. America's vast network of gas stations was constructed, and the requisite fossil fuels required to do so were burned, long ago. This was one of the major factors that Toyota Chairman Akio Toyoda considered when he concluded that hybrid vehicles were far more sensible for the environment than EVs. A hybrid such as the Toyota Prius greatly increases the fuel efficiency of the small, internal combustion engine by assisting it with a small, electric motor drawing from a small electric battery that is recharged whenever the driver applies the brakes. Toyoda argues that one electric vehicle may produce the same lifecycle carbon impact as three hybrids.[3]

Hybrid cars also do not require new infrastructure for fueling. Consider that building a nationwide network of charging stations in the United States, sufficient to support 33 million electric vehicles by 2030, will require massive quantities of construction materials and electrical grid upgrades. The project will require over 28 million charging ports ranging from home Level 1 to highway DC fast chargers.[4] The carbon footprint for this vast undertaking will be of an astronomical magnitude.

Generating electricity with wind turbines is another conspicuous example of an inefficient, environmentally harmful, and wasteful industry that has been erected with the purported goal of reducing carbon emissions. Currently in the United States, wind turbines generate approximately ten percent of the nation's total US utility-scale electricity. The claim that these gigantic industrial structures produce "zero emissions" is highly misleading.

First, there's the site preparation with excavators and bulldozers (burning diesel). Turbines in the one-to-two-megawatt range typically use 130 to 240 cubic meters of concrete for the foundation. This requires excavating and hauling cement, sand, and gravel for concrete, all of which require burning diesel. The concrete must then be hauled to site by cement trucks, burning more diesel. Then comes the massive, energy intensive business of building and hauling the gigantic turbine blades. This requires mining, refining, and manufacturing all the steel for the blades and the copper and aluminum for the transmission cables. Miles of the latter must be run underground—in trenches dug by diesel-powered excavators—to connect the turbines, often located in remote areas, to the power grid.

Then there's the terrible inefficiency of wind turbines, which only deliver significant power to the grid for a relatively small period per year. During winter storms in the northern hemisphere, when power is needed most to heat homes, wind turbine blades are inclined to icing. During the winter of 2014, an image circulated on the internet of a helicopter de-icing a wind turbine was taken at the Uljabuouda wind farm in Arjeplog, Sweden. During the February 2021 winter storm that struck Texas, the image was misleadingly circulated on the internet as evidence of state's absurd reliance on wind turbines to generate electricity. While this specific representation was misleading, it is nevertheless a fact that wind turbine blades are susceptible to icing when power is needed most, and there are multiple recorded instances of helicopter operators being called to spray de-icing agents on the gigantic blades. The blades have a lifespan of around twenty years, at which point they must be dismantled, hauled off and buried.

As Greenpeace co-founder, Dr. Patrick Moore, has persuasively argued, because wind and solar power are frequently interrupted, they cannot serve the power grid for much of the time. To achieve steady power delivery to the grid therefore requires equipping wind and solar infrastructure with enormous battery capacity. Using battery power to back up wind and solar not only generates an enormous carbon footprint for battery production; it also doesn't eliminate the frequently interrupted power generation from wind and solar. To compensate for power disruptions, it is necessary to build three times the total wind and solar capacity that can be achieved by constant production gas, coal, or nuclear power plants.[5]

In a controversial 2015 essay in the *New Yorker* titled "Carbon Capture," the renowned American author, Jonathan Franzen, argued that the overwhelming focus on global climate change was distracting attention from immediate, manageable, and local ecological issues, such as habitat loss and biodiversity conservation.[6] The essay resonated with me, because like Franzen, I am a lifelong lover and watcher of birds—a love that reminds me of Emily Dickenson's remark in an 1885 letter, "I hope you love birds, too. It is economical. It saves going to Heaven." Repeatedly in Franzen's essay, he references the environmental degradation and landscape blight caused by wind turbines, especially their destruction of wild birds. Because the human mind is overwhelmed by the prospect of global cataclysm from human-caused climate change, it struggles to consider immediate and local environmental impacts. "What were the eagles and the condors killed by wind turbines compared with the impact of rising sea levels on poor nations?" he asks rhetorically.

Franzen's essay drew widespread and harsh criticism from the climate-industrial complex and its propaganda division, which cannot tolerate a famous author talking about the significant environmental degradation caused by wind turbines. This begins with the conspicuous fact that they terribly mar the beauty of rural landscapes. Moreover, as Franzen mentions, wind turbines are extremely hard on migratory and non-migratory birds. The American Bird Conservancy recently estimated that 1.17 million birds, including endangered and protected species, are killed every year by wind turbines in the United States.[7]

I suspect the number is far higher and deliberately understated by wind power interests. As just one small example, the Auwahi Wind Farm on Maui, Hawaii, has acknowledged fatalities of birds and bats protected under the Migratory Bird Treaty Act (MBTA) and the Endangered Species Act (ESA) since operations began in 2012.[8] However, I know from a friend who regularly hikes the Lahaina Pali trail, which passes by the wind farm, that the number of birds and bats killed is far higher than what is conceded in published accounts. He told me that he regularly sees multiple dead birds and bats, even though the carcasses are gathered and concealed by personnel working for the wind farm. The Auwahi Wind Farm boasts that it provides power for ten thousand homes on Maui, but what contribution does this make to reducing human-caused climate change? How does the purported amount of C02 emissions spared by this wind farm compared to the greenhouse gas emissions from nearby Kīlauea, Maunaloa, Maunakea, Hualālai, and Kohala? These volcanoes release thousands of tons per day of water vapor, carbon dioxide, and sulfur dioxide. During a major eruption, Kīlauea emits between 30,000–40,000 tons per day of these gasses.[9]

The massive destruction of birds by terrestrial wind farms is an extremely odd twist in the environmental movement that initially concerned itself with wildlife and habitat conservation. Many pioneering environmentalists were bird lovers, and the first major conservation organization in American history was the National Audubon Society, founded in 1905 to stop the commercial slaughter of birds and the killing of herons for their feathers. Another pioneering environmental initiative was Greenpeace's 1975 "Save the Whales" campaign. I was reminded of this when I saw the news that on May 11, 2021, the Biden administration authorized the first major commercial offshore wind farm in US waters. The federal lease encompasses a vast stretch of coastal seabed between Martha's Vineyard and the New Jersey Shore for the construction of gigantic wind turbine farms.

According to a 2023 report by independent investigative journalist Linda Bonvie, the huge blitz of sonar for ocean bottom mapping may be responsible for an increasing number of whale and dolphin strandings along the affected shorelines.[10] The marine mammals flee from the maddening noise. Some dive to perilous depths; others run to the shoreline and beach themselves, suffering cruel and painful deaths. The climate-industrial complex seems to have lost all contact and feeling for actual nature—that is, the birds, whales, water, and sky, unmarred by the despoliation of man. The wind farms that are planned for the coast south of Martha's Vineyard and Nantucket are particularly distressing, as this is one of the richest coastal marine environments on Earth. For decades the cod were overfished, the oyster beds poisoned, and the whales were hunted almost to extinction. However, in recent years, all have made a comeback. Is it really time to wreck this environment again?

In yet another bizarre case of "destroying the environment in order to save it," in Scotland, the wind turbine industry has cut down an estimated 15.7 million trees since 2000, the equivalent of 1,700 per day, to clear sites for wind turbines. In 2023, rural affairs secretary Mairi Gougeon confirmed that nearly sixteen million trees had been felled to make room for the new project to make Scotland net zero over the next ten years.[11] During the 1980s, the environmental movement often expressed deep concern about the clear-cutting of tropical rain forests in Brazil and Southeast Asia. It therefore came as a surprise to many when the BBC reported on March 12, 2025, that a "new four-lane highway cutting through tens of thousands of acres of protected Amazon rainforest is being built for the COP30 climate summit in the Brazilian city of Belém."

> It aims to ease traffic to the city, which will host more than 50,000 people—including world leaders—at the conference in November. The state government touts the highway's "sustainable" credentials, but some locals and conservationists are outraged at the environmental impact. The Amazon plays a vital role in absorbing carbon for the world and providing biodiversity, and many say this deforestation contradicts the very purpose of a climate summit.[12]

Every year in Indonesia and Malaysia, millions of acres of forest are slashed and burned, much of it to clear land for palm oil plantations.[13] In 2022, the palm industry contributed $39 billion to the Indonesian economy. While this is a large sum of money for Indonesia, it is a small fraction of the $280 billion the western automotive industry invested in Electric Vehicle development in 2022. The carbon emission reduction of EVs—if there is any at all—is negligible compared to the one-two punch of burning millions of acres of forest and eliminating them as absorbers of carbon dioxide.

Of all industrialized nations that have been seized by "climate hysteria," Germany has proven to be the most irrational. Many of the German government's "climate" policies are so destructive that they strike the rational observer as an abnegation or even sabotage of the nation, its economy, and its environment. For decades, Germany has had an extremely productive manufacturing economy with an abundance of skilled, high-paying, creative, and rewarding jobs. A major contributing factor to its economic competitiveness has been its abundant supply of electrical power generated by its seventeen nuclear reactors with flawless safety records.

Despite these reactors producing vast amounts of clean energy—and despite none of them being in a tsunami zone—in 2011 the German government decided to shut them down after the Fukushima power plant in Japan was struck by a tsunami. As if this weren't weird enough, like Cortez burning his ships, the German government also decided to demolish the reactors in what struck many observers as something akin to a religious sacrifice. Only recently, as if awakening from an ecstatic trance, Chancellor Friedrich Merz announced that destroying Germany's perfectly good and safe and nuclear power plants had been a huge mistake.[14]

Since 2022, Germany has expressed a similar, suicidal impulse in its repudiation of its valuable natural gas infrastructure. As noted in the previous chapter, the German government didn't protest at all when agents of the US government bombed its Nord Stream pipeline and released approximately 778 million standard cubic meters of natural gas into the atmosphere.

On September 23, 2025, President Trump addressed the United Nations General Assembly in New York and made the following remarks about climate change.

> This "climate change," it's the greatest con job ever perpetrated on the world, in my opinion. All of these predictions made by the United Nations and many others, often for bad reasons, were wrong. They were made by stupid people that have cost their countries fortunes and given those same countries no chance for success. If you don't get away from this green scam, your country is going to fail.

Though his delivery was characteristically brash and provocative, he wasn't far off the mark in characterizing the climate-industrial-complex as perpetrating a confidence trick with many of its pronouncements. For example, in response to Trump's address, ABC News quoted a "climate scientist" named Adelle Thomas.

> For Adelle Thomas, a climate scientist who has published more than 40 studies and has a doctorate, climate change disasters are personal, too. A vice chair of the United Nations Intergovernmental

> Panel on Climate Change, the world's top body on climate science, Thomas is from the Bahamas and said she experienced firsthand "the devastation of the climate disaster" when Hurricane Sandy hit the Caribbean and New York City, the city Trump was speaking from, in 2012.[15]

This was a conspicuous example of the confidence trick of attributing dramatic weather events to human-caused climate change as though this is a proven fact and not speculation. In fact, there was nothing remarkable about Hurricane Sandy, a Category 3 hurricane (Category 1 equivalent when it made landfall in New York), that was weaker than hurricanes that struck New York City in 1821, 1893, and 1938. Hurricanes have been a regular occurrence in the Atlantic for all recorded history. Christopher Columbus noted two "violent hurricanes" in the years 1494 and 1495, the latter sinking three of his ships anchored in La Isabela harbor (now the Dominican Republic). Hurricanes were a headache for the Spanish Treasure Fleet, sinking multiple treasure galleons in the years 1622, 1715, 1733, and 1750.

By far the deadliest hurricane in history was the Great Hurricane of 1780, estimated to have killed twenty-two thousand in the Lesser Antilles when the storm blasted them between October 10 and 16.[16] The hurricane was likely a Category 5 when it struck Barbados with wind gusts that were estimated to have been as high as 200 miles per hour based on damage to solid structures and debris such as straw that was found embedded in tree trunks. Seasoned naval officers recorded their astonishment at the storm's strength. The hurricane then moved past Martinique, Saint Lucia, and Sint Eustatius, causing thousands of deaths. Because it struck during the American Revolution, it inflicted heavy damage and casualties on the British fleet that was on station in the area. The Great Hurricane eventually passed near Puerto Rico and over the eastern portion of Hispaniola, then turned to the northeast and was last observed on October 20, southeast of the Atlantic Coast of Canada.

CHAPTER 15

DEBILITATING YOUNG PEOPLE WITH FEAR OF CLIMATE CHANGE

In a 2024 survey of sixteen thousand US young people (aged sixteen to twenty-five), 85 percent reported being worried about the impact of climate change on their future. About 60 percent report that their anxiety about climate change impacts their daily functioning.[1] I sympathize with them, because for many years of my youth, I constantly fretted what was then characterized as "global warming." In 1988—just before my senior year in high school—I attended a college preparatory summer school at Tufts University. It was a blazing hot summer in Boston. Word went around our sweltering dorm building that it was the hottest June on record, and that our rooms weren't equipped with AC units because they'd never been necessary in the past. In fact, as I would learn years later, June of 1925 and 1952 were hotter. Frequent references to "record hot temperatures"—referencing historical records of air temperature measured by thermometers—never mention that reliable measurements have only been taken and recorded since about 1880, following major advances made in thermometer technology during the nineteenth century.[2] This means that "record hot temperatures" means very little.

During the summer of 1988, as part of my aspiration to broaden my horizons beyond my suburban upbringing in Dallas, I began dutifully reading the *New York Times*. On the morning of June 24, 1988, I read a front page story that seemed to explain why my dorm room was so stifling hot that I could scarcely sleep at night. The day before, NASA scientist James E. Hanson testified before the US Senate Committee on Energy and Natural Resources that rapid global warming was real and being caused by humanity's burning of fossil fuels. He cited the exceptionally hot weather at the time (it was 98 degrees that day in Washington, DC) as supporting evidence of his "high degree of confidence" in "a cause-and-effect relationship between the greenhouse effect and observed warming."[3]

I didn't understand his testimony. On the one hand, it seemed very gloomy. On the other hand, his numerical predictions—that the earth would warm around 0.7 degree or 1.0 degree Celsius by 2018, depending on carbon emission reductions—did not strike me as disastrous. He seemed to believe that this small amount of warming overall could cause extreme temperature swings in particular regions. Judging by the apparent gravity of this testimony, I got the impression that doom awaited us. I feared that much of the earth would soon become intolerably hot for humans, animals, and plants. This was dreadful news, and I was seized by the passionate desire to try to do something about it.

Upon my return to Dallas later that summer, I became an insufferable preacher about global warming and a proselytizer of others to join my crusade against it. To my maternal grandfather and uncle, who'd both worked in the Texas petroleum industry their entire lives, I announced the imperative to ditch our dependency on oil and gas and *immediately* adopt alternative energy forms. During the fall semester of my senior year, I founded a new environmental organization at my high school called the Salvation of the Earth Club, and I spoke with great fervor about the need to save our planet. Only years later did I realize that I was in the grip of something akin to religious passion. During the spring semester of my senior year, when I should have been having fun with friends during those special and fleeting few months, I was preoccupied with apocalyptic thoughts and made myself a bore.

During my freshman year at Boston University, I got a part-time job volunteering as a fundraiser at a Greenpeace office located about five miles from campus. On a few evenings per week, after my last class of the day, I rode my bike to the office and manned a phone, calling poor souls trying to enjoy their family dinners, preaching the need to help the cause *before it was too late*.

In retrospect, it seems to me that the two years I spent worrying about the end of the world hindered my personal, intellectual, social growth. During these formative years, young people should focus on developing their mind and character, and not fretting about gigantic global forces over which they have no control. As Jonathan Franzen pointed out in his 2015 New Yorker essay, "Carbon Capture," young people who get preoccupied with climate change resemble the young Alvy Singer in Woody Allen's 1976 comedy, *Annie Hall*. As a boy, Alvy stopped doing his homework after he read that the universe is expanding. Given that the world would break apart someday, he reasoned there was no point in doing his homework. His mother didn't buy it.

"You're here in Brooklyn!" she said. "Brooklyn is not expanding!"

I was reminded of my own youthful anxiety about climate change when I watched Gretha Thunberg's "How dare you?" speech to the United Nations Climate Action Summit in New York City on September 23, 2019. At the time, she was only sixteen years old, and her affect struck me as that of a deeply tormented adolescent. I wondered if it was morally wrong, perhaps even abusive, to fill a teenager's mind with such dread about her future, especially given the extreme flimsiness of the evidence on which her dread was predicated.

In rare but conspicuous cases, fear of climate change can result in extremely pathological behavior such as acts of climate change vandalism perpetrated by activist groups like Just Stop Oil and Letzte [Last] Generation. These organizations have targeted famous works of art to shock the public and demand government action. In recent years, vandals have thrown food and paint and glued themselves to the frames of icons of Western Civilization such as Leonardo's *Mona Lisa*, Vermeer's *Girl with a Pearl Earring*, and Van Gogh's *Sunflowers*. Though the paintings were shielded by protective glass, the symbolic violence still shocked onlookers. In October 2022, a Just Stop Oil activist glued his shaved head to the glass covering *Girl with a Pearl Earring*, while his companion glued his hand to the wall.

"How do you feel when you see something beautiful and priceless being apparently destroyed before your very eyes?" he asked the onlookers. "Do you feel outraged? Good. That is that same feeling when you see the planet being destroyed before our very eyes."[4]

While most of us naturally regard these vandals with loathing and a desire to see them severely punished, we must strive to bear in mind that they are genuinely terrified that the planet will soon be "destroyed before our very eyes." I was never that crazy, but once in the autumn of 1989, I made an embarrassing spectacle of myself at the Tower Records on Massachusetts Avenue in Boston. In those days, everyone who bought a CD was required to carry it out of the store in a single-use plastic bag. The sidewalk trashcan directly outside was always overflowing with bags that had been used for five seconds. Disgusted by the waste of it, I once gathered up several hundred, walked into the store, and deposited them on the checkout counter to the shock and dismay of the clerk.

Twenty-five years after I finished my education in Boston, I visited the city and my summer haunts on Cape Cod. My old friend's beach house was still there, unflooded by rising sea levels, the weather was cool enough to warrant wearing a sweater in the evenings, and the pine and oak woods looked the same. A major difference, according to a fellow windsurfer, was that the gray seal population had rebounded and was drawing in great white sharks, which made him a bit nervous while windsurfing. Likewise, after almost collapsing in the 1990s, the Cape's oyster beds had staged an astonishing revival since 2000.

In his 2010 TED Talk about climate change, Bill Gates opened by presenting the audience with an equation of what he claimed to be the primary factors causing human-induced climate change. On a gigantic projection screen appeared his formula $CO_2 = P \times S \times E \times C$, where *P* is population, *S* is services per person, *E* is energy per service, and *C* is CO_2 emitted per unit of energy. He then asserted that the challenge confronting humanity is to reduce carbon emissions to zero by 2050. He emphasized that cutting emissions by half isn't enough—that only zero carbon emissions would prevent severe environmental and economic impacts. He then proceeded to an exposition of how to reduce each of the factors, starting with *P* for population.

"First, we've got population," he said. "The world today has 6.8 billion people. That's headed up to about nine billion. Now, if we do a really great job on new vaccines, health care, reproductive health services, we could lower that by, perhaps, 10 percent or 15 percent."[5]

One wonders how Gates imagined that vaccines—which are supposed to prevent people from dying of infectious diseases—will help to reduce the world's population. It was also notable that he linked vaccines not only to public health, but also to his other great project for humanity and planet Earth—reducing carbon emissions. After making this strange statement, he explained the imperative to invest in technologies for generating power that do not require burning fossil fuels. He then asserted that, because markets forces aren't sufficient to make the changes fast enough, governments must fund research and provide other incentives for clean energy innovation. In other words, humanity had to make astronomical investments in reducing carbon emissions to zero or it would perish.

In 2015, Gates put his money where his mouth is by making multi-billion-dollar investments in clean energy technologies, mostly through his Breakthrough Energy Ventures (BEV) and Breakthrough Energy Catalyst. He also invested in $650 million in TerraPower for developing next-generation, small modular nuclear reactors. Though $2 billion was an impressive sum for Gates to invest in clean energy technologies, it was small potatoes compared to the $2 trillion the Biden administration proposed investing in the Green New Deal—a government funded program for overhauling US infrastructure, transportation, and housing with clean energy technologies. Though the administration fell short of persuading Congress to allocate $2 trillion, its key Congressional allies supported the Inflation Reduction Act that included $369 billion for climate and energy security. Apparently because John Podesta had done such a splendid job of allocating US government bailout funds for his friends in the banking industry, he was brought in to oversee the allocation of the Inflation Reduction Act's $369 billion in climate funding.[6]

In 2022, Bill Gates met with Senator Joe Manchin and others to build support for the Act. He frequently spoke with the Biden administration about climate policy, exhorting the administration to fund clean-energy technologies. to develop a "National Institutes of Energy Innovation" (modeled after the National Institutes of Health), and to offer tax credits for emerging technologies. Shortly after Biden took office, Gates publicly stated that he frequently spoke with the president about climate change and the pandemic.

Since 2022, Bill Gates and Microsoft (in which he and his foundation still hold large positions) have made major investments in companies developing artificial intelligence (AI) companies. For example, since 2019, Microsoft has invested $14 billion in OpenAI. In 2024, the International Energy Agency (IEA) estimated that data center electricity consumption could more than double by 2030, with AI as the primary driver.[7] In late 2024, the Department of Energy (DOE) announced that AI-driven data centers could consume up to 12 percent of total US electricity by 2028, up from approximately 4.4 percent in 2024.

In 2025, it became increasingly clear that alternative "clean energy" sources are not sufficient to meet the growing electricity demand to power AI data centers. Until new nuclear power plants are built, only natural gas and coal fired power plants will be able to meet the increasing demand. On October 28, 2025, Bill Gates published an essay titled "Three tough truths about climate" on his personal blog *Gates Notes*, just before the COP30 climate conference was held from November 10–22, 2025, in Belém, Brazil. The essay—a stunning volte face from Gate's 2010 TED Talk—contains the following highlights.

> There's a doomsday view of climate change that goes like this:
>
> *In a few decades, cataclysmic climate change will decimate civilization. The evidence is all around us—just look at all the heat waves and storms caused by rising global temperatures. Nothing matters more than limiting the rise in temperature.*
>
> Fortunately for all of us, this view is wrong. Although climate change will have serious consequences—particularly for people in the poorest countries—it will not lead to humanity's demise. People will be able to live and thrive in most places on Earth for the foreseeable future. . . . Although wind and solar have gotten cheaper and better, we don't yet have all the tools we need to meet the growing demand for energy without increasing carbon emissions. . . . Climate change is a serious problem, but it will not be the end of civilization.[8]

And just like that, one of the most powerful purveyors of climate alarmism for the last fifteen years proclaimed that there is nothing to be so alarmed at after all.

CHAPTER 16

THE CORONAVIRUS DISEASE OF 2019

Mind Virus: Extreme fear of COVID-19.
Proposed Remedy: Government lockdowns, suppression of early treatment, masking and social distancing mandates, vaccine mandates, and transfer of hundreds of billions of public funds to purveyors of countermeasures, especially vaccine manufacturers.

John Leonard Orr was a highly esteemed fire captain and arson investigator in Glendale, California. Unbeknownst to his colleagues, he was also the most active serial arsonist in US history, setting around two thousand fires over a thirty-year period. Before he was finally caught in 1991, he was widely regarded as a "fire genius" and "sage" for his uncanny ability to determine the cause of fires. The story of the Coronavirus Disease of 2019 (COVID-19) reminds me of John Leonard Orr.

In 1965, the British virologist David Arthur John Tyrrell—director of the Common Cold Unit—discovered a new virus. Under an electron microscope, the nucleocapsid appeared to be garlanded with a crown-like structure. As he related in his book *Cold Wars: The Fight Against the Common Cold*:

> We looked more closely at the appearance of the new viruses and noticed that they had a kind of halo surrounding them. Recourse

> to a dictionary produced the Latin equivalent, corona, and so the name coronavirus was born.[1]

As the title of his book indicates, Tyrrell regarded coronaviruses as pathogenic insofar as they caused the common cold—the most common infectious disease in humans. Reviewing the historical chronicles of infectious disease, it seemed that the deadly respiratory viral pandemics documented in the past were more likely caused by influenza viruses than coronaviruses.

However, about twenty years after Tyrrell first described human coronaviruses, a gifted and industrious microbiologist named Ralph Baric began obsessively studying coronaviruses and looking for additional ways in which they could cause disease, especially by creating recombinant variants of a coronaviruses—a process at which he became increasingly adept. Baric pursued this line of inquiry between 1985 and 2002. In April 2002, he and his colleagues at the University of North Carolina filed a patent application for their *Methods for Producing Recombinant Coronavirus.* The contents of the patent application revealed that he had come a long way in discovering how to manipulate coronaviruses in his lab. The purpose of his work, he claimed, was to create recombinant coronaviruses in order to develop vaccines against them.[2]

About seven months after Baric et al. filed their patent application, the first apparent cases of severe acute respiratory syndrome (SARS) were reported in Foshan, Guangdong China.[3] In February 2003, several people, including an American businessman, staying in a Hong Kong hotel, came down with the syndrome. The businessman then traveled to Hanoi, Vietnam, where he was hospitalized. Dr Carlo Urbani, a WHO scientist in Hanoi, visited the patient and suspected he was suffering from a novel disease. Urbani himself contracted the disease and died on March 29, 2003, in Bangkok. On April 1, 2003, the WHO announced:

> A new pathogen—a member of the coronavirus family never before seen in humans, is the cause of Severe Acute Respiratory Syndrome (SARS). The speed at which this virus was identified is the result of the close international collaboration of 13 laboratories from 10 countries.[4]

Between November 2002 and July 2003, SARS is estimated to have infected over 8,000 people from thirty countries and territories, and to have caused at least 774 deaths worldwide.

Looking back, it seems a remarkable coincidence that "a new pathogen—a member of the coronavirus family never before seen in humans"—emerged just seven months after Ralph Baric et al. filed their patent application for *Methods for Producing Recombinant Coronavirus.* Quickly this "new pathogen" became all the rage in pandemic planning circles, and a flood of NIH and private foundation money was made available to coronaviruses researchers like Ralph Baric at UNC Chapel Hill. In June 2005, Professor Baric gave at talk titled "Synthetic Coronaviruses. Biohacking: Biological Warfare Enabling Technologies" at a DARPA/MITRE-sponsored event in Washington, DC.[5]

In 2013— two years after influenza researchers Kawaoka and Fouchier made a splash by creating an H5N1 bird flu virus capable of respiratory transmission among ferrets—Professor Baric and a British zoologist named Peter Daszak, president of EcoHealth Alliance, teamed up to obtain a massive, multi-year NIH grant to study coronaviruses that purportedly had the potential to jump from bats into humans. Previously a wildlife conservation organization, EcoHealth under Daszak's leadership rebranded itself as an institution for studying emerging infectious disease threats in areas such as southern China. EcoHealth claimed that expanding human development is encroaching on tropical forest habitats of animal species that could be viral reservoirs. Its goal was to catalog these viruses and predict which ones are most likely to jump species and infect humans. Invoking the specter of the 2002 SARS outbreak in China, Daszak and Baric were able to sell their research project to US federal agencies, including the NIAID, USAID, and the US Army Medical Research Institute of Infectious Diseases (USAMRIID) in Fort Detrick, where alleged anthrax serial killer, Bruce Ivins had worked.[6]

The paper trail of Baric and Daszak's work to modify bat coronaviruses to make them infectious to humans is so vast that only a US Congressman or *New York Times* reporter could fail to see it. In 2013, Daszak and his collaborators at the Wuhan Institute of Virology published a paper (in *Nature*) titled "Isolation and Characterization of a Bat SARS-like Coronavirus That Uses the ACE2 Receptor."[7] As they put it, for the first time in history, they'd found two wild bat coronaviruses that would bind to the human ACE2 receptor. These two viruses were named,

1. Bat SL-CoV-WIV1
2. SHCOI4

Because these two virus species could (Daszak claimed) bind to human ACE2 receptors, they were (Daszak further claimed) of great interest to virologists who are in the business of anticipating which viruses could, in theory, mutate and evolve to infect and become transmissible among humans. Daszak's 2013 paper with his WIV colleagues Xing-Ye Ge and Zheng-Li Shi attracted much attention in virology circles.

The following year, Daszak and Baric obtained multiyear NIH funding for a research project under the grant title "Understanding the Risk of Bat Coronavirus Emergence." Continuing their work with Xing-Ye Ge and Zheng-Li Shi, Professor Baric performed gain-of-function work on the bat viruses SL-CoV WIV1 and SHCO15. They then published two papers in 2015 and 2016:

1. "A SARS-like Cluster of Circulating Bat Coronaviruses Shows Potential for Human Emergence" (published in *Nature Medicine*).[8]
2. "SARS-like WIV1-CoV Poised for Human Emergence" (published in *Proceedings of the National Academy of Sciences*, or *PNAS*).[9]

In the first paper, Baric and colleagues describe how they created a "chimeric virus expressing the spike of bat coronavirus SHC014 in a mouse-adapted SARS-CoV backbone" and named it SHC014-MA15. In the second paper, Baric and colleagues describe how they "also produced WIV1-CoV chimeric virus that replaced the SARS spike with the WIV1 spike within the mouse-adapted backbone" and named it WIV1-MA15. Regarding their first chimera (SHCOI4-MA15), Baric et al. made the bold claim that it

> . . . can efficiently use multiple orthologs of the SARS receptor human angiotensin converting enzyme II (ACE2), replicate efficiently in primary human airway cells and achieve *in vitro* titers

> equivalent to epidemic strains of SARS-CoV. Additionally, *in vivo* experiments demonstrate replication of the chimeric virus in mouse lung with notable pathogenesis.

These papers are just two pieces in the mountain of documentary evidence that SARS-CoV-2—the causative agent of COVID-19—was made in a laboratory by Ralph Baric and his Wuhan Institute of Virology colleagues. Another conspicuous document is Daszak's March 24, 2018, proposal to the Defense Advanced Research Projects Agency (DARPA), titled "Project DEFUSE: Defusing the Threat of Bat-borne Coronaviruses," seeking funding of $14,209,245. The reviewers at DARPA turned down the request because it proposed to do dangerous gain-of-function work on bat coronaviruses. Especially alarming was the proposal's statement:

> We will analyze all SARS-CoV gene sequences for . . . the presence of potential furin cleavage sites. SARS-CoV with mismatches in proteolytic cleavage sites can be activated by exogenous trypsin or cathepsin L. Where clear mismatches occur, we will introduce appropriate human specific cleavage sites and evaluate growth potential in Vero cell and HAE cultures.[10]

Two years later, when SARS-CoV-2—the causative agent of COVID-19—emerged, virologists all over the world marveled that its genome contained a sequence for a furin cleavage site. This is the component of the SARS-CoV-2 spike protein that enables the virus to dock onto human lung epithelial cells, thereby initiating the viral replication process. It is the key feature of SARS-CoV-2 that made it infectious to humans.

The official, stated reason for creating SARS-like bat coronaviruses in a lab was to develop countermeasures against them to protect humanity if such viruses were ever to evolve naturally to emerge in the wild. At a 2015 workshop hosted by the National Academies of Science, Daszak stated:

> Until an infectious disease crisis is very real, present, and at an emergency threshold, it is often largely ignored. To sustain the funding base beyond the crisis, we need to increase public understanding of the need for MCMs [Medical Countermeasures] such

> as a pan-influenza or pan-coronavirus vaccine. A key driver is the media, and the economics follow the hype. We need to use that hype to our advantage to get to the real issues. Investors will respond if they see profit at the end of process.[11]

In other words, in addition to being a beneficiary of the federal grant gravy train, Daszak also positioned himself to be an investment consultant in vaccine development for coronaviruses. During the years 2016–2019, multiple players in the bio-pharmaceutical complex prepared for the emergence or the lab release of a novel coronavirus. They correctly perceived that the opportunity to make a killing was in the offing.

CHAPTER 17

THE AMAZING PRESCIENCE OF ANTHONY FAUCI, STÉPHANE BANCEL, AND BILL GATES

As Dietrich Bonhoeffer observed in his 1943 essay "On Stupidity," the exertion of central power through fear and propaganda may render otherwise intelligent people "mindless tools" who are incapable of recognizing the evil that is being done right under their noses. The obvious corruption of the COVID-19 pandemic response brings Bonhoeffer's observation to mind.

On January 10, 2017, Dr. Anthony Fauci gave a speech at Georgetown University in which he stated that "there is no question that there will be a challenge to the coming administration in the arena of infectious diseases . . . there will be a surprise outbreak." About six months later, the new Wuhan National Biosafety Laboratory (BSL-4 lab) at the Wuhan Institute of Virology began conducting research on dangerous pathogens. The lab was conceived in 2003 during the SARS-CoV-1 outbreak and constructed by the French biotech company bioMérieux SA pursuant to a cooperative agreement between France and China.[1] The CEO of bioMérieux during the years 2007–2011 was Stéphane Bancel, who headed the company during the planning phase of the new lab and the training of its Chinese staff at bioMérieux's facilities in Lyon.

In 2011, it seemed like an extraordinary—perhaps even quixotic—decision for Bancel to leave his plum position at bioMérieux to become the CEO of the small, Cambridge, Massachusetts startup Moderna. At the time, the company had one employee and was exclusively focused on developing mRNA therapeutics.

"When I resigned from my last company, bioMérieux, to start on this journey at Moderna, I told my wife there was only a 5 percent chance it would work out," Bancel stated in a December 2020 interview.[2]

Two years after its founding, Moderna—short for "Modified RNA"—drew interest from DARPA, which awarded it a $25 million grant to develop messenger RNA (mRNA) therapeutics.[3] In 2016, Moderna began collaborating with the National Institute of Allergy and Infectious Diseases (NIAID) to develop mRNA vaccines against the SARS and MERS coronaviruses.[4] Moderna and its NIAID partner aspired to create the messenger RNA sequence of a protein of a pathogenic coronavirus and to inject it into the protein-making machinery of cells in the human deltoid muscle, instructing it to make this foreign protein.

A theoretical advantage of messenger RNA to produce viral proteins was that it could eliminate the so-called vaccine gap that had plagued earlier influenza vaccine developers—that is, the time between a new pandemic strain emerging and the mass production of vaccine by growing the new strain in embryonated chicken eggs. However, using mRNA to instruct human cells to produce a viral protein is different from a wild virus that invades a host cell and parasitically uses it to replicate. This action triggers the human immune system to respond with an array of complex biochemical processes—not merely antibody production—to neutralize the invader.

While creating an mRNA vaccine against a coronavirus seems like a godlike enterprise, an obvious shortcoming is that it would result in the production of only one viral protein (antigen) for the human immune system to recognize. This could impair the immune system's ability to recognize and respond to subsequent variants of the wild pathogen. Thomas Francis Jr. perceived this to be a form of imprinting of the first antigen on the immune system, and he (whose father was a Presbyterian minister) called it *original antigenic sin*. Closely related is the phenomenon of antibody-dependent enhancement, in which vaccine-induced antibody immune responses could result in *enhanced* SARS CoV- 2 acquisition or increased disease severity. The developers of Moderna's mRNA vaccine certainly understood this risk, as did Anthony Fauci, so it's hard to understand why they apparently ignored it.[5] At any rate, I suspect that Fauci understood all along that frequent boosters would need to be part of the product package.

On February 4, 2016, Moderna CEO Stéphane Bancel patented a 19-nucleotide genetic sequence that could, apparently, have value for an mRNA therapeutic application.[6] Six years later, this sequence was found to perfectly match the 19-nucleotide portion of the SARS-CoV-2 genome encompassing the 12-nucleotide furin cleavage site—the key feature of the virus that made it infectious to humans. The authors of the paper in which this finding was published (in the February 21, 2022, issue of *Frontiers in Virology)* stated, "Conventional biostatistical analysis indicates that the probability of this sequence randomly being present in a 30,000-nucleotide viral genome is 3.21×10^-11"—that is, 1 in 321 billion.[7] How did a Moderna patented, 19-nucleotide genetic sequence—one that codes for the feature that makes the virus infectious to humans—turn up in the SARS-CoV-2 genome? Shortly after the *Frontiers in Virology* paper was published, Fox News's Maria Bartiromo asked Bancel about this perfect match, and he replied that he would have his scientific team look into it.[8] No one, to my knowledge, has pursued this inquiry further.

Another organization that was, in 2016, positioning itself to invest in coronavirus vaccines was CEPI—Coalition for Epidemic Preparedness Innovations—founded principally by the Bill and Melinda Gates Foundation and the World Economic Forum. On November 16, 2016, CEPI published its "Preliminary Business Plan"—a prospectus that it sent out to donors and participants. Its executive summary set forth **The Challenge** and **The Opportunity:**

> **The Challenge**
> As the recent SARS, MERS, Ebola and Zika outbreaks demonstrate, new diseases can emerge quickly and unexpectedly. . . . To ensure robust and effective private sector participation in future outbreaks, industry will require a reliable risk/reward sharing

> system, a prioritization system for EIDs, and a clear development pathway for emergency-use vaccines.
>
> **The Opportunity**
>
> CEPI . . . will rationalize and accelerate research and development responses to new outbreaks by coordinating resources of industry, governments, philanthropic organizations and NGOs, prioritizing development goals, and facilitating the advanced development of vaccines for EIDs.[9]

The "Preliminary Business Plan" is dedicated entirely to vaccine development. Not once does the sixty-page document mention treating emerging infectious diseases. Treatment simply wasn't in the business plan. A prototype of CEPI—a nonprofit foundation that also serves as an investment vehicle—appears to have been by a 2011 proposal titled "Project Molecule" that Jeffrey Epstein submitted to Bill Gates and JPMorgan Chase for the creation of a donor-advised fund for investing in pandemic response technologies and financial instruments such as pandemic insurance.[10]

On August 30, 2019, the Gates Foundation purchased 3,038,674 ordinary shares of BioNTech—a Mainz, Germany startup developing mRNA therapeutics—for a pre-IPO price of $18 per share, totaling about $55 million.[11] On September 18, 2019—just nineteen days after the Gates Foundation took its huge position in BioNTech stock—a report titled "A World at Risk" was published by the Global Preparedness Monitoring Board, which was founded in 2018 by the World Bank Group and the World Health Organization. The report's title page is illustrated with an image of a coronavirus, and its text is an urgent call to action for the world to invest far more in preparedness for a respiratory viral pandemic. As the report states on page eight:

> A rapidly spreading pandemic due to a lethal respiratory pathogen (whether naturally emergent or accidentally or deliberately released) poses additional preparedness requirements. Donors and multilateral institutions must ensure adequate investment in developing innovative vaccines and therapeutics . . .[12]

The report mentions nothing about the need to invest in bolstering bio-laboratory safety. It warns about the threat of a lethal respiratory pathogen "accidentally or deliberately released," but its entire call to action is to invest a fortune to responding to such a pathogen instead of preventing it from being released in the first place. This was despite numerous urgent warnings from Rutgers University biology professor Richard Ebright and others that many of the world's bio-labs had a history of grave security lapses that were NOT being adequately addressed. In 2017, Professor Ebright expressed particular concern about the new BSL-4 lab in Wuhan, China.[13]

On October 19, 2019, the Johns Hopkins Center for Public Security, in collaboration with the Bill and Melinda Gates Foundation and the World Economic Forum, conducted a Pandemic Simulation Exercise. As Johns Hopkins described the event:

> The center's latest pandemic simulation, Event 201, dropped participants right in the midst of an uncontrolled coronavirus outbreak that was spreading like wildfire out of South America to wreak worldwide havoc.[14]

Many of the policy proposals presented at Event 201 for responding to the hypothetical coronavirus outbreak were put into real-world practice just three months later.

Another curious feature of the development timeline for Moderna's COVID-19 vaccine was a Material Transfer Agreement from NIAID/Moderna ("Provider") to Ralph Baric ("Research Recipient"). The Agreement specifies the transfer of "mRNA coronavirus vaccine candidates developed and jointly owned by NIAID and Moderna" to Dr. Baric "to perform challenge studies with the mRNA vaccine." The Agreement is signed by Ralph Baric on December 12, 2019—nineteen days before the Wuhan Municipal Health Commission announced the first cases of pneumonia that were subsequently identified as COVID-19.[15]

Why did NIAID and Moderna believe that Dr. Baric was equipped to challenge their "mRNA coronavirus vaccine candidates" that they were ready to deliver to him a month before the genome of SARS-CoV-2 was published on January 10, 2020? The timing of this agreement raises the suspicion that Dr. Baric already possessed samples of SARS-CoV-2 in his lab.

On January 10, 2020, the Chinese Centre for Disease Control and Prevention published the whole-genome sequences of SARS-CoV-2. On January 31, 2020, Secretary of Health and Human Services Alex Azar, declared COVID-19 a public health emergency. Pursuant to the 2005 PREP Act, liability immunity was granted to providers of "medical countermeasures" such as diagnostic tests and vaccines.

Between January 31 and February 8, 2020, Anthony Fauci exchanged a series of emails with Jeremy Farrar of the UK Wellcome Trust and the eminent virologists Kristian Anderson, Robert Garry, Eddie Holmes, and Michael Farzan about the genome of SARS-CoV-2. The virologists remarked in their private email correspondence that parts of the sequence "look engineered" and "are inconsistent with expectations from evolutionary theory." However, on March 6, 2020, the same virologists published a paper titled "The Proximal Origin of SARS-CoV-2" in *Nature Medicine* in which they stated the opposite. As they put it, "Our analyses clearly show that SARS-CoV-2 is not a laboratory construct or a purposefully manipulated virus."[16]

In early February, during the same time that Dr. Fauci and his virologist cronies were exchanging emails, Peter Daszak travelled to Wuhan, China as part of team commissioned by the WHO to investigate the origin of SARS-CoV-2. In March 2021, he and his team submitted their Joint Report on the Origins of the SARS-CoV-2 virus. The 120-page document gives the superficial impression of investigative rigor by presenting a long catalogue of genetic sequences of coronaviruses found in nature, but the researchers were unable to match any of them with SARS-CoV-2. Likewise, the researchers presented testing survey data on a wide array of wild animals and animals for sale at Chinese food markets, but were unable to find SARS-CoV-2 present in any of them.[17] In what may be the greatest act of willful blindness in history, the report dismisses the possibility of a lab leak as "extremely unlikely," even though the first cases of the illness were detected less than two miles from the Wuhan Institute of Virology, where Daszak's collaborators had been working on making bat coronaviruses transmissible to and among humans since 2013.

On February 27, 2020—twelve days before the WHO declared COVID-19 a pandemic, and before a single American had died of the illness—the *New York Times* published an Opinion piece by Peter Daszak titled "We Knew Disease X Was Coming. It's Here Now."[18] As he makes clear in the piece, Daszak already *knew*—down to the most precise detail—about the novel coronavirus's transmissibility and pathogenicity to humanity.

On March 16, 2020—just five days after the WHO declared SARS-CoV-2 to be the causative agent of the COVID-19 pandemic—NIAID issued a press release stating that it had commenced human trials of its mRNA-1273 vaccine, developed by NIAID scientists and their collaborators at Moderna. CEPI supported the manufacturing of the vaccine candidate for the Phase 1 clinical trial.[19]

CHAPTER 18

THERE'S NO BUSINESS LIKE PANDEMIC BUSINESS

The laboratory creation of SARS-CoV-2 (the causative agent of COVID-19) and the deliberate concealment of its origin are two elements of the greatest organized crime in history. Equally fraudulent and dangerous was the official pandemic response to this manmade disaster. The response was largely directed by the US Department of Defense and the Department of Health and Human Services. Their strategy consisted of the following components.

- Use mainstream media and social media to terrify the people of COVID-19.
- Impose lockdowns, social distancing, and masking to reinforce fear with isolation and distress that cherished social norms and freedoms have been lost.
- Ruthlessly suppress all early treatment modalities that could ease anxiety about the illness with the hopeful thought it can be treated at home.
- Fraudulently claim that natural immunity is inferior to vaccine immunity.
- Present a new and experimental genetic technology called Messenger RNA (mRNA) "vaccines" as the Liberator and Savior of humanity that will enable life to go back to normal.

- Aggressively censor anyone who questions the safety and efficacy of the experimental vaccines. Harass, fire, sue, and defame medical doctors who question the vaccine's safety and efficacy. Strip them of their medical licenses and board certifications.

Every element of the pandemic response was designed to maximize distress, disruption, and the feeling of being imprisoned until the new mRNA vaccines were rolled out. In March, US government agencies launched a campaign to "flood the zone"—that is, continuously broadcast messaging in all media channels with terrifying representations of the viral illness and the mortal threat it purportedly posed to the entire population, including the young and fit. This kind of propaganda campaign was prescribed by public relations experts who participated at the Event 201 coronavirus pandemic simulation in October 2019. The simulation planning board member, Matthew Harrington, CEO of Edelman global communications, expressly spoke about the need "to flood the zone."

On March 24, 2020, Rick Bright at BARDA and Janet Woodcock at the FDA took action to prevent doctors from prescribing, and pharmacies from dispensing hydroxychloroquine for early home treatment.[1] Bright's actions were part of a ruthless and coordinated campaign to suppress all early treatment modalities for COVID-19, including FDA-approved drugs such as hydroxychloroquine and ivermectin, which have some of the best safety profiles in all of medicine. On March 25, 2020, the New York State Department of Health issued a directive to nursing homes to accept residents returning from hospitals, including those who are coronavirus positive, which resulted in a massive spike of nursing home COVID-19 mortality.[2] This perverse and criminal decision helped to amplify fear, with media reports of Federal Emergency Management Agency (FEMA) deploying eighty-five refrigerated trucks to serve as makeshift morgues in New York City.

On March 27, 2020, Congress passed the Coronavirus Aid, Relief, and Economic Security (CARES) Act a $2.2 trillion economic stimulus bill equivalent to ten percent of US GDP. That the Act was hundreds of pages long raises the suspicion that the basic language had already been drafted, possibly for the event of a virulent influenza pandemic. To comply with the constitutional requirement that revenue-raising bills originate in the

House, Congress used H.R. 748—a bill originally introduced in January 2019 regarding tax repeals—as a shell. The authors removed the original language and replaced it with the three-hundred-plus page coronavirus relief package that President Trump signed on the same day. Hastily passed within the context of an emergency, the CARES Act is reminiscent of the Emergency Economic Stabilization Act of 2008 for bailing out Wall Street.

Shortly after NIAID and Moderna announced that their COVID-19 vaccine candidate, mRNA-1273 was entering human trials, Pfizer-BioNTech announced they were developing their own version of an mRNA vaccine. In July 2020—months *before* the vaccine had completed clinical trials—the Department of Defense and Department of Health and Human Services purchased an initial 100 million doses of the Pfizer product.[3] This was just one of many indications that the vaccine *would* receive an Emergency Use Authorization (EUA) approval, and that the clinical trials were largely a formality.

In the years that followed, the US government made six different bulk purchases from Pfizer, totaling 655 million doses, and five bulk purchases from Moderna, totaling 566 million doses, for a total of 1.2 billion doses. The European Union made even larger bulk purchases of these vaccines, with EU Commission President, Ursula von der Leyen, secretly negotiating the terms with Pfizer CEO Albert Bourla in April 2021—a scandal that came to be known as Pfizergate.[4] In 2021, Pfizer's COVID-19 vaccine generated $36.781 billion in revenue, thereby becoming the highest-selling pharmaceutical product in history.

With the governments of the world bulk purchasing these products and then forcing them on the citizens, Pfizer and Modern were relieved of the usual necessity of having to market the shots. The companies simply unloaded hundreds of millions of doses on governments, who assumed responsibility for distributing them and persuading the public to take them. The arrangement is exactly what the pharmaceutical industry wanted when it persuaded Congress to pass the PREP act—that is, a gigantic, liability free bonanza for their experimental products in the event of a public health emergency.

That the official pandemic response consisted of multiple elements of fraud was revealed by the following facts (just to name a few).

- By the end of March 2020, it was obvious that the respiratory viral illness had spread all over the world and was therefore far beyond containment, as Swedish state epidemiologist, Anders Tegnell, pointed out in a March 28, 2020, *New York Times* interview.[5] The initial stated rationale for lockdowns was that they could slow the rate of transmission, or "flatten the curve," to preserve hospital capacity. However, in many jurisdictions—even in those without strained hospital capacity—initial lockdowns were greatly extended with no clear rationale.
- By the end of April 2020, it was clear that COVID-19 was a highly risk-stratified illness that posed the greatest risk to the elderly as well as people suffering from obesity, prediabetes, and diabetes. Conversely, the illness posed little risk of hospitalization and death for otherwise healthy people under fifty, and no risk for healthy young people and children. Studies up to mid-2022 showed a median Infection Fatality Rate (IFR) of 0.0003 percent for ages 0–19, 0.002 percent for 20–29, 0.011 percent for 30–39, and 0.035 percent for 40–49.[6]
- Lockdowns were justified on the grounds of protecting the old and vulnerable, but their true objective was to slow down the rate of young people contracting the illness, discovering that it was mild, and acquiring natural immunity before the vaccine was rolled out.
- FDA-approved drugs such as hydroxychloroquine + azithromycin, as well as ivermectin, helped to reduce disease severity by impairing viral replication, reducing inflammation, and reducing hemagglutination (micro clotting). The deliberate withholding of these and other drugs from high-risk COVID-19 patients was an act of criminal negligence at best.[7]
- By the time the COVID-19 vaccines were rolled out to the public in the spring of 2021, at least 20 percent of the population had already been infected and recovered from the illness.[8] Nevertheless, this large cohort was also pressured or even required to receive the vaccine in flagrant violation of longstanding principles of immunology.
- The COVID-19 vaccines did not prevent transmission and infection, as CDC director Rochelle Walensky acknowledged on August

5, 2021.[9] With this admission, the rationale for COVID-19 vaccine mandates collapsed.

- In violation of standard legal procedure for a new pharmaceutical product, the FDA did not publish a ninety-day post marketing surveillance report for Pfizer BioNtech's new COVID-19 vaccine. Attorney Aaron Siri filed a lawsuit to compel the FDA to release the surveillance report. The FDA responded by announcing that the surveillance report would not be available for fifty-five years.[10] A judge ultimately ruled in Siri's favor. Eight months later, data started to trickle forth, revealing that 1,223 deaths had occurred shortly after vaccination with BNT162b2.[11] Historically, companies have voluntary withdrawn a product that caused between five and fifteen deaths during this ninety-day period, or the FDA has ordered the company to remove it. In 1976, the swine flu vaccine was removed from the market after twenty-five deaths and a few hundred cases of Guillain-Barré syndrome were reported. The mRNA Covid vaccine marks a total and criminal departure from established principles of safety and risk-benefit evaluations of a new medical product.

By May 2021, it had become clear that otherwise healthy children and teenagers were at virtually zero risk of suffering hospitalization and death from COVID-19, and were therefore not proper candidates to the receive the experimental, emergency shots. Nevertheless, on May 21, the FDA extended the Emergency Use Authorization to ages twelve to fifteen. During this same time, many American universities announced that students would be required to get vaccinations to attend classes in the fall.

The timing of this decision coincided with the European Medicines Agency (EMA) safety committee reviewing multiple cases of vaccine-induced myocarditis in young people. By the end of May 2021, 122 cases of myocarditis following the Pfizer/BioNTech vaccine had been reported to the European Union's EudraVigilance database. The risk was the highest for young athletic males. In July 2021, the EMA added a myocarditis risk warning to the product information.[12]

After the vaccine was rolled out to the public, millions of people were senselessly pressured into getting the vaccine *after* they recovered from COVID-19 illness. This was just one of many examples of tried-and-true medical practice being thrown out in the mad rush to embrace the new vaccine, which was represented as conferring *better* immunity than natural immunity. The shot, composed of synthetic mRNA delivered in a lipid nanoparticle, was designed to instruct the deltoid muscle to produce the toxic spike protein of the SARS-CoV-2 virus to induce the body's immune response to this protein. How could this convoluted process produce *better* immunity than exposure to the virus and *all* its antigens? This notion implied that the novel technology did not so much activate the human immune system as *improve* it, suggesting that its designers had somehow transcended nature. This was a ridiculous act of fraud to create a mendacious rationale for maintaining lockdowns for as long as possible and to persuade millions who'd recovered from the illness to still get a vaccine.

The spike protein is the pathogenic part of the virus that causes blood vessels to inflame and produce blood clots. This being the case, the rationale for an mRNA injection that induces the production of an uncontrolled quantity of this protein for an uncontrolled duration is highly questionable at best. The "emergency countermeasure" vaccine was a newly developed genetic biotechnology whose duration in the body and effects on the body were unknown. Though the motive remains unclear, it seemed that some overarching power had deemed it imperative for *everyone* to receive the shot. Never in the history of modern, science-based medicine had the claim been made that a drug was suitable for *everyone*, with zero contraindications.

Events in the winter and spring of 2021 reminded me of Aldous Huxley's 1931 novel *Brave New World* about a dystopian World State that engineers and controls every aspect of human life. Taking their cue from our public health agencies, our government representatives and our media told us daily that COVID-19 was the dominant natural force on Earth, and that responding to it was the key organizing principle of public policy and society. We were told that we were in a state of total war against the SARS-CoV-2 virus, and the only weapon at our disposal were the new mRNA vaccines. Scarcely a day went by without news of another time-tested principle of safe medical practice being tossed by the wayside.

Especially stunning was CDC Director Rochelle Walensky's April 2021 conversation with Dr. Eric J. Rubin (editor of *The New England Journal of Medicine*) in which she vehemently advocated COVID-19 vaccination for pregnant women, even though it hadn't been tested on pregnant women.[13] This was a flagrant violation of the "Golden Rule of pregnancy"—namely, that novel and/or potentially harmful substances are never used when new human life is being formed and nurtured within the womb—a lesson learned the hard way from the diethylstilbestrol (DES) and thalidomide disasters. After Walensky's approval, millions of pregnant women who wouldn't have dared drink a solitary glass of wine lined up to get an experimental genetic shot that had been developed "at warp speed."

By beginning of 2021, it had become clear that COVID-19 illness posed virtually zero risk to young athletes in top cardiovascular condition. Nevertheless, most college and professional leagues forced them to receive the experimental injections to participate in their sports. While such athletes were at the lowest risk of suffering severe COVID-19 illness, they (especially young males) were the highest risk cohort for suffering vaccine-induced myocarditis, or inflammation of the heart muscle. The first case of fatal, autopsy-proven mRNA COVID-19 vaccine myocarditis was reported in *The New England Journal of Medicine*, August 18, 2021.[14] This should have put a hold on the entire vaccine campaign until vaccine myocarditis was thoroughly investigated.

Extremely disturbing was the FDA's October 29, 2021, decision to authorize the Pfizer-BioNTech COVID-19 vaccine for emergency use in children five through eleven years of age (revised in June 2022 to include all children six months and older). By then it had become clear from the CDC's own data that COVID-19 illness posed virtually zero risk of hospitalization and death to children. Most healthy children, who have a large and very active thymus, completely recover from COVID-19 infection less than forty-eight hours after the onset of symptoms.

Dr. Eric Rubin, an adjunct professor of immunology and infectious diseases at Harvard University and editor-in-chief of *The New England Journal of Medicine*, played a key role in the deliberations of the Vaccines and Related Biological Products Advisory Committee. As was revealed in the transcript, Professor Rubin said the following:

> This is a much tougher one, I think, than we had expected coming into it. The data show that this vaccine works and it's pretty safe. . . . And yet, we're worried about a side effect that we can't measure yet,

> but it's probably real. And we see a benefit that isn't the same as it is in older age groups.

The "side effect" is myocarditis. "A benefit that isn't the same as it is in older age groups" was Rubin's mealy-mouthed way of saying that young people have a much lower risk of severe Covid illness. After acknowledging the myocarditis risk, Dr. Rubin made the following statement:

> So, for me, I think it's going to revolve around two questions, whether there is going to be a use for this vaccine in this age group, and then how the decision gets made within this age group. It's a very, sort of, personal choice. If I had a child who was a transplant recipient, I would really want to be able to use a vaccine. And there are certainly kids who probably should be vaccinated. The question of how broadly to use it, though, I think is a substantial one. . . . But I do think that it's a relatively close call . . . But we're never going to learn about how safe this vaccine is unless we start giving it. That's just the way it goes. That's how we found out about rare complications of other vaccines like the rotavirus vaccine. And I do think we should vote to approve it.[15]

"*But we're never going to learn about how safe this vaccine is unless we start giving it.*" What kind of reasoning was this? What could account for this monomaniacal desire for *everyone*, regardless of their risk profile, to get the shot? It was as though the public health agencies, medical profession, and public were in the grip of some wild enthusiasm for a new and untested technology. Often, I was struck by the thought that this mania was akin to a new religion.

CHAPTER 19

IN COVID-19 VACCINES WE TRUST

Mind Virus: Fear and loathing of SARS-CoV-2 virus harnessed to foster an unquestioning faith in the safety and efficacy of the COVID-19 vaccine, especially the mRNA products. Faith fosters reverence for the vaccine as the liberator and savior of humanity. Those who refuse to receive the vaccine are treated as dangerous heretics, unclean and unfit to participate in society, and scapegoated as responsible for the "pandemic of the unvaccinated."

After being locked down and systematically terrorized by the mass media for most of 2020, most of humanity anxiously awaited the vaccine that was heralded as their savior and liberator. As vaccine investor and enthusiast Bill Gates repeatedly stated in the spring, the world would only be able to go back to normal "when almost every person on the planet has been vaccinated against coronavirus."[1] This was an uncanny thing for anyone to say, but especially for the man who had, just twenty-two years earlier, been widely considered the most ruthless monopolist since John D. Rockefeller. The proclamation that "almost every person on the planet" needed to be injected with a novel substance about which they knew nothing seemed like something out of a dystopian science fiction novel.

When the emergency authorized mRNA vaccines were rolled out in December 2020, most of humanity was apparently unaware that they were *not* vaccines in the traditional sense of inactivated or attenuated pathogens that would induce an immune response. The new injections were the genetic code for instructing the body to create a foreign, toxic protein. Molecular biologists had been tinkering with messenger RNA since 1961, when Jacques Monod, François Jacob, and François Gros at the Institut Pasteur in Paris presented a paper about it for which they later won the Nobel Prize.[2] BioNTech was founded in 2008 and Moderna was founded in 2010 to create methods for using mRNA to intervene in disease processes such as cancer. Creating cancer therapies was the original concept of the founders of BioNTech.[3]

A major difference between natural mRNA—which is broken down by the body's enzymes soon after it performs its function—and the "modified" mRNA produced by Pfizer-BioNTech and Moderna, is that the latter has been chemically altered with methods created by Katalin Karikó and Drew Weissman, who won the Nobel Prize in physiology and medicine in 2023 for their work on these modifications. Both use N1-methyl-pseudouridine-modified mRNA encoding the SARS-COVID-19 spike protein delivered with a lipid nanoparticle (LNP) formulation.[4] These novel and experimental products were repeatedly injected into billions of people in 2021.

Because most of humanity did not understand what they were being injected with, the creators of this injection apparently perceived it necessary to erect something akin to a religion that deified the vaccines. This came naturally to them because many perceived that, with their new messenger RNA vaccines, they were using God's language to direct the cellular machinery of the human body to do their bidding. In his 2006 book, *The Language of God*, NIH director Francis Collins begins by quoting President Bill Clinton when he announced in early 2000 that the human genome had been sequenced. In fact, about 88 percent had been sequenced at that time, but as the leader of the Human Genome Project, Dr. Collins was apparently keen to make the big announcement sooner rather than later. At a press conference in the East Room of the White House, with Dr. Collins standing next to him, President Clinton announced:

> Today we are learning the language in which God created life. We are gaining ever more awe for the complexity, the beauty, and the wonder of God's most divine and sacred gift.[5]

Here it is worth recalling the archetypal "Scientist Playing God" whose lineage traces back to Mary Shelley's 1818 novel *Frankenstein: or, The Modern Prometheus* about a Swiss German doctor named Victor Frankenstein who applies his understanding of chemistry and electricity to create a living creature out of the dead. While this aspiration sounded interesting in theory, Frankenstein's creation is monstrous, and when he is rejected by society, he becomes a vengeful serial killer.

The code of life consists of the trinity of replication, transcription, and translation. Replication creates identical DNA strands; transcription converts DNA into messenger RNA (mRNA); translation decodes mRNA into amino acids, forming proteins essential for life functions. While this is an endlessly fascinating field, the practical applications of it are still in their infancy. Using modified (synthetic) mRNA to induce the deltoid muscle to produce a foreign protein was a deep intervention in the complex system of the human body.

One of many unintended and unforeseen consequences of receiving multiple mRNA shots was the marked shift toward IgG4 antibodies against the spike protein—going from around 0.04 percent to over 19 percent of the total spike-specific Immunoglobulin G (IgG) antibody pool—an unexpected finding associated with impaired immunity.[6] Many immunologists candidly expressed their surprise about this development, revealing that they didn't know how the mRNA shots would affect the immune system.

Within academic circles and publications, immunologists acknowledged that this was an unforeseen development. However, most medical universities and large medical centers have remained silent about all the other negative consequences of injecting billions of people with synthetic mRNA coding to produce a foreign, toxic spike protein. These include an array of autoimmune pathologies, inflammation of the heart and blood vessels, and impairment of tumor suppression. There are now more than four thousand peer reviewed manuscripts in the medical literature concerning fatal and nonfatal COVID-19 vaccine injuries, including those recognized by regulatory agencies around the world. These include myocarditis, neurologic injury, thrombosis, and immunologic syndromes.

As of April 25, 2025, 19,403 American deaths have been reported to the Vaccine Adverse Event Reporting System (VAERS), mostly by health-care professionals who believe these deaths are vaccine related. Approximately 1,134 deaths on the day of vaccination have been reported, and 1,266 on the day after vaccination.[7] A study published in 2010 by principal investigator Lazarus, Ross, MBBS, MPH for Harvard Pilgrim Health Care, Inc. found that "fewer than 1 percent of vaccine adverse events are reported" to VAERS.[8] Using the far more conservative estimate of 3.3 percent, or a 1 in 30 under-reporting factor, 19,403 yields a nationwide estimate of 582,090 US vaccine deaths.

It appears the gods of biotechnology understood that there could be unforeseen consequences of injecting billions of people with an experimental genetic product. It is likely that top mRNA vaccine advocates initially expected far more resistance from the lay public to receiving the experimental shots. In October 2021, Bayer Pharmaceuticals Division president Stefan Oelrich gave a speech to the World Health Summit in which he expressed his surprise at how many people had been willing to be experimented on. As he put it:

> I always like to say: If we had surveyed two years ago the public, 'Would you be willing to take a gene or cell therapy and inject it into your body?' we probably would have had a 95 percent refusal rate. I think this pandemic has opened many people's eye to this innovation.[9]

From the outset of the pandemic, those who were said to be working "at the speed of science" to create a new vaccine were presented as high priests of molecular biology and vaccinology. Anthony Fauci was presented by the adoring media as the pope of the COVID-19 vaccine program. He frequently stated the mantra "follow the science," which consisted of his edicts, issued like papal bulls, that no one was allowed to question. On June 9, 2021, Dr. Fauci implicitly invoked the doctrine of papal infallibility when he proclaimed, "Attacks on me, quite frankly, are attacks on science."[10]

Those who did question Fauci in public forums and on the internet quickly ran afoul of an army of censors who worked for various internet policing organizations that resembled the Holy Office of the Inquisition during the Counter-Reformation. Doctors who advocated treating

COVID-19 with old, safe, and effective repurposed drugs like hydroxychloroquine and ivermectin were branded as heretics and excommunicated from the college of physicians and from the rest of society. The safe medicines they recommended were banned as anathema that could not, under any circumstances, be dispensed, even to a patient dying in hospital to whom nothing else was being offered.

This religion wasn't entirely new in that it appropriated existing religious iconography and symbols in the same way the early Roman Catholic Church overlaid Christian symbols and rituals onto existing religions throughout the Roman empire. I was reminded of this in 2022 when Vatican City issued a 20 Euro silver coin commemorating the COVID-19 vaccine. As the Numista catalogue describes it:

> The coin depicts a doctor, a nurse and a young person who is ready to receive the vaccine. The Holy Father has repeatedly stressed the importance of vaccination, recalling that healthcare is "a moral obligation", and it is important to "continue efforts to immunize even the poorest peoples.[11]

Note that the formulation "a young person who is ready to receive the vaccine" is identical to the formulation for a communicant "who is ready to receive the host"—in Italian "*pronto a ricevere l'Eucaristia.*" The obverse of the coin bears the name Franciscus, the year 2022 ("Anno MMXXII") and the Coat of Arms of Pope Francis. With this commemorative silver coin, issued in the name of Francis, the Holy Father officially endorsed the COVID-19 vaccine and bestowed upon it his sublime authority and prestige, thereby suggesting that the vaccine is something like the Savior of Mankind. On February 10, 2024, Pope Francis appointed Katalin Karikó as a member of the Pontifical Academy for Life, which had been founded in 1994 by Pope John Paul II "to represent the various branches of the biomedical sciences and those that are most closely related to problems concerning the promotion and protection of life."[12]

Some churches suggested that the vaccine was a more powerful protector than Christ himself. A Methodist church in Cape Town South Africa draped itself with an enormous banner proclaiming "The Blood of Jesus will not save you from Covid. Get vaccinated. The words "Blood" and "vaccinated" were both printed in red script, suggesting that the vaccine resembles the Blood of Christ, only it possesses more protective power.

An especially disturbing manifestation of the Vaccine Religion was that the vaccine was repeatedly administered to people even after they suffered violent, adverse reactions to it. It didn't matter that each shot in the primary series and subsequent boosters had clearly made them gravely ill. Because the vaccine had been deemed as an infallible savior, its administration was still deemed essential. In 2021, multiple individuals suffered increasingly severe reactions, including some that required hospitalization, to each subsequent booster.

The Covid Vaccine Religion quickly resulted in a division of society between the **Elect**—that is, those who received the vaccine and would be saved by it—and the **Reprobate** who had not received it. This characterization is no exaggeration, as was evidenced by late night host Jimmy Kimmel's performance on September 7, 2021, during a massive propaganda campaign to suppress ivermectin as a treatment for COVID-19. This wasn't the first time that late-night comedy hosts participated in the COVID-19 vaccine propaganda campaign. In June 2021, Stephen Colbert produced a bizarre musical segment called "The Vax-Scene," featuring dancers outfitted as syringes, singing a musical number that encouraged viewers to get vaccinated. The segment was a shocking expression of just how much Colbert had agreed to serve as a propagandist. It also suggested that the show's producers regarded his audience as responsive to the crudest kind of showbiz manipulation.

Three months later, Jimmy Kimmel continued the pro-vaccination campaign by smearing ivermectin because it was a treatment favored by unvaccinated people. As he stated,

> Fauci has said that if the hospitals get any more overcrowded, they're going to have to make some very tough choices about who gets an ICU bed. That choice doesn't seem so tough to me. Vaccinated person having a heart attack, yes, come right on in, we'll take care of you. Unvaccinated person who gobbled horse goo, rest in peace, wheezy.[13]

In Kimmel's view, which he propagated among his fans, those reprobates who refused salvation by the COVID-19 vaccine deserved to die.

Yet another, deeply disturbing feature of the COVID-19 vaccination campaign was the extreme persecution of admired public figures who chose not to receive the shots. Top professional athletes such as Green Bay Packers quarterback Aaron Rogers[14] and world champion tennis player Novak Djokovic were quarantined, ostracized, abused, and harassed, even after the CDC admitted that the vaccines didn't prevent infection and transmission. Djokovic's treatment at the hands of Australia's authorities was one of the most shameful moments in the entire sorry saga. After he contracted and recovered from a COVID-19 infection in December 2021, he was issued a visa to travel to Australia to compete in the 2022 Australian Open. However, upon his arrival in Melbourne, his visa was canceled because he was unvaccinated, and he was placed in a quarantine hotel.

After Djokovic was deported from Australia, he gave an interview with BBC media editor Amol Rajan, who asked, "Ultimately, are you prepared to forgo the chance to be the greatest player to ever pick up a racquet statistically because you feel so strongly about this jab?" Djokovic replied that he was indeed prepared to forgo this chance and was willing to skip the French Open and Wimbledon in 2022 if vaccination was a requirement for entry. Responding to Rajan's expression of incredulity, he reiterated that forgoing the chance to be the greatest player in tennis history was "the price that I'm willing to pay" for maintaining the individual's right to choose what he puts in his body.[15]

Watching this appalling interview, I was reminded of the scene in the New Testament (Matthew 4:9, Luke 4:7) when the devil promises Jesus worldly power, glory, and all kingdoms if Jesus will bow down and worship him. As Rajan saw it, all Djokovic had to do was submit to the COVID-19 vaccine and all tennis glory would be his. With consummate grace, Djokovic replied that maintaining his individual freedom and bodily autonomy was more important to him than tennis glory.

Djokovic and Rogers were not persecuted because they posed a risk to others, but because they rejected the orthodoxy of the Covid Vaccine. Refusing to take it was the equivalent of an infidel refusing to convert to the One True Faith. In their case, their high status made their public repudiation of the vaccines especially threatening to the religion. The persecution of Rogers and Djokovic also highlighted a paradoxical notion that lay at the heart of this fanatical enterprise to vaccinate everyone. Millions of people believed that the vaccine would protect them. However, they were also terrified of being in the presence of someone who wasn't vaccinated.

The most astonishing feature of the Vaccine Religion was that the fervent faith of its votaries was not in the least shaken by the fact that the vaccine did not—as originally promised by its creators—prevent infection and transmission of the disease. Millions of vaccinated people noticed this when they repeatedly came down with Covid even after they received multiple boosters, probably due to antibody-dependent enhancement. Apparently recognizing that there was no way to obscure this reality, CDC director Rochelle Walensky publicly admitted on August 5, 2021, that the vaccines do not prevent transmission of SARS-CoV-2.[16]

With this admission, the entire rationale for COVID-19 vaccine mandates in various professions, among federal workers, in the military—and for traveling, attending public functions, and even visiting hotels and restaurants in cities such as Washington, DC—collapsed. Nevertheless, these mandates were maintained by the Biden administration for several months after Walensky made her announcement. Why? Was doing so a symbolic expression of faith in the vaccines and their miraculous benefaction, even though they didn't prevent infection? Or was there some other motive?

I couldn't help wondering if the fanatically pursued global mass vaccination program was an expression of a much bigger plan for all of humanity. But what exactly was the plan, and who was behind it? As best as I can figure, the objective of the campaign was to propagate deep faith in the vaccines so that all of humanity would *agree* to receive the shots on faith alone, without questioning what is in the substance they receive into their bodies. Here it is important to distinguish the willing submission of the faithful from the coerced obedience of the persecuted. The faithful line up to be injected because they are frightened of the illness and have been persuaded to place their *faith* in the vaccine as their Liberator and Savior. The disbelievers—those who are guilty of the heresy of "vaccine hesitancy"—must be persecuted into submission.

The final purpose of this ambitious project remains unclear, but its primary purpose was to use the COVID-19 vaccine as an instrument for acquiring global dominion. When Bill Gates's proclaimed that the world would only go back to normal when everyone on Earth received the vaccine, he envisaged all of humanity eagerly receiving an injection, most without questioning what is in it. Such would be the ultimate act of submission to an idol that he played a key role in creating.

CHAPTER 20

THE US PROXY WAR AGAINST RUSSIA IN UKRAINE

Mind Virus: Fear and loathing of Russia harnessed to create an irrational, Manichean reverence for the Ukrainian government and President Volodymyr Zelensky. The Ukrainian nation (of which most Americans know nothing) and its president are idealized in heroic terms and deemed worthy of unquestioning and virtually unlimited support from the US government, whose officials turn a blind eye to the gross corruption within Ukraine's oligarchic society and government. The costs and risks of the US proxy war against nuclear-armed Russia are dismissed in a cavalier way that was unthinkable during the Cold War.

On February 15, 2022, Washington, DC and other US cities abruptly dropped their indoor mask and vaccine mandates for indoor dining. This resulted in an immediate relaxing of tension, and to millions of Americans, it felt like a major step in putting the COVID-19 trauma behind us. Right when news of this broke, I had a powerful premonition that we would not be able to relax for long because, I sensed, a new crisis would soon be upon us. Nine days later, on February 24, Russia invaded Ukraine.

I wondered if top decision makers at the Departments of Defense and Health and Human Services knew that war was coming and wanted to clear space in the media and in people's heads to change the subject from

COVID-19 to the Russian invasion of Ukraine. Even so, I was surprised by how quickly millions of Americans became so captivated by this new crisis in Eastern Europe. People who had expressed mortal terror of catching Covid now expressed avid enthusiasm for supplying Ukraine with sophisticated US military hardware, thereby waging a proxy war against nuclear armed Russia. Many of the same people who posted vaccine syringe emojis on their social media profiles added a Ukrainian flag.

The response of the US government and the American people to Russia's military action in Ukraine starkly contrasted with the Eisenhower administration's response to the Soviet invasion of Hungary in 1956 and the Johnson administration's response to the Soviet invasion of Czechoslovakia in 1968. Both condemned the invasions but chose to avoid military confrontation with the Soviets because it risked escalation over countries that were not of vital interest to the peace and prosperity of the American people. Eisenhower and Johnson would have been shocked by Washington's response to the Ukraine crisis, which was apparently guided by the conviction that maintaining the territorial integrity of Ukraine was America's single most vital interest. How did this irrational obsession with Ukraine come about?

Until around 2002, Ukrainian nationalism had, in foreign policy circles, been viewed with suspicion and distaste. Since Walter Duranty's mendacious *New York Times* reporting in the 1920s and '30s, American intellectuals had shown little interest in the Holodomor. Holocaust historians regarded the wartime alliance of Ukrainian nationalists with Hitler's SS as beyond the pale. Hitler's Operation Barbarossa in 1941 was launched from Poland and went through Ukraine, with around 250,000 Ukrainian nationalist soldiers joining the German Army to attack Russia. Ukraine's Azov Brigade traces its lineage to the Organization of Ukrainian Nationalists. Its leader, Stepan Bandera, was a notorious Nazi collaborator.

Those familiar with this dark history were shocked in September 2023 when the Canadian House of Commons gave a standing ovation to Nazi Waffen-SS veteran Yaroslav Hunka, who was invited to attend an address by Ukrainian President Zelensky. Hunka was praised as a "Canadian hero" for fighting the Soviet Union. Members of the House apparently didn't know that the Waffen SS was declared a criminal organization by the International Military Tribunal in Nuremberg, which found it guilty of committing atrocities in Poland, Ukraine, Russia, and Serbia, including atrocities against Jewish civilians. The ovation seemed all the odder, given that President Zelensky is Jewish. Apparently, many Canadians had forgotten that the Soviet Union was an ally of Canada during World War II and did the lion's share of fighting against Nazi Germany.

Within US foreign policy circles, the attitude towards Ukraine shifted during the Bush administration, when so-called neoconservative intellectuals such as Robert Kagan and his wife, Victoria Nuland, exerted their influence. Nuland is the granddaughter of Meyer Nudelman, who immigrated to New York from the Ukrainian region of the Russian Empire. In the years 2003–2005, she served as deputy national security advisor to Vice President Dick Cheney. She then held ranking State Department positions in the Obama and Biden administrations. During the Biden years, she worked closely with Secretary of State Antony Blinken, whose paternal ancestors were also from Ukraine. Nuland, Blinken, Kagan, and other neoconservative advisors in Washington pursued the policy of extricating Ukraine from the Russian sphere of influence in which it had been situated—on and off—since around 882, when Kiev was the capital of Kievan Rus,' a medieval state generally regarded as the predecessor to modern Russia, Ukraine, and Belarus.

Washington's relationship with Kiev intensified during the Obama administration. Secretary of State Hillary Clinton deepened her relationship with the Ukrainian billionaire oligarch, Victor Pinchuk, who donated $13.1 million to the Bill, Hillary & Chelsea Clinton Foundation between 2006 and 2014[1]. Vice President Joe Biden served as the Obama administration's envoy to Ukraine, with a mandate to promote economic stability and push for energy reform and combat the country's endemic corruption. In a 2016 report issued by Transparency International, Ukraine tied with Russia as the most corrupt country in Europe,[2] but by then, the American political class's love affair with Ukraine was in full swing, and in 2017, Anne Applebaum published a book about the Holodomor.[3]

For Vice President Biden, combatting corruption meant interacting with the oligarchs who have owned and run the natural resource–rich country since 1991. Who are Ukraine's oligarchs, and what is the nature of their relationship with Russia and the United States? To answer this question, it is useful to review a bit of Ukrainian history. For centuries, the peoples of Russia and Ukraine have been closely related, though the territory of what is now Ukraine was often contested by the ruling classes of Austria, Lithuania, and Poland. In 1783, Russian empress Catherine the Great annexed most of Ukraine, including the Crimea. During the nineteenth century, a Ukrainian nationalist movement developed, emphasizing its ethnic and linguistic identity. After fighting a war for independence in 1917, the nation was subsumed by the Soviet Union.

With the fall of the Soviet Union in 1991, Ukraine became an independent nation, though it maintained strong ties with Russia. Since the end of the Cold War, both countries have been shaped by oligarchies who own the lion's share of real estate and mineral assets. According to 2008 report, the combined wealth of Ukraine's fifty richest oligarchs was equal to 85 percent of Ukraine's GDP.[4] For decades, six billionaires wielded an outsized influence in its politics in a nation that had, in 2021, a per capita annual income of roughly $2,470.

Generally, Ukraine's oligarchs have been somewhat agnostic in their personal and political attachments. Over the years, they have done deals together, and later accused each other of corruption. In international politics, Victor Pinchuk has advocated building better relations with Russia while at the same time hobnobbing with the Clintons. Likewise, Ihor Kolomoisky has vacillated between advocating better relations with Russia and exchanging amusing insults with President Putin. In 2014, he called Putin a "schizophrenic of short stature" and accused him of having a "messianic drive" to recreate the Russian Empire or the Soviet Union. Putin responded by calling Kolomoisky

> a unique crook who even managed to cheat our Roman Abramovich two or three years ago. Scammed him, as our intellectuals like to say. They signed some deal, Abramovich transferred several billion dollars, while this guy never delivered and pocketed the money. When I asked him [Abramovich]: "Why did you do it?" he said: "I never thought this was possible."[5]

Kolomoisky was the chief patron of Ukrainian President Volodymyr Zelensky. Kolomoisky's 1+1 Media Group distributed *Servant of the People*, a TV comedy series in which Zelensky played a schoolteacher who—to everyone's surprise including his own—is elected president on an anti-corruption platform. With Kolomoisky's media and financial support, Zelensky registered his *Servant of the People* party in 2018 and rode the wave of the show's popularity to being elected president of Ukraine in 2019.[6] And although Kolomoisky is Jewish, he was a primary, early financier of the neo-Nazi, ultra-nationalist Azov Battalion, founded in 2014 to fight Russian separatists in eastern Ukraine.[7]

For reasons obscured in the nation's murky politics, Kolomoisky's fortunes took a turn for the worse after Zelensky entered office, with law enforcement agencies in Ukraine and the US investigating him for an array of crimes including fraud, embezzlement, international money laundering, and contract murder. According to the Pandora Papers—a collection of leaked documents exposing the offshore banking activities of many politicians and celebrities—President Zelensky also has significant and questionable offshore holdings. Following the Russian invasion of Ukraine in 2022, Zelensky came under pressure to dump his patron. Kolomoisky is currently *persona non grata* in the United States and remains under federal investigation.[8]

Another colorful Ukrainian oligarch is former President Petro Poroshenko (in office from 2014–2019). During the 2016 US presidential election, Poroshenko's government favored Hillary Clinton. Ukrainian agents worked with a Ukrainian American Democratic operative named Alexandra Chalupa, who had served in the White House Office of Public Liaison during the Clinton administration. Chalupa then worked as a consultant for the Democratic National Committee and disseminated claims of Trump's allegedly close ties with the Putin regime. In 2022, Poroshenko was arrested by Zelensky's government on charges of high treason. Though Poroshenko presented himself as pro-Western and anti-Russian, he is alleged to have (treasonously) facilitated the sale of large amounts of coal that helped finance Russian-backed separatists in eastern Ukraine in 2014–15.[9]

In December 2015, Vice President Joe Biden traveled to Kiev to meet Poroshenko and Prime Minister Arseniy Yatsenyuk. During this meeting, Biden threatened to withhold a $1 billion US loan guarantee if Ukrainian Prosecutor General Viktor Shokin was not removed from office. As he later recounted, he told them, "I'm leaving in six hours. If the prosecutor is not fired, you're not getting the money."[10] Of special interest to Vice President Biden was Shokin's investigation of the Burisma gas company. Biden's son, Hunter, was a company board member—a position for which he was paid a handsome monthly salary.

Hunter Biden's Ukraine adventure began in 2014, when he was invited to join the board of Burisma Holdings, purportedly to assist the company with "corporate compliance"—an odd position for Hunter, who hadn't practiced law in years and had no understanding of the Ukrainian code or even the ability to read it in the language in which it was written.

A couple of months after Vice President Biden issued his ultimatum to Ukrainian President Poroshenko to fire Prosecutor General Shokin, the owner of Burisma, Mykola Zlochevsky, met an FBI Confidential Human Source (CHS) at a cafe in Vienna. The CHS was apparently posing as an experienced businessman who wanted to do deals with Zlochevsky and help him realize his dream of expanding Burisma's operations into the United States. However, as he stated, the ongoing corruption investigation in Ukraine would likely impede his plan. With surprising candor, Zlochevsky told the CHS that this was why he had Joe and Hunter Biden on his payroll. As the CHS noted in his FBI report:

> CHS told Zlochevsky that due to Shokin's investigation into Burisma, which was made public at this time, it would have a substantial negative impact on Burisma's prospective IPO in the United States. Zlochevsky replied something to the effect of, "Don't worry Hunter will take care of all of those issues through his dad." . . . CHS advised Zlochevsky it would be problematic to raise capital in the U.S. given Shokin's investigation into Burisma, as nobody in the U.S. would invest in a company that was the subject of a criminal investigation. CHS suggested it would best if Burisma simply litigate the matter in Ukraine and pay some attorney $50,000. Zlochevsky said he/Burisma would likely lose the trial because he could not show that Burisma was innocent; Zlochevsky also laughed at CHS's number of $50,000 (not because of the small amount, but because the number contained a "5") and said that "it cost 5 (million) to pay one Biden, and 5 (million) to another Biden."

> CHS told Zlochevsky that any such payments to the Bidens would complicate matters, and Burisma should hire "some normal U.S. oil and gas advisors" because the Bidens have no experience with that business sector. Zlochevsky made some comment that although Hunter Biden "was stupid, and his (Zlochevsky's) dog was smarter," Zlochevsky needed to keep Hunter Biden (on the board) "so everything will be okay." CHS reiterated CHS's opinion that Zlochevsky was making a mistake, and he should fire Hunter Biden and deal with Shokin's investigation directly so that the matter will remain an issue in Ukraine, and not turn into some international matter. Zlochevsky responded something to the effect of, "Don't worry, this thing will go away anyway."[11]

Go away it did. On March 29, 2016—shortly after this intriguing meeting in Vienna—Prosecutor General Shokin was fired by the Ukrainian Parliament. Three years later, in July 2019, President Trump asked Ukrainian president Volodymyr Zelensky to investigate Joe and Hunter Biden's business activities in Ukraine. When President Trump's request came to light, House Democrats acted as though the mere request was an outrage and they impeached him on December 18, 2019. The lesson was clear: When it comes to US politicians engaging in questionable business in Ukraine, it's best not to ask too many questions.

Shortly after President Biden was sworn into office in January 2021, tensions between the United States and Russia began to ratchet up over various disagreements. In the autumn of 2021, Russian intelligence told President Putin that, in addition to the ongoing training and equipping of the Ukrainian military, CIA and British intelligence (MI6) were essentially controlling Ukrainian intelligence and turning it into a "springboard for operations against Moscow." President Putin found these reports highly alarming, and he quickly submitted a proposal to NATO for Ukrainian neutrality. As NATO secretary Jens Stoltenberg later recounted to the EU Parliament:

> In the autumn of 2021, Russia actually sent a draft treaty that they wanted NATO to sign to promise no more NATO enlargement. That was what they sent us, and that was a precondition for not invading Ukraine. Of course we didn't sign that.[12]

Why wasn't Stoltenberg at least willing to *try* an Austrian style neutrality deal for Ukraine? Given that the Russians proposed it, they had a strong motive to abide by it. If they subsequently violated the terms of their own proposal, the West would have a clear cause for war with Russia. Implied in Stoltenberg's statement is that, in December 2021, he found the prospect of imminent war with Russia in Ukraine preferable to making a concession to Russia to avert war for an indeterminate period, perhaps for as long as Austria had remained at peace with Russia.

Stoltenberg was apparently guided by the same logic as that of the US Army Major in Vietnam who told war reporter Peter Arnett that, during the 1968 Battle of Bến Tre, "It became necessary to destroy the town to save it." This raises the suspicion that President Biden's foreign policy advisors *wanted* Russia to commit to military action in Ukraine. They apparently reasoned that, with the Ukrainian army equipped with sophisticated US weaponry and targeting assistance, the Russian army would suffer the same kind of humiliating defeat it had suffered in Afghanistan at the hands of the US-armed Mujahideen, who succeeded in getting the Soviet Army to withdrawal from in the country in February 1989. Hillary Clinton explicitly made this comparison in a February 28, 2022, MSNBC interview in which she said:

> Remember, the Russians invaded Afghanistan back in 1980. It didn't end well for the Russians . . . but the fact is, that a very motivated, and then funded, and armed insurgency basically drove the Russians out of Afghanistan.[13]

Later in the interview, Clinton conceded that arming the Afghan Mujahideen had produced unintended consequences like the Taliban and Al-Qaeda. The actions of these groups resulted in the US government sending the American military to Afghanistan and occupying the country for twenty years. After getting thousands of American servicemen killed and maimed and spending $2.3 trillion, the US government made its own chaotic withdrawal from Afghanistan on August 30, 2021, leaving the country *back* in the hands of the Taliban that was supposed to have been vanquished twenty years earlier.

It didn't seem to bother Clinton that an Afghan-style quagmire in Ukraine would likely kill hundreds of thousands of people and inflict great suffering on the Ukrainian people, just as the Afghan people had suffered during the Soviet Afghan War. Implied in Clinton's statement was her apparent assumption that the Ukrainian people view the Russian people as enemies. In fact, most Ukrainians and Russians have long had close and affectionate relations, and many have extended family members in both countries. For decades, ordinary Ukrainians have—because of the country's location, history, and rich natural resources—been caught in the middle of oligarchies in Kiev and Moscow who have much in common but also frequently squabble over natural gas deals. Washington, London, and Brussels have sought to bring Ukraine into the western sphere of influence. Most disturbing to Moscow has been the aggressive foreign policy clique in Washington that has aspired to make Ukraine a forward operating base against Russia in the same way it aspired to make Iraq a forward operating base against Syria and Iran.

Many reasonable critics have pointed out that in early 2022, Putin still had several nonviolent options he could have pursued before taking military action. While this may indeed be the case, he was likely under severe pressure from hawkish factions within Russian military, intelligence, and government circles to take a harder stance against US military and intelligence agencies that were turning Ukraine into a base of operations close to the Russian capital. An open and fair-minded reader should ask himself how the United States government would react if Russian military and intelligence advisors heavily trained and equipped the Mexican army and elite commando units to operate out of bases near the US border.

On February 24, 2022, a Russian military force estimated to be between 150,000 and 200,000 soldiers advanced simultaneously from the north (from Belarus toward Kiev), the northeast (toward Kharkiv and Sumy), the east (along the Donbas front), and the south (from Crimea into southern Ukraine). The apparent objective of the initial campaign was to neutralize Ukraine's military command and air defenses, and pressure Zelensky's government to negotiate a security arrangement with Russia. The small invasion force obviously wasn't large enough to manage a protracted occupation of Ukraine.

In March 2022, President Zelensky agreed to send a Ukrainian delegation to a conference in Istanbul to negotiate a ceasefire and settlement with a Russian delegation. Around this time, he gave a video-recorded interview with the British *Economist* magazine in which he stated, "There are those in the West who don't mind a long war because it would mean exhausting Russia, even if this means the demise of Ukraine and comes at the cost of Ukrainian lives."[14]

Talks held on March 29, 2022, in Istanbul produced initial optimism, with Russia indicating a reduction in military activity around Kiev as a gesture. However, upon learning that the Ukrainians and Russians might quickly settle their differences, British Prime Minister Boris Johnson made a surprise visit to Kiev on April 9, 2022, where he urged President Zelensky to keep fighting. Johnson argued that even if Zelensky's government was ready to sign an agreement with Russia, the "collective West" was not.[15]

During this time, the "collective West" was rapidly becoming fervently obsessed with Ukraine and the drama into which it had been swept. Hillary Clinton's fantasy of turning the country into an Afghan-style quagmire for the Russian army became official policy, and the US government's mainstream media propaganda organs flooded the zone with anti-Russian propaganda, thereby unleashing a virulent mind virus into the general population. Suddenly, millions of people in the West who'd never given Ukraine any thought, and probably could not have located it on an unmarked map, became passionately animated with the conviction that defending it from Russia was, to quote Senator Mitch McConnell, "the number one priority for Americans."

The far southeast (Russian-speaking) provinces of Ukraine—Donetsk, Luhansk, Kherson and Zaporizhzhia—were suddenly conceived as sacred territory, to be defended till the last *Ukrainian* man, like Colonel Travis and his 180 Texans who defended the Alamo. As a native Texan, I often thought about the Alamo during these passionate years, and the irony that our own border with Mexico was not being maintained. Seeking a negotiated settlement with Russia was, in the minds of millions of Americans, deemed out of the question, even though it could possibly spare the lives of hundreds of thousands of young men. Extreme examples of this mental derangement included the following incidents:

- 2022–2025: Congressional approval of $175 billion in total aid to Ukraine. This contrasts with Congress's reluctance to allocate funding for critical US infrastructure such as $32 billion to upgrade of

America's antiquated air traffic control system, widely deemed as under immense strain and producing a growing number of near misses.
- September 2022: Deliberate detonation of Nord Stream pipeline from Russia into Germany, causing the largest amount of methane (greenhouse gas) pollution in history.
- September 2023: Senate Minority Leader Mitch McConnell states that "the number one priority for Americans is providing assistance for the Ukrainians to defeat the Russians."
- April 2024: Just a few days after Americans pay their taxes, Congress erupts in jubilation and Ukrainian flag waving as the final vote in favor of another aid package ($61 billion) for Ukraine was tallied.
- June 2025: Massive Ukrainian drone swarms attack of Russia's strategic bomber fleet, part of its nuclear triad and therefore an essential component of its nuclear deterrence doctrine.
- US Congressmen such as Senator Bob Casey sign bombs to be shipped to Ukraine and used on young Russian soldiers.

Within the United States, the psychic epidemic of extreme adulation for the *idea* of Ukraine—combined with little concern for actual human beings in Ukraine—and hatred for Russia peaked in 2024 and gradually cooled over the course of 2025. In November 2025, Zelensky's regime was embarrassed when Ukraine's National Anti-Corruption Bureau (NABU)—established by the Obama administration to facilitate USAID to Ukraine— announced it had discovered evidence that senior figures in Zelensky's inner circle took $100 million of kickbacks on construction projects to protect power stations from Russian missile attacks. At the center of the investigation was Zelensky's friend and business associate, Timur Mindich. Investigators characterized Mindich as the "co-organizer" of the alleged scheme, and that approximately $100 million of illicit funds were siphoned through his office.[16]

"He controlled the work of the so-called 'laundry room,' where criminally obtained funds were laundered," a NABU spokesman said.

Mindich was co-owner of production company Kvartal 95 Studio (owned by billionaire oligarch and accused international money launderer, Ihor Kolomoisky) which Zelensky co-founded. Kvartal 95, in association with 1+1 Media Group, produced the popular *Servant of the People* television show. As previously mentioned, the show starred Zelensky as a Ukrainian schoolteacher who runs for president on an anti-corruption platform. *Servant of the People* ran for three seasons between 2015 to 2019, and its popularity greatly helped Zelensky to win the 2019 presidential election.

According to a report in *Politico*, Timur Mindich was tipped off about the forthcoming raid and fled to Israel. NABU released images of his opulent apartment in Kiev, replete with a golden toilet and bidet with a matching golden toilet brush.[17] Because ordinary Ukrainians are increasingly suffering from power outages due to Russian attacks on their energy infrastructure, they found it especially distasteful that Zelensky's inner circle had been siphoning funds that were supposed to bolster energy infrastructure defenses.

Such blatant corruption within Zelensky's inner circle—as well as the oligarchic state's longstanding reputation for money laundering—naturally raise the question: Where exactly have the tens of billions of monies and munitions sent to Ukraine ended up? The question is especially germane when one considers that the US Department of Defense has failed its department-wide audit for eight consecutive years and cannot properly account for a significant portion of its $4.1 trillion in assets.[18] How exactly does the DoD keep track of what happens to the billions of weapons and munitions it delivers to Ukraine? How does the DoD know that all this Materiel is being delivered to the front and used for military operations, and not being sold on the international arms market? Can American taxpayers really rest assured that USAID during the Biden administration kept track of the billions of dollars that were disbursed in Ukraine?

Of all the mind viruses characterized in this book, the fanatical advocacy for waging a US proxy war against Russia in Ukraine may be the most dangerous. Western propaganda frequently characterizes Vladimir Putin as suffering from delusions of grandeur and a desire to conquer Europe, even though he still hasn't fully mobilized against Ukraine. At the same time, western governments express their bold confidence that he would never use a nuclear weapon—not even a low-yield tactical nuclear weapon against military targets. This is a radical departure from the Cold War doctrine of avoiding confrontations with nuclear-armed Russia that could trigger escalation.

During the Cold War, men like George Kennan would have regarded the June 1, 2025, drone attacks on Russia's strategic bomber fleet as an unthinkable provocation, and it would have elicited traumatic memories of "Black Saturday," October 27, 1962, when a U-2 plane was shot down over Cuba. A U-2 plane also accidentally flew over Russia, and US Navy destroyers dropped signaling depth charges on a Soviet submarine. As was the case back then, with both sides on high alert, in a state of hyper-vigilance, the situation could spin out of control with catastrophic consequences. This being the case, everyone in the West has an existential interest in looking for ways to deescalate this war and seek a negotiated settlement.

I conclude this chapter with a recounting of the events on September 26, 1983, when Soviet Lieutenant Colonel Stanislav Petrov, stationed near Moscow, prevented a potential nuclear exchange by identifying a satellite warning system of incoming US ICBMs as more likely a system malfunction. Rather than following protocol to report the attack immediately, Petrov made the gut decision to classify the alert as a false alarm. His hunch was later confirmed to be a satellite malfunction that misinterpreted cloud reflections as missiles. For trusting his intuition and making his bold decision to err on the side of caution, he was known as "the man who saved the world."[19] Petrov was born in 1939, and lived through many of the most dangerous years of the twentieth century, and died in 2017. I hope there are still men like him managing Russia's nuclear weapons systems.

CHAPTER 21

TRANSGENDER

For all human prehistory and history, it's likely that some men have had persistent fantasies of being women, and some women have had persistent fantasies of being men. Philosophers such as Arthur Schopenhauer have argued that being a woman is much harder than being a man because the labor of reproducing the species—pregnancy, childbirth, nursing, and taking care of infants—falls on the female sex. However, prior to late twentieth century, most of the recorded examples of people who fantasized about being the opposite sex were men.

A conspicuous example was the Roman Emperor Marcus Aurelius Antoninus, whose short reign was from 218–22 AD. Posthumously known as Elagabalus from his activities as a high priest of the Syrian sun god Elagabal (known as Baal among the ancient Hebrews), he became infamous in Rome for his eccentric and extravagant sexual behavior. The Roman Senator and historian, Cassius Dio, wrote that Antoninus was briefly married to an ex-slave and charioteer named Hierocles, and that he delighted in being called Hierocles's mistress, wife, and queen. The emperor enjoyed wearing makeup and wigs, liked to be called a lady, and offered a large sum to any physician who could surgically provide him with a vagina. After incurring widespread disgust in Rome, he was assassinated at the age of eighteen.[1]

Until recently, it was universally understood that eccentric fantasies are one thing, the unavoidable facts of life another. One of the hard facts of life is that the divide between male and female is as impassable as the divide between the living and the dead. The ancient Greeks thought the divide between the sexes is the greatest of all, as even the immortal gods were stuck with being either male or female.

The only exception in Greek mythology was Tiresias, a blind seer from Thebes, who is a character in Sophocles's *Oedipus the King* and Ovid's *Metamorphoses*. Born a man, Tiresias was transformed into a woman after striking two mating snakes with his staff. She then lived as a woman for several years before being restored to a man when she again struck a pair of mating snakes with a staff. Following this totally unique experience, he was drawn into a dispute between Zeus and his wife Hera over whether men or women experience greater pleasure in sex. Tiresias's answer, "woman," angers Hera, who punishes him with blindness. Zeus compensates him with the gift of prophetic sight. Tiresias's unique transcendence of the divide between the sexes symbolizes his total knowledge. While all other humans and gods are limited to single perspective, he has experienced both. However, as everyone (until recently) has always understood, Tiresias's experience was mythical.

During the late sixteenth century, surgeons in the Norcia region of Italy performed illegal orchiectomies (surgical removal of testicles) on boys who had exceptionally beautiful singing voices before they reached puberty. Several "castrati" became famous for the angelic quality of their voices, and they sang to papal audiences in the Sistine Chapel. The last known castrato in history was Alessandro Moreschi (1858–1922), who was called the "Angel of Rome" and served in the Sistine Chapel choir until his retirement in 1913.

In Berlin in 1922, a thirty-year-old man named Rudolf Richter underwent an orchiectomy—performed by the Berlin surgeon Erwin Gohrbandt—to try to realize his longstanding fantasy of becoming a woman. Early in childhood, Richter showed a tendency to act in a feminine way. When he was six, he apparently tried to remove his penis with a tourniquet. In his late twenties, he consulted with the renowned "sexologist," Magnus Hirschfeld, who referred him to Gohrbandt for the surgery. In 1931, Richter had a penectomy performed by Institute physician Ludwig-Levy-Lenz. Dr. Gohrbandt then performed a vaginoplasty operation on Richter, thereby helping him to fulfill his fantasy of becoming more like a woman.

When the Nazi Party came to power in 1933, they destroyed Hirschfeld's Institute for Sexual Science, characterizing it as un-German and degenerate. Hirschfeld, who was on an international speaking tour, never returned to Germany. Dr. Erwin Gohrbandt went on to hold ranking medical positions during the Nazi era, including that of Chief Medical Advisor of the Luftwaffe (Airforce), and was a consulting physician for high-altitude and freezing medical experiments conducted on prisoners in Dachau concentration camp.[2]

George William Jorgensen Jr. was born in 1926 and grew up in New York City. From a young age, he felt himself to be "a woman in a man's body." After serving in the US Army, he traveled to Copenhagen, Denmark in 1950 (when he was twenty-four) to consult with the endocrinologist, Dr. Christian Hamburger, who quickly understood that the isolation and synthesis of estrogen and testosterone in the 1930s held great promise for altering sex characteristics.

Following hormone injections, Jorgenson received an orchiectomy in 1951 and a penectomy in 1952. Upon returning to the United States in December 1952, a report on his "transsexual journey" was featured on the front page of the *New York Daily News.* Jorgenson then became a prominent transsexual advocate and worked as an actress, singer, and popular nightclub entertainer. He also developed a working relationship with Dr. Harry Benjamin. Born in Berlin and part of Magnus Hirschfeld's circle, Benjamin was originally an infectious disease doctor who, because of his German nationality, got stranded in New York in 1914 with the outbreak of World War I. He initially worked as an assistant for Dr. Friedrich Franz Friedmann, who did a tour of the United States to promote his "turtle cure" for tuberculosis—that is, what Dr. Friedmann claimed was a strain tuberculosis bacillus he had passed through a turtle in the Berlin Zoo, thereby (he claimed) rendering it benign but immunogenic for humans.[3]

Later, despite Dr. Benjamin's lack of formal training in endocrinology, he established an endocrinology practice in New York, and ultimately became the foremost advocate of transsexual medical procedures in the United States. His greatest benefactor was a woman named Rita Alma Erickson who was the daughter of a wealthy industrialist and the first female graduate of Louisiana State University's school of mechanical engineering. A skilled investor, she greatly augmented her inheritance. In 1963, at the age of forty-six, she consulted with Dr. Benjamin, received hormone treatments and surgery, and changed her name to Reed. With her Erickson Educational Foundation, she made large donations to the Harry Benjamin Foundation and the Johns Hopkins University Gender Identity Clinic, founded in 1966 by John Money, a pioneer in transsexual procedures for children. Toward the end of her life, Reed became addicted to illegal drugs and fled to Mexico to evade US federal drug indictments.

With his high-profile, pioneering patients and funding from Erickson, Dr. Benjamin published his book, *The Transsexual Phenomenon* in 1966.[4] The book presented his thesis of "transsexualism," which he characterized as a true medical condition resulting from biological or physiological causes. He claimed that the condition presents on a spectrum, with medical intervention using hormones and surgery indicated for severe cases, which he called "true transsexuals"—that is, people who feel that they were "born in the wrong body." Benjamin's book generated the new discipline of "transsexual medicine."

In 1979, Dr. Richard Green and other transsexual advocates founded the Harry Benjamin International Gender Dysphoria Association (HBIGDA) in Benjamin's honor. In 2007, the organization changed its name to the World Professional Association for Transgender Health (WPATH), which claims to be the leading authority in the field. In 1994, what Dr. Benjamin called "transsexualism" was changed to "gender identity disorder" (GID) in the Fourth Edition of the Diagnostic and Statistical Manual of Mental Disorders (DSM), which defined the disorder as

> having deeply rooted feelings of persistent discomfort with one's current biological gender and having the desire to be of the opposite gender to the extent that "the disturbance causes clinically significant distress or impairment in . . . important areas of functioning.[5]

In 1994, GID was considered a rare condition. The prevalence of those seeking sex reassignment surgery (SRS) in Western countries was estimated to be 1 in 30,000 natal males and 1 in 100,000 natal females. In 2013, the name "gender identity disorder" was changed to "gender dysphoria" in the *DSM* (Fifth Edition), purportedly "to reduce stigma and focus on distress rather than pathologizing identity." In 2013, the estimated prevalence of the condition was still low—approximately 5–14 per 100,000 natal males and 2–3 per 100,000 natal females.

Transsexualism was initially thought to be an adult phenomenon, and transsexual procedures were only offered to adults. For several years after the field was established, providers of transsexual procedures continued to regard childhood and adolescence as periods of rapid change and unstable identity, marked by awkward and confusing phases between the ages of twelve and eighteen, and then stabilizing between the ages of eighteen and thirty. The idea of deeply intervening in this complex developmental process with a potent medical procedure was therefore not countenanced by doctors or parents.

The first well-known doctor to break this taboo was John Money, founder of the Johns Hopkins University Gender Identity Clinic, where he developed his bogus theory of "gender neutrality"—that is, that gender identity emerged more from social conditioning than biological sex. In 1967, he was presented with a male child named Bruce Reimer whose penis had been mutilated by a botched circumcision. Money persuaded the distressed parents that the best option was to use hormones and surgery to "reassign" the child's sex from male to female. And so, little Bruce Reimer became the subject of the ugliest, most shocking, and patently illegal medical experiment since the Nuremberg Code was published in 1947. The investigative journalist, John Colpinto, meticulously documented the story in his 2000 book, *As Nature Made Him: The Boy Who Was Raised as A Girl.*[6]

After the sex "reassignment" procedures were inflicted on Bruce, his name was changed to Brenda, and he was raised as a girl. However, Bruce's biology proved conspicuously recalcitrant to Dr. Money's experiment. The boy never felt or acted like a girl—despite his girl's clothing and haircut—and nor did his classmates perceive that he was a normal girl. They often teased him, calling him "cave girl." Dr. Money tried to encourage the boy to have a female sexual identity by showing him pornographic images and telling him that his role was that of the female in the pictures. He also forced the boy and his twin brother, Brian, to perform what he called "childhood sexual rehearsal play." Later in life, Brian revealed that he and his brother were forced to act out sexual gestures, with Bruce playing the female role. On at least one occasion, Money photographed the children performing these acts that he commanded them to do. Revealing a high degree of sadistic psychopathy, Dr. Money was always courteous in the company of the boys' parents, but cruel and imperious to the boys when he had them alone in his office. Brian's account of what the doctor did to him and his brother is shocking in the extreme. Dr. Money's perverse experiments with the identical twin boys recall Dr. Joseph Mengele's notorious experiments with twins in the Auschwitz concentration camp.

Long after it became evident that Money's experiment was an abject failure, he continued to publish favorable reports about it in medical journals, describing it as his "John/Joan case" of successful female gender development. As Bruce Reimer entered puberty, Money injected him with high doses of estrogen to induce female breast development and other female sex characteristics. However, at this point, the boy rebelled and told his parents he would commit suicide if they made him see Money again.

The next year they told him the truth they'd so long concealed from him. Quickly he tried to reverse what Money had done to him. He changed his name to David—the boy who slew Goliath—to symbolize the great challenge he was up against. In 2002, his twin brother Brian committed suicide by overdosing on psychiatric medication. Two years later, in 2004, David committed suicide by shooting himself in the head with a shotgun.

The catastrophic and heartbreaking failure of Dr. Money's monstrous experiment on the Reimer twins did not diminish his influence until it was exposed in 1997. One of his pupils at Johns Hopkins was a Dutch endocrinologist named Louis Gooren, who founded the Center of Expertise on Gender Dysphoria at the VU University Medical Center Amsterdam in 1975. He then studied with Money at Johns Hopkins in 1976–1977. For years, Gooren's clinic in the Netherlands only treated adult transsexuals, but in 1987, it opened a clinic for adolescents in Utrecht. In 1996, Gooren and the pediatric endocrinologist, Henriette A. Delemarre-van de Waal, published a paper titled *The Feasibility of Endocrine Interventions in Juvenile Transsexuals*. In their paper's Introduction, they presented their reasoning for breaking the taboo against transsexual medical interventions in children.

> A large number of adult transsexuals recall that their gender dysphoria started early in life, well before puberty. They remember puberty with abhorrence, since the hormones of puberty precisely

> induced the body characteristics they perceived as improper in relation to their gender identity. The latter often reinforced their determination to rid themselves from the primary and secondary sex characteristics. For most of them, the time and period they grew up in provided not much room for the expression of their gender dysphoria; they themselves often would not even know how to label themselves until they learned about the phenomenon of transsexuality. They all agree that this period in their lives has been a vexation.[7]

Note the unscientific character of the opening sentence. What is a "large number," and how reliable are the recollections of biologically altered adults looking back on their childhood feelings? Did they grow up in stable households with mentally healthy parents, or were their parents afflicted with poor mental health and unstable identities? It is now generally accepted among cognitive psychologists that memory is highly fallible and heavily colored by present conceptions, emotions, and knowledge. Based on the authors' claim of evaluating an unquantified cohort of patients—with no details of their personal, familial, and medical history presented in the paper—the authors recommend administering a luteinizing hormone-releasing hormone (LHRH) agonist to block the onset of puberty to prevent the development of "the body characteristics they perceived as improper." After proposing this extraordinary intervention into a complex, developmental, biological process, the authors then rationalized it with the following untestable claim:

> The effects of LHRH analogues are fully reversible; in other words, no lasting undesired effects are to be expected. Upon discontinuation of the LHRH analogues, the hormonal activity of the own puberty is resumed within three months. Side effects are few, particularly when there is usage only for a limited period of 3–18 months, as will be the case with adolescent gender dysphoric persons. In their case, the issue is often that they themselves are highly motivated to start with cross-sex hormones, but the psychotherapist sometimes needs more time to work with this person, or parental approval is pending or the personal educational situation of the

> youngster makes it undesirable to start on cross-sex hormones now or legal regulations prevent a start on cross-sex hormones at this age.[8]

There is no way to know how a child *would have* developed had he not taken puberty-blocking hormones for three to eighteen months. Even if the basic hallmarks of puberty appear with the cessation of the hormones, one cannot know if the child's development is comparable to what it would have been had the natural progression of puberty not been blocked. Indeed, a recent study by Grigoria Betsi et al. found that puberty blockers cause a range of side effects, including headaches, mood swings (65 percent), increases in fat, decreases in growth and height, bone loss, worsened cardiovascular risk factors (glucose, lipids, blood pressure), and, most importantly, sterility and potential impairment of brain function.[9]

Despite the tragic reality of administering puberty blockers, the 1997 paper by Gooren and Delemarre-van de Waal laid the foundation and built the basic edifice for transsexual medicine for minors. The authors then teamed up with child psychologist Peggy Cohen-Kettenis to formulate what came to be known as the Dutch Protocols for transsexual medicine for minors. The protocols prescribed puberty blockers followed by cross sex hormones, ultimately advancing to surgery. About a decade after the protocols were published, they were adopted by medical universities, societies, and major medical centers all over the world. That transsexual medicine was propagated by a handful of doctors publishing unscientific studies recalls Carl Jung's observation that under certain circumstances, a small number of abnormal people may have an enormous influence by encouraging "chimeric wish fantasies" in the broader population of people who possess little self-awareness or critical reasoning ability.

The entire transgender enterprise is based on the proposition that endocrinologists and surgeons can physically change the sex of a human being. In fact, all that endocrinologists and surgeons can do is inject a boy or girl with the hormones of the opposite sex and cut off his or her sex and secondary sex organs. The argument that performing such procedures is justified because the patient believes it will satisfy his craving is also not tenable. As the Dutch American doctor and psychoanalyst, Joost Meerloo, put it:

> Unwittingly, many a physician does not treat the disease as such but treats, rather, the fantasy a patient develops about his disease. . . . I believe the surgical treatment of transsexual yearnings easily falls into this trap. . . . What about our medical responsibility and ethics? Do we have to collaborate with the sexual delusions of our patients?[10]

Sex is just one of many physical characteristics with which we are born that are not amenable to medical intervention. Many features that are advantageous or disadvantageous in life are determined by one's genetic inheritance from one's parents. The painful process of growing up involves coming to terms with the fact that many things in life are beyond our control and that our best strategy is to make the most of what we do have. Those who identify what lies within their control and focus on it are the most likely to succeed in life because they don't waste their precious time, effort, and resources on things that are beyond their control.

Telling a little boy that he can, if he so desires, become a little girl, or vice versa, is a lie and a false promise. Insofar as sex is a defining feature of one's life, it is inherently connected with physical attractiveness, sexual prowess, and ultimately (for most men and women) reproductive capability. Life is hard enough—with more than enough challenges in finding an attractive and satisfying mate—when one is a man or a woman by birth. A prepubescent or pubescent boy has no idea what it's like to be a girl and the psychological and social pressures with which girls must contend. Likewise, a prepubescent or pubescent girl has no idea what it's like to be a boy, competing with other boys in the social, athletic, masculine, and sexual hierarchy. Thus, telling a boy that medical doctors can make him into a girl or vice versa is as meaningless as it is it false.

Even if it were possible for endocrinologists and surgeons to change a person's sex, no child or adolescent has the experience, intellect, and judgement to consent to undergoing such radical medical interventions. This basic fact is enshrined in our legal concept of the age of consent for sexual activity. If our civilization maintains that a child does not have sufficient understanding to consent to sexual relations, how can it maintain that a child can consent to being injected with powerful body and brain altering hormones?

The World Professional Association for Transgender Health (WPATH) is widely considered the premier institution for publishing Standards of Care for children and adolescents diagnosed with gender dysphoria. The latest edition (number eight) states that adolescents who have been diagnosed with "gender incongruence" should receive access to puberty blockers, cross-sex hormones, and surgeries so long as the young person "demonstrates the emotional and cognitive maturity required to provide informed consent/assent for the treatment."

In this official declaration, WPATH implies that the thousands of children who receive these treatments do indeed possess the "emotional and cognitive maturity to provide informed consent/assent for the treatment." And yet, in leaked video footage of an internal WPATH panel discussion titled "Identity Evolution Workshop," held on May 6, 2022, panelists spoke candidly about how their young patients did *not* understand what hormone treatments would do to their bodies. Environmental Progress, a research and policy institute founded by investigative journalist, Michael Shellenberger, recently published a meticulous exposé and analysis of the leaked footage.[11]

One of the panelists, Dr. Daniel Metzger, a Canadian endocrinologist (whose surname is the German word for "butcher") admitted it was impossible to obtain informed consent from most adolescents seeking this medical treatment. He reminded the panelists that they are "often explaining these sorts of things to people who haven't even had biology in high school yet." He further noted that even many patients often have little medical understanding of the effects of the interventions. In his experience, young patients want to pick and choose the physical effects of hormone therapy, with some wanting a deeper voice without facial hair or to take estrogen without developing breasts. This revealed their poor understanding of how the body works.

"It's hard to kind of pick and choose the effects that you want," Metzger remarked. "That's something that kids wouldn't normally understand because they haven't had biology yet, but I think a lot of adults as well are hoping to be able to get X without getting Y, and that's not always possible." As Metzger put it (with an undertone of cynical humor), "I tell my patients that they may not be binary, but hormones are binary." He often explained to children and adults that "you can't get a deeper voice without probably a bit of a beard" and "you can't get estrogen to feel more feminine without some breast development."

Other panel members agreed that many children are unable to comprehend the potent effects of the hormone treatments they seek. Dianne Berg, a child psychologist and coauthor of WPATH's Standards of Care number eight, concurred that they wouldn't expect children and young adolescents to comprehend the effects of hormone treatments because it is "out of their developmental range to understand the extent to which some of these medical interventions are impacting them. . . . They'll say they understand, but then they'll say something else that makes you think, oh, they didn't really understand that they are going to have facial hair."

Such is the way WPATH's medical officers speak in private. In public, they never make such admissions. Metzger and Berg are like the eminent virologists who privately pointed out to Dr. Fauci that the SARS-CoV-2 genome bears features of lab manipulation, but publicly proclaimed that the virus emerged from nature.

Full institutional respectability was bestowed on transgender procedures in 2007, when the first pediatric gender clinic was established at Boston Children's Hospital under the direction of endocrinologist, Dr. Norman Spack. His biography, posted on a public speaking agency website, is revealing in its shallowness.

> Dr. Spack's interest in patients with gender variance was kindled in 1974 as a volunteer on a medical van serving homeless youth. . . . His experience treating adults convinced him that starting hormonal treatment in late puberty was too late for an optimal physical and psychosocial outcome. His first patients from the UK were treated according to the Amsterdam protocol using pubertal suppression. . . . In 2007 he co-founded the Gender Management Service" ("GeMS") at Boston Children's Hospital, an interdisciplinary clinic for Transgender adolescents. GeMS the only program of its kind outside of Europe and soon became the model for 70 comparable clinics currently operating throughout North America, including three who became partners in a 4-site \$6 million NIH collaborative longitudinal outcome study.[12]

What inferences did Dr. Spack make from working with homeless youth that he applied to the general population? Two years after he co-founded the Boston's Children unit, the Endocrine Society, under the direction of Dr. Wylie C. Hembree, published clinical guidelines that adopted the "Dutch method" of blocking puberty followed by cross sex hormone administration. After Boston Children's broke the ice, seventy other pediatric clinics opened in the United States, creating an entirely new medical industry. The American Academy of Pediatrics was apparently reluctant to give its full blessing to transgender procedures for minors until 2018, when it finally issued a full-throated endorsement for the procedures.[13]

The explosive epidemic of gender dysphoria in American adolescents began after 2014, when the Affordable Care Act (ACA) went into effect. In May 2014, the HHS Departmental Appeals Board invalidated the longstanding (1981/1989) National Coverage Determination that categorically excluded "transsexual surgery." Coverage then shifted to case-by-case decisions by local Medicare contractors. The ACA prohibited discrimination based on sex. Section 1557, which interpreted "sex" discrimination to include gender identity and barred categorical exclusions of transition-related care, was finalized in May 2016. This led to multiple insurance plans lifting blanket exclusions of covering medical procedures for the treatment of "gender dysphoria." It is almost certainly no coincidence that diagnoses of gender dysphoria rapidly increased after insurance policies began covering the medical procedures for treating it.

The mercenary motive for treating so-called "gender dysphoria" was candidly revealed by a leaked video recording of a staff meeting of Vanderbilt University Medical Center's Clinic for Transgender Health, founded in 2018 by Dr. Shayne Taylor. In the recording, Dr. Taylor, proclaims that female-to-male bottom surgeries are "huge money makers," elaborating that a single phalloplasty could bring in up to $100,000, and that even routine hormone treatments generate steady revenue for the hospital. Another leaked video clip showed a staff member stating that employees with religious or personal objections to participating in these procedures "probably shouldn't work at Vanderbilt" and could face "consequences" for refusing.[14]

At heart of the twenty-first-century transgender industry is a total and absurd contradiction. On the one hand, confused and impressionable children are told that biological sex is not a significant determinant of one's identity. On the other hand, they are told that if they feel "dysphoric" with their (purportedly insignificant) "sex assigned at birth," they can undergo long, gruesome, and painful procedures to be shorn of the characteristics of their biological sex and to acquire the characteristics of the opposite sex. This project becomes the all-consuming focus and purpose of their entire lives. As the transgender researcher and critic, Mia Hughes, has pointed out, the obsessive pursuit of irreversible body modification is a pathological fixation rather than an innate identity.

Nonprofit foundations have also played a substantial role in generating transgender propaganda and introducing transgender ideology into American education, law, and politics. Billionaires such as Jon Stryker (heir of the Stryker medical device fortune) and Hyatt Hotel heir Jennifer Pritzker—who was born James Pritzker and "transitioned" in 2013—have given enormous sums to transgender advocacy organizations and medical universities, who have been happy to adopt transgender ideology.[15] Pritzker is a major donor to WPATH.

Starting around the year 2018, many prestigious American medical universities, including Harvard, adopted the concept of "assigned sex" instead of "biological sex" in their basic medical curricula. In June 2021, the American Medical Association (AMA) issued a report in which it proclaimed its endorsement of the concept of "assigned sex," and advocated removing sex designations from the public portion of birth certificates.[16]

With increasing insurance coverage after the Affordable Healthcare Act went into effect in 2014, the number of transsexual procedures performed on minors exploded. By 2015, clinics were reporting fourfold and fivefold increases of trans-identifying kids seeking their services, including thirteen- and fourteen-year-old girls clamoring to get double mastectomies. Between 2013 and 2020, the University of California San Francisco medical center reported thirteen-fold increase of mastectomies performed on adolescent girls (fourteen to seventeen years old).[17] One wonders about the psyche of a surgeon who is willing to take a knife to the healthy breasts of a fifteen-year-old child.

The transgender bonanza has coincided with four other major developments that have profoundly affected the mental health of millions of American children.

- Approximately 23 to 25 percent of US children under age eighteen—around nineteen million—live in a household with a single mother, which makes the United States the leading country in the world for children raised by a single mother. The absence of a strong and stable father in the household leaves these children without a masculine role model. Although the rise of single motherhood preceded the sharp rise of gender dysphoria, the absence of fathers to help mothers in rearing children may have resulted in many children being more susceptible to the other factors that are causing the social contagion. In a 1974 book titled *Sexual Identity Conflict in Children and Adults*, the transgender researcher, Richard Green, observed that, in the case of young boys fantasizing about being girls: "What comes closest so far to being a necessary variable is that, as any feminine behavior begins to emerge, there is no discouragement of that behavior by the child's principal caretaker."
- The meteoric rise of smart phones and social media sites that broadcast extremely captivating content, including pornography, that can influence and shape the developing minds of children and adolescents.
- The introduction of gender ideology (of the sort formulated by John Money) into the American school curriculum. Many school children are taught to think of their gender as something separate from their biological sex. Many school libraries are stocked with graphic novels about "gender identity" that contain sexually explicit images.
- The stunning increase of autism spectrum disorder (ASD) from an estimated 1 in 150 American children (aged eight years) in the year 2000 to 1 in 31 children (aged eight years) in the year 2025. As has become increasingly apparent to diligent, perceptive, and moral medical researchers, autistic children are especially confused and vulnerable to being influenced by transgender ideology.

The result of this perfect storm has been a psychic epidemic of American children who identify themselves as transgender. According to a 2024 CDC report, over 3 percent (1 in 33) of high schoolers identify as transgender, with another 2.2 percent questioning their gender identity.[18] Note that this estimated prevalence almost exactly matches the CDC's estimated prevalence (1 in 33) of American children suffering from autism spectrum disorder.[19]

A key driver of this psychic epidemic has been the brainwashing of parents into accepting the subversion of social norms and of their parental authority. Parents who maintain a stable and wholesome household must still contend with their children being subjected to influences online and at school that encourage them "to explore their gender identities." If a child goes through a phase in which he becomes curious about "exploring" the identity of the opposite sex, he will likely find encouragement online, at school, and among his peers and even their parents. If a child expresses dislike of his sex and interest in being the other sex, his parents may find themselves having to contend with a deranged pediatrician or pediatric psychologist who bullies them into supporting the child's cross-gender behavior.

The most malignant expression of this perverse enterprise is the threat that parents had better support their child's transition or they will run the high risk of the child committing suicide. As the constitutional law professor, David Smolin, remarked in a 2025 essay in the *Harvard Journal of Law & Public Policy*:

> The risks of suicide and suicidality have been repeatedly invoked in defenses of pediatric medical transition and its specific interventions of puberty blockers, cross-sex hormones, and surgery, which are often labeled a part of "gender-affirming care." The message to parents has often been stark, as admonitions such as "[w]ould you rather have a dead daughter or a live son?" warn parents that a failure to consent to and support medical transition risks the death of their child by suicide.[20]

In public schools in California, Oregon, New York, Maryland, and Minnesota, children are taught that if they ever feel uncomfortable with their gender "assigned at birth," they should talk with a counselor about the possibility of getting their gender reassigned. Official guidelines direct students who question their gender to speak with a school counselor or a so-called GSA (Gender & Sexuality Alliance) advisor. Counselors are trained to affirm the student's asserted identity immediately and develop a "Gender Support Plan" to facilitate social transition at school with respect to their name, pronouns, restroom and locker room access. Many of these policies frame this as creating a "safe space."[21] In Oregon, minors aged fifteen or older may consent to certain hormone therapy under specific conditions without parental consent.

Such school policies remind one of Hamelin in Lower Saxony, Germany. Town records from 1384 note "100 years since our children left" and a 1602 inscription confirms that 130 children disappeared on June 26, 1284. Who took the children away remains a mystery. The Brothers Grimm fairytale, *The Pied-Piper of Hamelin* was inspired by this true historical event.

The Biden administration was an avid super spreader of the transgender mind virus, starting with its appointment of the pediatrician Richard Levine—who underwent transgender procedures to become Rachel Levine—as Assistant Secretary of Health. While in office, Levine (who was also made a four-star admiral) was a vocal supporter of gender-affirming care for minors, describing it as evidence-based, vital, and medically necessary health care. Another flamboyant Biden administration hire was Sam Brinton, who worked in the Department of Energy nuclear division in 2022. The nuclear engineer and gay activist was touted as "the first openly genderfluid individual in federal government leadership," and uses singular "they" pronouns. Brinton's tenure was cut short when he was caught stealing designer luggage from airport carousels for the third time.

On March 31, 2024, which happened to be Easter Sunday, President Biden issued Proclamation 10724—Transgender Day of Visibility, 2024, in which he proclaimed:

> On Transgender Day of Visibility, we honor the extraordinary courage and contributions of transgender Americans and reaffirm our Nation's commitment to forming a more perfect Union—where all people are created equal and treated equally throughout their lives.

The key passage in President Biden's proclamation took aim at proposed legislation for restricting transgender procedures for minors.

> But extremists are proposing hundreds of hateful laws that target and terrify transgender kids and their families—silencing teachers; banning books; and even threatening parents, doctors, and nurses with prison for helping parents get care for their children. These bills attack our most basic American values: the freedom to be yourself, the freedom to make your own health care decisions, and even the right to raise your own child. It is no surprise that the bullying and discrimination that transgender Americans face is worsening our Nation's mental health crisis, leading half of transgender youth to consider suicide in the past year.

The phrase "the freedom to make your own health care decisions" was particularly rich coming from a president who had, just three years earlier, issued COVID-19 vaccine mandates for federal employees, federal contractors, and large private employers. His phrase "and even the right to raise your own child" was especially mendacious, given the recent passage of state laws mandating that minors receive access to gender-affirming counseling even without their parents' consent or knowledge.

On the same day that President Biden issued his proclamation, the Department of Defense announced the publication of revised policies to allow transgender Americans to serve in the military by prohibiting discrimination and encouraging recruits to join in their self-identified gender. President Biden also sent a video speech to the National Center on Transgender Equality's "Trans Equality Now Awards" ceremony, emphasizing his support for the Equality Act—a proposed law for amending the Civil Rights Act of 1964 to explicitly prohibit discrimination based on sexual orientation and gender identity in the domains of employment, housing, public accommodations, education, credit, and federal funding.

On September 15, 2022, WPATH published its Standards of Care Version 8 (SOC 8), which officially dropped the requirement for those seeking transgender procedures, including surgery, to receive professional mental health evaluations.[22] This raises the concern that young men suffering from profound mental illness may undergo transgender procedures that do not address the true causes of their illness and may exacerbate their negative feelings and aggression. In some cases, boys may be disappointed, frustrated, and even enraged by the outcome of their "reassignment."

Karl Avati, who grew up in Perth, Australia, was a gifted student. In his late teens, he underwent transgender procedures and changed his name to Evie. His "transition" did not improve his poor mental health and substance abuse. One night in 2017, after suffering rejection from a woman he'd met on Tinder, he went on a rampage with an axe in a convenience store and inflicted massive injuries with lifelong consequences on two people.[23] At trial, his defense attorney argued that his transgender operation caused him immense pain and contributed to his attempt to kill strangers.

On August 27, 2025, a twenty-three-year-old man named Robert Westman, who claimed to be a trans woman named Robin, barricaded the doors of the Annunciation Church in Minneapolis, Minnesota and shot to death two people and wounded seventeen. Just before he committed the mass shooting, he scheduled the publication of his diary on his YouTube channel. In one diary entry, he wrote the following:

> I am sick of my hair, I want to chop it off! I only keep it because it is pretty much my last charade of being trans. I am tired of being trans, I wish I never brain washed myself. I can't cut my hair off now as it would be an embarrassing defeat, and it might be a concerning change of character that could get me reported.[24]

Mass shootings in Aberdeen, Maryland (in 2018), Denver, Colorado (in 2019), and Nashville, Tennessee (in 2023) were committed by transgender individuals. On February 10, 2026, eighteen-year-old Jesse Van Rootselaar, who also went by the name Jesse Strang, killed his mother and stepbrother at his family home in Tumbler Ridge, British Columbia. He then went to the town's secondary school, where he shot and killed a female teacher and five students between the ages of twelve and thirteen. Local police alerts described the shooter as a "female in a dress with brown hair." In later press conferences, the police initially referred to the shooter as a woman and as a "gunperson." Eventually the truth came out that the shooter was a biological male who had undergone hormone and possibly other transgender procedures six years earlier.[25]

These tragic stories remind one of the tormented serial killer Jame Gumb—a.k.a., "Buffalo Bill"—in the 1988 novel *The Silence of the Lambs*, adapted for cinema in 1991. Gumb obsessively fantasizes about metamorphosizing from male to female, but he has an extremely distorted image of the feminine. In the novel, it is revealed that he had sought to undergo transsexual procedures at the Johns Hopkins Gender Identity Clinic. However, his psychiatric evaluation found that transsexual procedures were not likely to cure his Anti-Social Personality Disorder and other mental disturbances resulting from severe childhood trauma.

A bizarre variant of the transgender mind virus has been the normalization of biological males competing in women's sports. Especially disturbing was the spectacle of Imane Khelif—the Algerian women's division gold medalist at the 2024 Olympic Games in Paris—beating the hell out of "her" opponents, punching Italian boxer Angela Carini so hard that she withdrew from the bout after forty-six seconds.[26] The year before, the International Boxing Association (IBA) disqualified Khelif from its 2023 world championships based on what media reports deceptively characterized as "unspecified eligibility tests." IBA's then-president, Umar Kremlev, claimed that DNA tests had revealed Khelif to have XY chromosomes.[27]

The International Olympic Committee (IOC) claimed the International Boxing Association had not provided evidence to back this claim. This dispute arose within the context of the IOC claiming that the IBA was under undue Russian influence due to its Gazprom sponsorship—a conspicuous example of the anti-Russia mind virus combining with the transgender mind virus.

In May 2025, the World Boxing federation announced a new mandatory policy requiring a PCR test to determine chromosomal sex for athletes to compete in its matches. The organization specifically mentioned Khelif in its statement of the new policy. This triggered a paroxysm of virtue-signaling outrage, which prompted World Boxing to issue a public apology for "singling out" Khelif.[28] Rather than simply getting an inexpensive PCR test, Khelif protested the new requirement and appealed to the Court of Arbitration for Sport (CAS) seeking to overturn the decision and to be allowed to compete without taking the chromosome test.[29] The CAS dismissed "her" request to suspend the decision while "her" appeal is being heard.

This development is of great significance to the young women who competed against Khelif at the 2024 Olympics. The International

Olympic Committee cleared Khelif to compete in the Paris Olympics under its own regulations, which did not require the chromosome test at the time. On average, male professional boxers punch approximately 160 percent harder (with about 2.6 times more force) than female professional boxers of similar weight. On average, male professional boxers can move and react considerably faster than female professional boxers of similar weight. Allowing a biological male boxer to compete against women at the Olympic Games subverted every principle of fair sportsmanship, and it raises the suspicion that at least some members of the IOC have contempt for women's sports and possibly a sadistic streak as well.

Just as it was a small number of medical doctors who led our civilization so horribly astray, an equally small number of good people are now working diligently to lead it back to reason. Doctors such as Stanley Goldfarb, Myriam Grossman, and Peter McCullough have taken principled stands against transgender medical madness. Journalists Mia Hughes and Michael Shellenberger have both done tremendous work in exposing WPATH's deceptions and false claims.

In 2023, Texas State Senator Donna Campbell (R-New Braunfels) introduced Senate Bill 14 (SB 14) to ban transgender procedures for minors in Texas. Attorney General Ken Paxton strongly advocated for the bill, arguing that puberty blockers, hormone therapies, and surgical interventions for transgender minors constitute "child abuse," laying the legal groundwork banning the practice. Dr. Peter McCullough supported the bill, and submitted an affidavit to AG Paxton's office, enumerating the terrible physical and psychological harms being inflicted on Texas children by transgender procedures. The bill was passed in May 2023 and upheld by the Texas Supreme Court on June 28, 2024.

In April 2024, the renowned British pediatrician, Dr. Hilary Cass, submitted her *Independent Review of Gender Identity Services for Children and Young People* to the National Health Service (NHS), which commissioned the review. Though the language of her report is clinical and diplomatic, its message is clear: The entire project of "gender-affirming care" in children and adolescents is built on assertions and assumptions that have no basis in the scientific method. Highlights from Dr. Cass's report are as follows:

- While a considerable amount of research has been published in this field, systematic evidence reviews demonstrated the poor quality of the published studies, meaning there is not a reliable evidence base upon which to make clinical decisions, or for children and their families to make informed choices.
- The rationale for early puberty suppression remains unclear, with weak evidence regarding the impact on gender dysphoria, mental or psychosocial health. The effect on cognitive and psychosexual development remains unknown.
- The use of masculinizing/feminizing hormones in those under the age of eighteen also presents many unknowns, despite their long-standing use in the adult transgender population. The lack of long-term follow-up data on those commencing treatment at an earlier age means we have inadequate information about the range of outcomes for this group.
- Clinicians are unable to determine with any certainty which children and young people will go on to have an enduring trans identity.
- For most young people, a medical pathway will not be the best way to manage their gender-related distress. For those young people for whom a medical pathway is clinically indicated, it is not enough to provide this without also addressing wider mental health and/or psychosocially challenging problems.
- Innovation is important if medicine is to move forward, but there must be a proportionate level of monitoring, oversight and regulation that does not stifle progress, while preventing creep of unproven approaches into clinical practice. Innovation must draw from and contribute to the evidence base.[30]

The Cass Review prompted the National Health Service (NHS) to stop the routine prescription of puberty blockers for minors (under eighteen). Shortly after the Review's publication, a group of twenty-one Republican attorneys general, led by Montana Attorney General Austin Knudsen and Idaho Attorney General Raúl Labrador, sent a letter to the American Academy of Pediatrics (AAP), challenging its guidance on gender dysphoria care for minors. The attorneys general accuse the AAP of violating state consumer protection laws by making the "misleading and deceptive" statement that puberty blockers are fully reversible—a claim that is "scientifically unsupported" and contradicted by emerging evidence such as that enumerated in the Cass Review.[31]

In late 2025 and in early 2026, the US Department of Health and Human Services announced it has taken steps to restrict gender-affirming care for minors, including proposed rules by the Centers for Medicare & Medicaid Services (CMS) to prohibit federal funding like Medicaid and the Children Health Insurance Program (CHIP) from covering these treatments for individuals under eighteen years of age.

And so, the transgender mind virus appears to be losing institutional and financial support, which likely marks the beginning of the end of this abominable psychic epidemic. The prestigious doctors, medical centers and societies who participated in this organized crime of promoting and performing transgender procedures on minors should be subjected to severe civil and criminal penalties. The end of the epidemic should also prompt the American people to do some deep soul-searching about why they tolerated and even embraced the mutilation of children on an industrial scale. Like the COVID-19 vaccine mind virus, the transgender mind virus induced a trancelike state in millions of otherwise reasonable adults, rendering them unable to think critically about the delusional nonsense we are told by our corrupt medical and government authorities.

Transgender ideology is an expression of the diabolical ambition to subvert human civilization and its ability to perpetuate itself. The transgender mind virus is a species of what KGB defector, Yuri Bezmenov called "ideological subversion." As he stated in a 1984 interview with American author G. Edward Griffen, the goal of ideological subversion is:

> To change the perception of reality of every American to such an extent that despite the abundance of information, no one is able to come to sensible conclusions in the interest of defending themselves, their families, their communities, and their country.[32]

To combat ideological subversion and the tyrants it serves, a free people must never surrender its right to free speech. They must always speak out against tyrannical nonsense before it becomes so entrenched in minds and institutions that it cannot be expunged. An especially potent weapon for disarming tyranny and deflating its bloated power is humorous ridicule. In the United States, comic Dave Chapelle has been a leader in exploding the self-righteous absurdities of transgender ideology. In the UK, former Member of Parliament, Andrew Bridgen, attained comic immortality during a 2022 Sky News interview in the Victoria Gardens, overlooking the House of Lords. During the conversation about various issues, reporter Beth Rigby asked him in a deadly serious tone, "Is it possible for a woman to have a penis?"

"Yes, of course it is," Bridgen replied. "But only if she asks for one very nicely."

CHAPTER 22

THE DEATH OF CHARLIE KIRK

On September 10, 2025, the conservative activist and Turning Point USA founder Charlie Kirk gave a talk to an audience of about three thousand people in an outdoor amphitheater at Utah Valley University in Orem, Utah. The theme of his address was the "American Comeback," in which he outlined his vision for restoring traditional Christian values. He emphasized his belief in the sacredness of human life, including that of the unborn, and his dedication to preserving free speech, especially on college campuses. After his initial talk, he gave his customary question and answer session.

Just before 12:23 p.m. Mountain Daylight Time (MDT), an audience member identified as a man named Hunter Kozak engaged him in a dialog about mass shootings.

"Do you know how many transgender Americans have been mass shooters over the last ten years?" Kozak asked.

"Too many," Kirk replied.

"Do you know how many mass shooters there have been in America over the last ten years?

"Counting or not counting gang violence?" Kirk asked.

"Great," Kozak replied, at which point a shot rang out, inflicting what appeared to be a high velocity gunshot wound on the left side of Kirk's neck. He reacted with a decorticate posture—a flexion of the upper limbs caused by severe trauma to the central nervous system—as blood poured from the neck wound. He then went limp and collapsed.

While most of the audience screamed in horror and reflexively ducked down in case subsequent shots were fired, a bearded young man in a black T-shirt and backward baseball cap rose from his seat with a broad grin, pumped his fists, threw his arms triumphantly into the air, and began chanting "USA! USA! USA!" while looking back toward the direction of the gunshot. In the terrorized crowd, his apparent jubilation was deeply disturbing and perplexing. Was he exulting in Kirk's violent death or expressing defiance in the direction from which the shot was fired? Later he explained in a post on his X account, "I stood and shouted 'USA,' not as a provocation, but to project strength, encourage others, and create a distraction that might help calm panic or even save lives."[1] The following day, a viral video on TikTok circulated of what appeared to be a male college student in a public place, using a bullhorn to lead a group jubilantly chanting "We got Charlie in the neck! We got Charlie in the neck! Who's next!"[2]

The spectacularly violent murder of Charlie Kirk in public while he was discussing transgender mass shooters seemed emblematic of all the instability, division, and emotional dysregulation documented in this book. Conservatives reacted with grief and outrage. President Trump, Vice President JD Vance, and Republican leaders framed the murder as the inevitable fruit of "radical left" lunacy. Vigils were held nationwide, and Kirk was eulogized as a martyr for free speech and traditional values. Their reaction starkly contrasted with people like the young man with a bullhorn leading the exultant chant, who responded with glee, dark humor, or callousness. Posts declaring "karma's a bitch," labeling Kirk a "divisive hatemonger," or pronouncing that he "got what he deserved" rapidly proliferated online. A CloudResearch poll found that 12 percent of all respondents said they believed Kirk's murder was "justified." Among young Americans under thirty, 22 percent said they believed that his murder was justified. Among young Democrats, 32 percent said they believed his murder was justified.[3]

Kirk's murder was also emblematic of another conspicuous feature of American public life that traces back to the assassination of President John F. Kennedy—namely, the widely shared, persistent perception that official accounts of high-profile political assassinations are not trustworthy. In the case of Charlie Kirk, the official account is that twenty-two-year-old Tyler James Robinson was a lone gunman who fired the single, deadly accurate shot from a rooftop approximately 142 yards away, fled on foot, and was arrested the next day after a manhunt. According to federal and state investigators, Robinson had a romantic, live-in relationship with a young man named Lance Twiggs who was transitioning to become a female. Robinson claimed that Charlie Kirk was expressing and inciting hate against transgender persons and other minorities. As he put it in a text message to Twiggs, "I had enough of his hatred. Some hate can't be negotiated out."

Robinson's text exchange with Twiggs has struck many observers as one of the strangest features of this story. He purportedly sent the texts while waiting for the police to clear out so that he could retrieve his rifle from a nearby wooded area. As he put it in a text message, "I had planned to grab my rifle from my drop point shortly after, but most of that side of town got locked down. It's quiet, almost enough to get out, but there's one vehicle lingering."[4]

Police investigators have never explained why Robinson sent an extremely detailed confession—referencing every element of the crime—by text message to his live-in romantic partner instead of waiting until he got home to confess in person. Robinson is an intelligent young man who almost certainly understood that if he fell under suspicion, the police would subpoena his cell phone records. His texts, composed in complete sentences in formal and even florid diction, have a theatrical quality that suggest he wrote them not just to communicate with his partner, but for an audience.

Space does not allow for a full account of all the strange and anomalous elements of Charlie Kirk's violent death—elements that seem inconsistent with the official narrative. Many commentators found it very strange that Kirk's security detail apparently took no measures to secure or even just to scan the rooftop with a direct line of sight that was only 142 yards from the stage. The question seems even more pressing when one considers the assassination attempt on presidential candidate Donald Trump the previous year in Butler, Pennsylvania in which a sniper was able to perch on an unsecured rooftop 142 yards from the stage. Securing nearby rooftops is standard procedure at outdoor speaking events for high-profile, controversial political figures.

Authorities maintain that the murder weapon was a .30-06 rifle that belonged to Robinson's grandfather. Given the velocity and energy of a .30-06 cartridge (approximately 2,500 feet per second, generating around 2,000 foot-pounds of energy) it is very difficult to understand why the bullet did not pass through Kirk's neck and exit the back of it. Turning Point USA spokesman and executive producer of the *Charlie Kirk Show* Andrew Kolvet, addressed this anomaly in a post on X.

> I just spoke with the surgeon who worked on Charlie in the hospital. . . . He said the bullet "absolutely should have gone through, which is very very normal for a high powered, high velocity round. I've seen wounds from this caliber many times and they always just go through everything. This would have taken a moose or two down, an elk, etc." But it didn't go through. Charlie's body stopped it. I mentioned to his doctor that there were dozens of staff, students, and special guests standing directly behind Charlie on the other side of the tent, and he replied: "It was an absolute miracle that someone else didn't get killed." "His bone was so healthy and the density was so so impressive that he's like the man of steel. It should have just gone through and through. It likely would have killed those standing behind him too." In the end, the coroner did find the bullet just beneath the skin. Even in death, Charlie managed to save the lives of those around him. Remarkable. Miraculous.[5]

This is a very strange and implausible communique. Also strange was the behavior of Kirk's chief of staff, Michael McCoy. In the minutes before the shot was fired, he was standing a few feet behind Charlie Kirk, slightly behind the back of the tent. In video footage he can be seen looking at his phone, which he is grasping with his right hand. Just before the shot was fired, he was holding the face of the phone against his chest, with his left arm crossed over his right. When the shot was fired, he instantly raised his phone to his right ear, turned, and walked away.

From where McCoy was standing—behind and to the left of Charlie Kirk—he had no means of knowing where Kirk was shot, the severity of the injury, or his prospects for surviving. Nevertheless, McCoy instantly turned around and walked away, *before* Kirk slumped back into his chair, and *before* blood issued from the wound. McCoy then passed behind the tent, talking on his phone, while others ran past him. Unlike the people who ran past him, he didn't seem concerned that additional shots could be fired in his direction as he walked behind the tent and through the line of fire of the shot just taken. From there, he kept walking, past the SUV to which Kirk was taken shortly thereafter, apparently never looking back to assess the situation. All the above raises the suspicion that McCoy had foreknowledge of the assassination.

Joe Kent, former director of the National Counterterrorism Center (NCTC) under the Trump administration, stated that his team identified multiple instances of apparent foreknowledge of Kirk's assassination—that is, social media posts and online discussions *before* the shooting at Utah Valley University that predicted or referenced Kirk being killed at the event. Kent's team also detected evidence of potential foreign ties. He found this troubling, given that, in June 2025, Kirk visited the White House and urgently tried to dissuade President Trump from attacking Iran. This was consistent with multiple occasions in which he spoke to his large following about US foreign policy in the Middle East and declared it would be a "catastrophic mistake," and not in the interest of the American people, for the United States to go to war with Iran.[6]

Less than one month after Kirk was assassinated, the Trump administration began discussions and preparations for additional US strikes on Iran. On October 5, 2025, while visiting the Naval Station Norfolk to celebrate the 250th anniversary of the US Navy, Trump stated that he would bomb Iran again if they restarted their nuclear program. Charlie Kirk was an exceptionally thoughtful, informed, and articulate young man. Had he not been assassinated, he would have again tried to dissuade President Trump from attacking Iran a second time. The rotating cast of hosts who took over his show, most notably Andrew Kolvet and Blake Neff, have expressed mild caution against the Iran War that began on February 28, 2026, but they have not opposed the strikes.

CHAPTER 23

IRAN

Mind Virus: Fear and loathing of Iran and its theocratic state
Proposed Remedy: Attacking Iran on February 28, 2026

In his Farewell Address of 1796, printed in *Claypoole's American Daily Advertiser* on September 19, 1796, President George Washington wrote:

> Europe has a set of primary interests which to us have none or a very remote relation. Hence she must be engaged in frequent controversies, the causes of which are essentially foreign to our concerns. . . . Our detached and distant situation invites and enables us to pursue a different course. If we remain one people, under an efficient government, the period is not far off when we may defy material injury from external annoyance.

As Washington saw it, the key to avoiding "material injury from external annoyance" was to avoid political alliance with any particular nation.

> In the execution of such a plan nothing is more essential than that permanent, inveterate antipathies against particular nations and passionate attachments for others should be excluded, and that in place of them just and amicable feelings toward all should be cultivated. The nation which indulges toward another an habitual hatred or an habitual fondness is in some degree a slave. It is a slave to its animosity or to its affection, either of which is sufficient

> to lead it astray from its duty and its interest. Antipathy in one nation against another disposes each more readily to offer insult and injury. . . . So, likewise, a passionate attachment of one nation for another produces a variety of evils. Sympathy for the favorite nation, facilitating the illusion of an imaginary common interest in cases where no real common interest exists, and infusing into one the enmities of the other, betrays the former into a participation in the quarrels and wars of the latter without adequate inducement or justification.[1]

Underlying Washington's address is a profound understanding of human nature, which is always prone to passion, hostility, pride, ambition, "and other sinister and pernicious motives." As in all human affairs, it is often difficult for everyone, including the conflicting parties, to comprehend fully the roots of longstanding antipathy that "disposes each more readily to offer insult and injury, to lay hold of slight causes of umbrage, and to be haughty and intractable when accidental or trifling occasions of dispute occur." And so, President Washington asked the rhetorical question, "Why entangle our peace and prosperity in the toils of European ambition, rivalship, interest, humor, or caprice?"

If President Washington were alive today, he would regard his thesis as even more apt with respect to the various nations and religious sects of the of the Middle East that are given to constant quarreling. The US government's "passionate attachment" to Israel—a country that has long existed in a state of implacable enmity with Iran—is precisely what Washington counseled the republic to avoid. He would also recognize that Iran's long history of political instability, despotic government, and theocratic state institutions are not the responsibility of the US government to correct. Finally, he would understand that the history of British, Soviet, and US meddling in Iranian affairs since 1941 has contributed to the pathologies its regime.

In 1941, during World War II, Britain and the Soviet Union invaded Iran to secure oil and supply routes to the Soviet Union.[2] The British and Soviets forced Reza Shah Pahlavi to abdicate and cede the throne to his son, Mohammad Reza Shah Pahlavi. The Allies occupied the country until 1946, while the Anglo-Iranian Oil Company (now known as

BP) dominated the nation's oil industry, fostering widespread resentment among Iranians who enjoyed little benefit from the exploitation of their natural resources. For example, in the year 1947, the company took approximately 82 percent of the profits from the oil it extracted from Iran.

Widespread popular discontent resulted in the rise of Mohammad Mosaddegh, a nationalist politician who became prime minister in 1951 and who proposed that Iran acquire a much larger share of the profits. Following failed attempts by the Iranian government in the years 1948–1950 to negotiate a 50/50 deal with the company, as Saudi Arabia had recently done, the government of Prime Minister Mosaddegh nationalized the company. Two years later, in 1953, the CIA and Britain's MI6 orchestrated a coup that overthrew Mosaddegh and restored Shah Mohammad Reza Pahlavi—who briefly fled the country in August 1953— to absolute power.[3]

The coup deepened resentment among ordinary Iranians who regarded the United States as the usurper of their sovereignty. The Shah ruled Iran as a dictator, enforcing his will against dissidents with his SAVAK secret police and intelligence agency that often tortured and executed dissidents. The US government backed the Shah with billions of dollars of military assistance, and Israel maintained friendly relations with his government.

In 1963, two years after President John F. Kennedy was sworn in, he warned Israeli Prime Minister David Ben-Gurion that Washington would not tolerate an Israeli atomic bomb. In a sternly worded letter, Kennedy demanded regular inspections of Israel's Dimona reactor, and he warned that an Israeli nuclear weapon would likely trigger a dangerous nuclear arms race across the Middle East.[4] Unlike Iran, Israel never signed or ratified the Nuclear Non-Proliferation Treaty (NPT). It is one of the few nations outside the treaty, which allows it to maintain its policy of "nuclear ambiguity"—that is, neither confirming nor denying the possession of nuclear weapons. However, by 1967, many analysts strongly suspected that Israel had produced weapons-grade plutonium at its Dimona nuclear site.

The 1979 Islamic Revolution overthrew the Shah and ended Iran's friendly relationship with the US government. This event, along with the American embassy hostage crisis and the Ayatollah Khomeini's characterization of the US as the "Great Satan," placed the two countries in the hostile state in which they have existed ever since. When the Iraqi dictator Saddam Hussein invaded Iran in September 1980, the United States equipped his regime with intelligence, economic credits, and dual-use chemical and biological agents such as anthrax and bubonic plague. The eight-year war devastated both countries and left Iran convinced that Washington would always side with its enemies.

In 1982, Israel invaded Lebanon with the stated objective of dismantling the Palestine Liberation Organization (PLO) that was operating in the country's southern region. The Israeli invasion prompted the founding of a Lebanese Shia militia that called itself Hezbollah ("Party of God"). Iran provided the paramilitary group with substantial financial support and military training to counter the Israeli invasion and occupation.

With the US using Iraq as a proxy to attack Iran, and Iran using Hezbollah as a proxy to attack Israel, hostility deepened and was further aggravated by reports that Iran was trying to develop nuclear weapons. In 1992, the then Israeli parliamentarian, Benjamin Netanyahu, gave an address to the Knesset in which he asserted that Iran was "three to five years" away from reaching nuclear weapons capability, and that this danger needed to be "uprooted by an international front headed by the US." In his 1995 book, *Fighting Terrorism*, he made a similar claim, as he did in addresses to Congress in 1996 and in 2002. During the latter address, he claimed that Saddam Hussein was also close to getting a nuke.

A 2009 US State Department cable released by Wikileaks reported that the then prime ministerial candidate Netanyahu had assured a visiting congressional delegation that Iran was "probably one or two years away" from developing nuclear weapons capability. Another 2009 cable reported the reelected prime minister telling another delegation of American politicos that "Iran has the capability now to make one bomb . . . [or] they could wait and make several bombs in a year or two." In a 2010 interview with Jeffrey Goldberg at *The Atlantic*, he asserted "You don't want a messianic apocalyptic cult controlling atomic bombs . . . that's what is happening in Iran." In 2012 Netanyahu said in talks reported by Israeli media that Iran is just "a few months away" from attaining nuclear capabilities. Later in 2012, he addressed the United Nations and asserted that Iran would be able to build a nuke in roughly one year.

In 2015, the five permanent members of the United Nations Security Council (China, France, Russia, United Kingdom, United States) plus Germany entered the Joint Comprehensive Plan of Action (JCPOA) deal with Iran to limit its nuclear program in exchange for sanctions relief. The plan explicitly required extensive International Atomic Energy Agency (IAEA) supervision. The IAEA was tasked with independently verifying and monitoring Iran's compliance with nuclear-related commitments. However, in 2018, the first Trump administration withdrew from the agreement, claiming that the arrangement was inadequate. By withdrawing from JCPOA, Trump returned the US to a state of overt hostility with Iran, which responded by limiting the agreed upon IAEA inspections.

According to former Secretary of State Antony Blinken, Netanyahu repeatedly tried to pressure the Obama administration to attack Iran, but President Obama made it clear that if Israel attacked Iran, it would be on its own. In 2023, Israel claimed it was facing an imminent attack from Hezbollah and therefore intended to launch a preemptive attack on the paramilitary group's positions in Lebanon. The Biden administration told the Israelis that if they attacked first, they would be on their own.[5]

In June 2025, the Trump administration launched Operation Midnight Hammer to destroy three key Iranian nuclear sites—Natanz, Fordow, and Isfahan. Following these strikes, President Trump proclaimed that the US had "completely and totally obliterated" Iran's nuclear enrichment capability. However, in late January 2026, he sent a large naval fleet to the Arabian Sea, off the coast of Oman, to apply pressure on Iran to give up its stockpile of 60 percent enriched uranium (approximately 30 percent below weapons grade).

On February 6 in Muscat, Oman, President Trump's special envoys, Steve Witkoff and Jared Kushner, met the Iranian Foreign Minister, Abbas Araghchi, to discuss how Iran could avoid being attacked again by the United States. Following this initial talk, Witkoff and Kushner met with Araghchi in Geneva, Switzerland on February 26, with Omani Foreign Minister Badr Al Busaidi mediating. The following evening, Al Busaidi appeared on CBS's *Face the Nation* and stated that a nuclear deal was "within our reach."[6] Specifically, the Iranian Foreign Minister stated that Iran would consider giving up its 60 percent enriched uranium in exchange for concessions from the United States. Al Busaidi encouraged the Trump administration to give the US envoys and the Iranian Foreign Minister more time to strike a deal.

Britain's national security adviser, Jonathan Powell, attended the talks in Geneva and subsequently stated his belief that progress had been made. Unnamed British sources told the *Guardian* newspaper that "the UK team were surprised by what the Iranians put on the table. It was not a complete deal, but it made progress and was unlikely to be the Iranians' final offer."[7] The British team expected the next round of negotiations—in Vienna on Monday, March 2—to go ahead as planned. However, despite Omani Foreign Minister Al Busaidi's encouraging news on the evening of February 27, the armed forces of Israel and the United States launched airstrikes against Iran at 8:10 local time the next morning. The strikes—code-named Operation Epic Fury—halted all diplomatic negotiations. Omani Foreign Minister Al-Busaidi flew to Washington to protest that US special envoys Witkoff and Kushner had misrepresented Iranian concessions.

On March 17, Joe Kent, director of the National Counterterrorism Center, resigned with the assertion that "Iran posed no imminent threat to our nation."[8] The following day, US Director of National Intelligence Tulsi Gabbard submitted a written report to the Senate Intelligence Committee stating that Iran made "no efforts" to rebuild its nuclear enrichment program following the 2025 strikes.[9] In her oral testimony on the same day, she added an element of ambiguity to her written report by stating that the intelligence community believed that Iran was trying to recover from "severe damage" to its nuclear infrastructure.

One often hears the assertion that Iran's Supreme Leader, Ali Khamenei, was a religious fanatic for whom the Cold War doctrine of Mutually Assured Destruction (MAD) did not apply. However, this appears to be more of an assertion than an established fact. Khamenei issued an oral fatwa (religious decree) against the production of nuclear weapons in October 2003 and reiterated it in April 2010 and October 2019. He was also known to be strongly dedicated to his wife, six children, in-laws, and seven grandchildren.

The Iranian regime has a forty-seven-year track record of pragmatic survival behavior. It has not invaded neighbors, and it has used proxies and deniability to avoid direct regime-ending confrontations. The regime has adapted to sanctions, negotiated the JCPOA (2015) to ease pressure, and reacted to provocations with calibrated responses such as limited direct strikes on Israel after assassinations. In a 2012 *60 Minutes* interview, former Mossad chief Meir Dagan characterized the regime as "very rational" and he said it weighs implications carefully.[10]

Rarely if ever mentioned in the western media is the possibility that if the Iranian regime indeed wishes to acquire nuclear weapons, it is for the rational purpose of deterring aggression from Israel and the United States, both of which are armed with nuclear weapons. Here it is useful to compare Iran to Pakistan. The latter country is often accused by the United States of sponsoring terrorism and is strongly suspected of having provided a haven for Osama bin Laden for five years in a secure compound in Abbottabad, a military garrison town close to Islamabad. Following India's acquisition and testing of a nuclear bomb in 1974, Pakistan began developing its own nuclear weapons against strong Israeli opposition. In 1981, the Mossad sent letter bombs to firms in West Germany and Switzerland that were assisting in the effort. Though Pakistan succeeded in acquiring and testing nuclear weapons in 1998, it has never threatened Israel with an atomic bomb attack. The government of Pakistan believes that possessing nuclear weapons is a deterrent against aggression from India and other nations in the region. Given that Israel once regarded Pakistan's nuclear ambition as a grave threat, it's a remarkable irony of history that the recent ceasefire negotiations between US and Iranian envoys were conducted in Islamabad, Pakistan and organized by Pakistani mediators.

In 2006, North Korea began successfully testing nuclear weapons. Since then, its dynastic dictator, Kim Jong Un—widely regarded as aggressive and unpredictable—has repeatedly threatened "shocking and unimaginable disaster," and "total destruction" of the United States if it takes military action against North Korea. Despite his threats, most military analysts believe he is a rational actor who understands the MAD doctrine and therefore maintains nuclear weapons as a means of deterrence rather than suicidal aggression. With the US and Israel now waging war on Iran after killing Ali Khamenei and several of his family members in the opening bombardment, it seems likely the Iranian government will now try to move forward with enriching its 60 percent uranium to full weapons grade.

The American and Israeli airstrikes were apparently conceived as a rapid "decapitation" maneuver that would quickly result in the end of the Iranian regime. However, as of this writing in April, the US-Israel war has not been resolved. Iran's widely predicted closure of the Strait of Hormuz in the event it was attacked is already causing fuel shortages in Asia and Australia. Steadily rising oil prices have already caused gasoline, diesel, and jet fuel cost to rise significantly, which will likely result in significant hardship for the working and middle classes that were already being hurt by inflation. Each passing day of death and destruction seems to vindicate Charlie Kirk's warning that war with Iran would be a "catastrophic mistake." And so, "We the People" of the United States are now left trying to figure out why President Trump joined Israel in attacking Iran after proclaiming dozens of times since 2015 that he would never drag the United States into another immensely destructive and costly war in the Middle East.

Millions of Americans must somehow come to terms with the bitter realization that President Trump not only broke his promise not to drag the United States into another foreign war; he also tricked us into reestablishing our undue bond with the central state and our erroneous belief that our freedom and prosperity will be safeguarded by someone who holds high office. Our experience with the Biden and Trump administrations resembles what psychologists call trauma bonding.

Trauma bonding describes the way in which a victim develops an unhealthy attachment to his abuser, characterized by a repetitive pattern of intense abuse followed by periods of affection and kindness. Coined by Dr. Patrick Carnes, this bond is rooted in fear, dependency, and intermittent reinforcement, making it difficult for victims to leave, even when they recognize the relationship's toxicity. For four years, the American people were abused by the madness of the Biden administration and the preposterous insistence that the senile Joe Biden was our true executive. Trump succeeded in getting reelected president because he seemed to understand and sympathize with his supporters' distress about censorship, the COVID-19 vaccine mandate, and the US proxy war in Ukraine against nuclear-armed Russia. The bond between the abused (We the People) and the abuser (the US government) was thereby reconstituted.

After entering office, President Trump:

- refused to acknowledge that the mRNA COVID-19 vaccines are toxic
- honored Pfizer CEO Albert Bourla by inviting him to the White House
- did NOT demand a full investigation of the origin of SARS-CoV-2
- did NOT end the US proxy war against Ukraine as he promised
- did NOT demand the full disclosure of the Epstein Files
- attacked Thomas Massie and Marjorie Taylor Greene for demanding the full release of the Epstein Files
- did NOT demand that Google-YouTube cease running its vigorous shadow-banning program on dissident voices
- did NOT in the slightest tame the voracious beast of runaway federal spending
- did NOT reduce the undue influence of the national security state

Now, despite his dozens of promises of no new wars since he announced his candidacy in 2016, President Trump has started a war with Iran—a country four times the size of Iraq with twice the population and a standing army of 610,000 active-duty personnel.

Like the proverbial abused wife who can't break free from her abusive husband, tens of millions of Trump supporters cannot see that he reconstituted their bond with the US federal government, which is now abusing them again.

The only way this country could reclaim its health and vitality is through a widespread movement to reassert limits on federal power, which is the key underlying concept of the US Constitution. Only when "We the People" tell the US government—regardless of who is president—that we reject the continuous expansion of its size and power, and especially its abominable wars, will the cycle of abuse end. In the meantime, it appears that the US constitutional republic is in for a great deal of pain.

CHAPTER 24

THE DEVIL AND THE GREAT UNDOING

During the 1950s, while reflecting on the catastrophes that had happened during the first half of the twentieth century, Carl Jung wrote:

> Indeed, it is becoming ever more obvious that it is not famine, not earthquakes, not microbes, not cancer but man himself who is man's greatest danger to man, for the simple reason that there is no adequate protection against psychic epidemics, which are infinitely more devastating than the worst of natural catastrophes.[1]

As Jung saw it, only a large stratum of reasonable, responsible, and self-aware adults, working with each other, could prevent further manmade disasters from happening.

The events of the last twenty-five years indicate that this critical stratum of reasonable and responsible adults has worn perilously thin in the United States and in the other nations of the West. The mind viruses characterized in this book have rapidly infected our civilization not because they are especially virulent, but because we are so weak and susceptible to them.

During the COVID-19 pandemic, shortly before Dr. Peter McCullough gave his first Senate testimony about the official pandemic response, he had a conversation with his church pastor, Andrew Forrest, about medical centers refusing to administer certain safe and effective treatments to desperately ill patients.

"It's as though, for the first time in history, our medical system is opposed to caring for the sick," McCullough said. "What on Earth is going on?"

Pastor Forrest wasn't surprised.

"There are times when evil prevails over good in a large way," he said. "We know from the dark periods of history that this has happened before, and now it's happening again. What you describe is Satan working in the hearts and minds of people, sowing fear, confusion, and anger. All you can do is keep trying to do good until it turns the tide."

At the time that Dr. McCullough related this conversation to me, I doubted Forrest's supernatural explanation for what we were observing, which I figured could be explained by fear, greed, and other atavistic emotions. However, the further I got into my research, the more I thought about traditional, metaphysical concepts of evil. Especially perplexing to me was the way in which hospitals steadfastly refused to administer ivermectin and other safe old drugs to critically ill patients to whom nothing else was offered. Many hospital administrators went as far as defying court orders to administer the drugs, preferring to engage in costly lawsuits instead of allowing ivermectin—an FDA-approved "wonder drug" whose discoverers had received the Nobel Prize in 2015—to be administered to dying people. How could one explain this nihilistic behavior that caused patients and their families to experience total despair?

I don't know if the devil exists, or if he is merely the mythical personification of the madness and malevolence that may, under certain circumstances, spread like a contagion, causing masses of humans to commit extremely destructive behavior. I find it fascinating that the Greek word for devil, diabolos, derives from the verb *diaballein* ("to slander" or "to attack") which literally means "to throw across" or "to throw apart.") Since 2001, our civilization has been barraged by a series of purported threats that have thrown us apart from each other, dividing us into hostile camps, and causing rifts even among old friends and family members.

As was recently revealed in vivid and astonishing detail in the extended release of the Epstein Files on January 30, 2026, our current ruling class is as deluded, self-serving, and irresponsible as it has ever been in history. The disclosures seemed to confirm the thesis set forth by investigative journalist Whitney Webb in her 2022 book, *One Nation Under Blackmail:*

The Sordid Union Between Intelligence and Organized Crime That Gave Rise to Jeffrey Epstein. As Webb conceptualized it, Epstein's sexual blackmail and trafficking operation was not the work of a lone actor, but the latest manifestation of a long-standing nefarious relationship between US (and Israeli) intelligence agencies and transnational organized crime networks.

In his email correspondence, Epstein himself referenced the intoxicating power of his insubordination to all spiritual and legal authority. In a cryptic September 19, 2018 email to Steve Bannon regarding a news report about the Vatican supporting mass immigration, Epstein wrote, "great, they forgot to mention lucifer himself," followed by a quote from John Milton's *Paradise Lost* in which Satan rallies his fallen angels after being cast out of Heaven: "Here we may reign secure, and in my choice / To reign is worth ambition though in Hell: / Better to reign in Hell than serve in Heav'n."[2]

The callousness and corruption on display in Epstein's correspondence recall Jordan Peterson's interview with Charlie Kirk shortly before Kirk's death. Reflecting on the current situation, Peterson pointed out that about 4 percent of every society is composed of predatory, parasitic psychopaths.[3] It's a notable fact that notorious psychopaths described in the literature of criminal psychology resemble the characters in Dostoevsky's novel *Demons* in their ruthlessness, moral nihilism, and lack of empathy.

In early 2026, the Epstein Files seemed to provide us with a unique opportunity to usher our overlords into disgraced retirement—something akin to Napoleon's final exile on the island of Saint Helena—in which they will be limited in their ability to do further harm. The disclosures provided us with clear evidence that we cannot blindly trust our institutional leaders to represent our interests. The files reminded us that unless our rulers are closely watched and held accountable for the gigantic messes they make, such as the 2008 financial crisis, they will continue yielding to the temptation to serve their own interests and those of their elite friends at the expense of everyone else.

Of great significance was the February 26 resignation of Børge Brende, a Norwegian politician, diplomat, and World Economic Forum (WEF) president and CEO from 2017 to 2026.

"After careful consideration, I have decided to step down as President and CEO of the World Economic Forum," he announced in a published statement. "My time here, spanning 8-1/2 years, has been profoundly rewarding." Prior to the release of the Epstein Files, Brende claimed, "I had nothing to do with Epstein" and he further stated that he didn't know about Epstein's 2008 criminal conviction. However, the release of emails from September 2018 revealed that Epstein had corresponded with Brende about working together to "create a new global architecture."

On September 16, Epstein wrote, "davos can really replace the UN. cyber, crypto, genetics . . . intl coordination. like my stint at the trilateral. Issues now need to deal with the distributed trust, and internet fallout." Brende replied in agreement: "Exactly—we need a new global architecture. World Economic Forum (Davos) is uniquely positioned—public private."[4] In other words, Epstein proposed that he work with Brende to make the World Economic Forum the preeminent institution for directing global affairs, including revolutionary technologies and the power of the internet to erode trust in government institutions.

Jeffrey Epstein's correspondence recalls Arnold Toynbee's theory of how civilizations rise and fall, which he presented in his book *A Study of History*. As he saw it, civilizations grow when a "creative minority"—an elite group of leaders—meets military and social challenges. The majority follows not from coercion but through willing imitation. Growth continues so long as the minority retains its creative vitality and inspires collective effort.

Decline begins when this creative minority degenerates into a "dominant minority." Proud and complacent about its past successes, the erstwhile creative minority idolizes its own power and prestige, loses moral authority, and begins to rule by force rather than from care, responsibility, and desire to build and create. Hubris, nationalism, militarism, and the pursuit of material comfort replace creative innovation. Society fractures into a "schism" between the alienated "internal proletariat" (the masses that withdraw their trust and faith in the elite), and the elite that is increasingly detached from the reality of the people it rules. Toynbee's thesis aligns with Frédéric Bastiat's 1850 essay titled *The Law*, in which he observed, "When plunder becomes a way of life for a group of men living together in society, they create for themselves in the course of time a legal system that authorizes it and a moral code that glorifies it."[5]

When World Economic Forum President Børge Brende resigned on February 26, many perceived that the release of the Epstein Files was having an enormous salutary effect in dismantling the "dominant minority" of the globalist elite. Two days later, in what may be the greatest misdirection trick in history, the military forces of Israel and the United States attacked Iran. Soon after the war began, internet searches and mainstream media coverage of the release of the Epstein Files dropped 90–95 percent.

As I stated in the preface, my objective in writing this book is to show how mind viruses are produced and transmitted to the public. I hope that revealing the anatomy of this diabolical project will immunize readers against the next mind virus that is unleashed on us. Strengthening our immunity begins with a careful examination of ourselves and our susceptibility to being manipulated by propaganda and driven by fear. We must take seriously our responsibility to educate ourselves and our children—to fortify our minds against the constant assault of distractions and confusing nonsense.

On September 17, 1787, at the conclusion of the Constitutional Convention, Benjamin Franklin walked out of Independence Hall. There he was approached by a prominent Philadelphia socialite named Elizabeth Willing Powel, who asked, "Well, Doctor, what have we got, a republic or a monarchy?"

"A republic, if you can keep it," Franklin replied.

Franklin's admonition has never been more apt than it is today.

NOTES

Prologue

1 F.M. Lur'e, *Nechayev: Creator of Destruction,* Moscow: *Molodaya Gvardiya,* 2001.
2 Jeffrey Meyers, "Portraits of a Terrorist: Dostoevsky, Conrad, and Coetzee," *Antioch Review*, Vol. 72, No. 1, Generations: Passing the Torch? (Winter 2014), pp. 61–80.
3 Sergey Nechayev, The Revolutionary Catechism, 1869, Marxist Internet Archive.
4 Fyodor Dostoevsky, *Demons*, translated by Richard Pevear and Larissa Volokhonsky (New York, Vintage Books, 1994).
5 V.I. Lenin, "The Tasks of the Youth Leagues" delivered at the Third All-Russian Congress of the Russian Young Communist League (Komsomol) in Moscow, October 2, 1920.
6 See Robert Conquest's two books, *The Great Terror* (Oxford University Press, 40th anniversary edition, 2007) and *Harvest of Sorrow* (Oxford University Press, 1987).
7 Z.A.B. Zeman (ed.), *Germany and the Revolution in Russia, 1915–1918*: Documents from the Archives of the German Foreign Ministry (London: Oxford University Press, 1958).
8 Winston Churchill, House of Commons, 5 November 1919, in Richard M. Langworth, ed., *Churchill in His Own Words* (New York, Rosetta, 2015.) p. 355.

Chapter 1

1 Tomás Irish, *The University at War* (London: Palgrave Macmillan, 2015).
2 Madison Debates, June 29, 1787, reproduced by the Avalon Project, Yale University Law School.
3 President Dwight D. Eisenhower's Farewell Address (1961), National Archives.

Chapter 2

1 Brian Fagan, *The Little Ice Age: How Climate Made History 1300-1850* (New York, Basic Books, 2001).

2 Christopher S. Mackay, An *Unusual Inquisition: Translated Documents from Heinricus Institoris's Witch Hunts in Ravensburg and Innsbruck* (Leiden, Brill, 2020).

3 Heirich Kramer, *Malleus Maleficarum: Hammer of Witches*, translated by Montague Summers and Paul Tice, New York: Dover, 1971).

4 George Lincoln Burr, *The Fate of Dietrich Flade* (New York: GP Putnams, 1891).

5 Brian P. Levack, *The Witch Hunter in Early Modern Europe* (London, Routledge, 2015).

6 Carl Jung, *Collected Works, Volume 10, Civilization in Transition* (Princeton University Press, 2024).

7 Rachel Walker, *Salem Witch Trials in History and Literature*, "Cotton Mather," University of Virginia, 2001. https://salem.lib.virginia.edu/people/c_mather.html.

8 Carl Jung, *Collected Works*, Volume 10, "The Undiscovered Self," Princeton University Press, 2024.

9 Ibid.

10 George S. Messersmith, U.S. Consul General in Berlin, June 26, 1933, letter to Under Secretary of State William Phillips, reproduced in "Peace and War: United States Foreign Policy, 1931–1941," U.S. Department of State.

Chapter 3

1 *"The Battle of Los Angeles,"* Military Museum. Retrieved 6 November 2015.

2 Executive Order 9066: Resulting in Japanese-American Incarceration (1942) National Archives.

3 *Korematsu v. United States*, 323 U.S. 214 (1944).

4 James Madison, "Political Observations," 1795.

5 *Korematsu v. United States*, 323 U.S. 214 (1944).

6 Bonhoeffer, Dietrich. "Von der Dummheit": *Widerstand und Ergebung. Briefe und Aufzeichnungen aus der Haft*. S. 17–20. Muenchen, Christian Kaiser Verlag, 1951.

7 Cosmides, L., Tooby, J., & Price, M. E, "Groups in Mind: The Coalitional Roots of War and Morality," *Cognition and Culture*, 2010.

8 Hart et al., "Differential response in the human amygdala to racial outgroup vs ingroup face stimuli." *NeuroReport*, 2000 Aug 3;11(11):2351-5.

9 Balliet et al. "Ingroup favoritism in cooperation: a meta-analysis" in *Psychological Bulletin*, 2014. Nov;140(6):1556-81.

10 Helgason et al. "mtDNA and the origin of the Icelanders: deciphering signals of recent population history," *American Journal of Human Genetics*, 2000 Feb 23;66(3):999–1016.

Chapter 4

1 James Madison, "letter to W. T. Barry, 4 August 1822," *The Founders' Constitution* (University of Chicago Press Web Edition).

2 "Thomas Jefferson, letter to Charles Yancey, 6 January 1816," Founders Online (National Archives).
3 "John Adams, letter to Massachusetts Militia, 11 October 1798," Founders Online (National Archives).
4 Madison Debates, June 29, 1787, reproduced by the Avalon Project, Yale University Law School.
5 Admiral Hyman G. Rickover, *How the Battleship Maine Was Destroyed,* (Washington: Naval History Division, Dept. of the Navy, U.S. Govt. Print. Off., 1976).
6 Edward L. Bernays, *Propaganda* (New York: Horace Liveright, 1928).
7 Edward L. Bernays, *Biography of an Idea: Memoirs of Public Relations Counsel* (New York: Simon and Schuster, 1965).
8 Letter from Supreme Court Justice Felix Frankfurter to President Franklin D. Roosevelt, 1934, Franklin D. Roosevelt Presidential Library and Museum, President's Personal File correspondence.
9 John Curatola, "Lend-Lease to the Eastern Front," The National World War II Museum, June 19, 2024.
10 S.J. Taylor, *Stalin's Apologist: Walter Duranty: The New York Times's Man in Moscow* (Oxford University Press, 1990).
11 Robert Conquest, *Harvest of Sorrow* (Oxford University Press, 1987).
12 Church Committee Final Report (1976, Book I and related volumes on intelligence activities) and Carl Bernstein, "The CIA and the Media," *Rolling Stone,* October 20, 1977.
13 Matt Taibbi, Written Statement submitted to "Hearing on the Weaponization of the Federal Government on the Twitter Files" Select Subcommittee on the Weaponization of the Federal Government Committee on the Judiciary United States House of Representatives March 9, 2023.
14 See court documents for *Missouri v. Biden*.

Chapter 5

1 "President Dwight D. Eisenhower's Farewell Address (1961)," National Archives.
2 Gilbert King, "Fritz Haber's Experiments in Life and Death," *Smithsonian Magazine*, June 6, 2012.
3 Margit Szöllösi-Janze, "Pesticides and war: the case of Fritz Haber," *European Review*, Cambridge University Press, 2001.
4 Malcolm Gladwell, *The Bomber Mafia* (New York: Little, Brown and Company, 2021).
5 Clay Blair Jr., "The Passing of a Great Mind," *LIFE*, February 25, 1957, p. 96.
6 *Hitler's Table Talk, 1941–1944: His Private Conversations.* Translated by Norman Cameron and R. H. Stevens, (New York: Enigma Books, 2000).

Chapter 6

1 National Security Archive (George Washington University), "NATO Expansion: What Gorbachev Heard," December 12, 2017 and Mary Elise Sarotte, *Not One Inch: America, Russia, and the Making of Post-Cold War Stalemate*, (New Haven: Yale University Press, 2021).
2 Osama bin Laden, "Declaration of Jihad Against the Americans Occupying the Land of the Two Holiest Sites," *Al-Quds Al-Arabi*, August 23, 1996.
3 See recorded episode of *60 Minutes* on YouTube.
4 See copy of "A Clean Break: A New Strategy for Securing the Realm," posted on Douglas J. Feith's website.
5 Osama bin Laden, "Declaration of Jihad Against the Americans Occupying the Land of the Two Holiest Sites," *Al-Quds Al-Arabi*, August 23, 1996.
6 Bernard Lewis, "License to Kill: Usama bin Ladin's Declaration of Jihad," *Foreign Affairs*, November 1, 1998.

Chapter 7

1 Declassified 28 pages (Part Four: "Finding, Discussion, and Narrative Regarding Certain Sensitive National Security Matters") of the Joint Inquiry into Intelligence Community Activities Before and After the Terrorist Attacks of September 11, 2001.
2 Ibid.
3 Ibid.
4 CNN, "Congress releases '28 pages' on alleged Saudi 9/11 ties" July 15, 2016.
5 "The Intelligence Community's Knowledge of the September 11 Hijackers Prior to September 11, 2001," Eleanor Hill, Staff Director, Joint inquiry Staff, September 20, 2002.
6 U.S. District Judge George B. Daniels (Southern District of New York) Memorandum Decision and Order, August 28, 2025.
7 Tucker Carlson, "The 9/11 Files," Tucker Carlson Network, September 23, 2015.
8 Catharine Herridge, "Straight to the Point: Exposing Epstein's Saudi 9/11 Connection," *Los Angeles Times* Studios, March 26–27, 2026.
9 ABC News "Were Israelis Detained on Sept. 11 Spies?" June 21, 2002.
10 LaHadashot (The News), Channel 2, Israel, November 2021. See segment on YouTube.
11 Neta C. Crawford, "United States Budgetary Costs of the Post-9/11 Wars Through FY2019: $5.9 Trillion Spent and Obligated," Brown University, November 14, 2018.
12 James Bennet, "A Day of Terror: The Israelis; Spilled Blood Is Seen as Bond That Draws 2 Nations Closer," *New York Times*, Section A, Page 22, September 12, 2001.
13 Burnham, Riyadh, et al. "Mortality after the 2003 invasion of Iraq: a cross-sectional cluster sample survey" *The Lancet*, October 11, 2006.

14 See Brown University's "Cost of War" project.
15 Jannace, Pompeii, et al., "Occupation and Risk of Traumatic Brain Injury in the Millennium Cohort Study," *Military Medicine*, August 29, 2023.
16 Mazzetti, Mark; Goldman, Adam; Schmidt, "Behind the Sudden Death of a $1 Billion Secret C.I.A. War in Syria" *The New York Times*, (2 August 2017).
17 Ramy Inocencia et al., "Trump meets with Syrian President Ahmed Al-Sharaa after U.S. removes him from terrorist list," CBS News, November 10, 2025.
18 Mostafa Salem, "Syria's jihadist-turned-president caps extraordinary transformation with White House visit," CNN, November 12, 2025.

Chapter 8

1 Thomas E. White, Secretary of the Army, Memorandum: "Slowdown of the Anthrax Vaccine Immunization Program" (AVIP), June 8, 2001.
2 Decker, R. Scott. *Recounting the Anthrax Attacks: Terror, the Amerithrax Task Force, and the Evolution of Forensics in the FBI*: Lanham, MD, Rowman & Littlefield, 2018.
3 H.R.3448 - Public Health Security and Bioterrorism Preparedness and Response Act of 2002, 06/12/2002 Became Public Law No: 107-188. https://www.congress.gov/bill/107th-congress/house-bill/3448.
4 United States District Court for the District of Columbia Thomas L. Rempfer, et al., *Plaintiffs, v. U.S. Department of Air Force Board for Correction of Military Records, et al.*, Defendants. pp. 18-19. https://ecf.dcd.uscourts.gov/cgi-bin/show_public_doc?2005cv2350-31.
5 NBC NEWS, "U.S. officials: Scientist was anthrax killer," Aug. 6, 2008. https://www.nbcnews.com/id/wbna26054859.
6 See "How Saddam Happened," Congressional Record Volume 148, Number 120 (Friday, September 20, 2002), Senate, Pages S8987-S8998.
7 H.R. 2863, Department of Defense, Emergency Supplemental Appropriations to Address Hurricanes in the Gulf of Mexico, and Pandemic Influenza Act, 2006. Public Law 109–148—DEC. 30, 2005, Division C—Public Readiness and Emergency Preparedness Act, PDF pp. 139-153. https://www.congress.gov/bill/109th-congress/house-bill/2863/text.
8 United States Senate. Roll Call Vote 109th Congress - 1st Session, H.R. 2863 (DOD, Emergency Supplemental Appropriations to Address Hurricanes in the Gulf of Mexico, and Pandemic Influenza Act, 2006 https://www.senate.gov/legislative/LIS/roll_call_votes/vote1091/vote_109_1_00366.htm.
9 Phlip M. Boffey, "Soft Evidence and Hard Sell," *New York Times*, Sept. 5, 1976.
10 Neustadt RE, Fineberg HV. "The Swine Flu Affair: Decision-Making on a Slippery Disease." Washington (DC): National Academies Press (US); 1978. C, Swine Flu Chronology January 1976—March 1977.
11 *New York Times*, October 30, 1977. https://www.nytimes.com/1977/10/30/archives/article-12-no-title.html.

12 Katie Drummond, "Once Scarce, H1N1 Vaccines Now Getting Dumped," AOL news, April 1, 2010.
13 Herfst, S.; Schrauwen, E.J.A.; Linster, M.; Chutinimitkul, S.; de Wit, E.; Munster, V.J.; Sorrell, E.M.; Bestebroer, T.M.; Burke, D.F.; Smith, D.J.; et al. "Airborne Transmission of Influenza A/H5N1 Virus Between Ferrets." *Science* 2012, *336*, 1534–154.
14 Imai, M., Watanabe, T., Hatta, M. et al. "Experimental adaptation of an influenza H5 HA confers respiratory droplet transmission to a reassortant H5 HA/H1N1 virus in ferrets." *Nature* 486, 420–428 (2012).

Chapter 9

1 See Wikileaks "Podesta Emails."
2 United States Department of the Treasury Initial Section 105(A) Troubled Asset Relief Program Report To Congress for the Period of October 6, 2008 to November 30, 2008.
3 John Carney, "Citi and Morgan Stanley Borrowed Over $2 Trillion From Fed," CNBC, July 22, 2011.
4 Andrew Huszar, "Confessions of a Quantitative Easer," *Wall Street Journal*, Nov. 11, 2013.
5 Committee for a Responsible Federal Budget, "Debt Ceiling Q&A," January 7, 2025.

Chapter 10

1 Zach Goldberg, "How the Media Led the Great Racial Awakening," Tablet, August 4, 2020.
2 Alexis de Tocqueville, *The Old Regime and the Revolution*, 1856.
3 Neil Gotanda, "A Critique of "Our Constitution is Colorblind," *Stanford Law Review*, Nov. 1991.
4 See transcript posted on Famous Trials (University of Missouri-Kansas City School of Law).
5 See trial transcript posted on Famous Trials (University of Missouri-Kansas City School of Law).
6 See Department of Justice Report Regarding the Criminal Investigation into the Shooting Death of Michael Brown by Ferguson, Missouri Police Officer Darren Wilson, March 4, 2015.
7 See Press Release Summary of Hennepin County Medical Examiner's Office Autopsy Report (ME No. 20-3700) performed by Dr. Andrew M. Baker on May 26, 2020.
8 See trial testimony of Dr. Andrew M. Baker on April 9, 2021. "What Caused George Floyd's Death?" Famous Trials (University of Missouri-Kansas City School of Law).
9 See Open letter advocating for an anti-racist public health response to demonstrations against systemic injustice occurring during the COVID-19 pandemic.

10 Jamiles Lartey and Abbie VanSickle, "'Don't Kill Me': Others Tell of Abuse by Officer Who Knelt on George Floyd," *New York Times*, Feb. 2, 2021.
11 Cary Aspinwall and Dave Boucher, "'You're gonna kill me!': Dallas police body cam footage reveals the final minutes of Tony Timpa's life," *Dallas Morning News*, July 31, 2019.
12 ACLED, "Demonstrations and Political Violence in America: New Data for Summer 2020," Sept. 3, 2020.
13 Major Cities Chiefs Association (MCCA), "Report on the 2020 Protests and Civil Unrest."
14 Sean Campbell, "Black Lives Matter Secretly Bought a $6 Million House" *New York Magazine*, April 4, 2022.
15 DoD Press Release, "Executive Director of Black Lives Matter OKC Charged with Wire Fraud and Money Laundering," December 11, 2025.
16 Thomas Sowell, *Discrimination and Disparities* (New York: Basic Books, 2019).
17 DEI Spending in the Biden Administration Functional Government Initiative (FGI) and the Center for Renewing America (CRA), March 10, 2025.
18 National Museum of African American History and Culture (NMAAHC) online educational portal, "Talking About Race," subsection on "Whiteness," 2020. Chart removed July 16–17, 2020 after public criticism.
19 Thomas Sowell, *Discrimination and Disparities* (New York: Basic Books, 2019).
20 "A Pathway to Equitable Math Instruction," May 2021.
21 Corinne S. Kennedy, "Palm Springs starts removal of controversial tamarisk trees between neighborhood, golf course," *Palm Springs Desert Sun*, May 24, 2018.

Chapter 11

1 Ellen Nakashima, "Russian government hackers penetrated DNC, stole opposition research on Trump" *Washington Post*, June 14, 2026.
2 Peter Hermann and Clarence Williams, "Slain Democratic National Committee staffer 'wanted to make a difference,'" *Washington Post*, July 11, 2016.
3 Randy Smith, "Where, when, and why: A guide to homicides in 2016," D.C. Policy Center, February 20, 2017.
4 Metropolitan Police Department, "Homicides in the District of Columbia," October 2001.
5 Metropolitan Police, "Major Case/Unsolved Homicides - 2016."
6 Zaid Jilani, "DNC Staffers Mocked the Bernie Sanders Campaign, Leaked Emails Show," *The Intercept*, July 22, 2016.
7 Donna Brazile, *Hacks: The Inside Story of the Break-ins and Breakdowns That Put Donald Trump in the White House* (New York: Grand Central Publishing, November 2017). An excerpt titled "Inside Hillary Clinton's Secret Takeover of the DNC," *Politico*, November 2, 2017.

8 Duncan Campbell and James Risen, "CIA Director Met Advocate of Disputed DNC Hack Theory—at Trump's Request," *The Intercept*, November 7, 2017.
9 Adam Entous et al. Clinton campaign, "DNC paid for research that led to Russia dossier," *Washington Post*, October 24, 2017.
10 National Security Archive (George Washington University), "NATO Expansion: What Gorbachev Heard," December 12, 2017.
11 George F. Kennan, "A Fateful Error," *New York Times*, February 5, 1997.
12 The Department of Defense's Cooperative Threat Reduction Program—Biological Threat Reduction Program Activities in Ukraine FACT SHEET.
13 Jeremy Kuzmarov, "National Endowment for Democracy deletes records of funding projects in Ukraine," *Monthly Review*, March 8, 2022.
14 Ivan Katchanovski, *The Maidan Massacre: The Mass Killing that Changed the World* (London: Palgrave MacMillan, 2024).
15 BBC News, "Ukraine crisis: Transcript of leaked Nuland-Pyatt call," Feb. 7, 2024.
16 Adam Entous and Michael Schwirtz, "The Spy War: How the C.I.A. Secretly Helps Ukraine Fight Putin," *New York Times*, February 28, 2024.
17 Elias Yousif, "U.S. Security Assistance to Ukraine Breaks All Precedents," Stimson Center, Congressional Research Service (CRS), October 20, 2022.
18 Rolf Steininger, *Austria, Germany, and the Cold War: From the Anschluss to the State Treaty, 1938-1955*, (Oxford: Bergbahn Books, 2003).
19 The Ministry of Foreign Affairs of the Russian Federation, "Press release on Russian draft documents on legal security guarantees from the United States and NATO," December 17, 2021. Biden's rejection reported by Amanda Macias, "Biden didn't accept Putin's 'red lines' on Ukraine," CNBC, December 8, 2021.

Chapter 12

1 Ben Knight, "The History of Nord Stream," *Deutsche Welle*, July 23, 2021.
2 Danish Energy Agency, "The possible climate effect of the gas leaks from the Nord Stream 1 and Nord Stream 2 pipelines," September 29, 2022.
3 PBS News, "Gas leaks in Baltic Sea could equate to 1/3 of Denmark's CO2 emissions, official says," September 28, 2022.
4 Leslie Palti-Guzman et al. "U.S. LNG: Remapping Energy Security," CSIS, January 17, 2023.

Chapter 13

1 John von Neumann, "Can We Survive Technology," *Fortune*, June 1, 1955.
2 See Quaternary Period, Science Direct for excerpts from multiple standard reference works.
3 Kjær, K.H., Winther Pedersen, M., De Sanctis, B. et al. "A 2-million-year-old ecosystem in Greenland uncovered by environmental DNA." *Nature* 612, 283–291 (2022).

4 Hannah Devlin, "DNA from 2m years ago reveals lost Arctic world," Dec. 7, 2022.
5 See Portland State University, "Glaciers and Glacier Change."
6 NASA, "Milankovitch (Orbital) Cycles and Their Role in Earth's Climate," Feb. 27, 2020.
7 NASA, "Milankovitch (Orbital) Cycles and Their Role in Earth's Climate," Feb. 27, 2020.
8 Rebecca Lindsey, "How do we know the build-up of carbon dioxide in the atmosphere is caused by humans?" NOAA, October 12, 2022.
9 Berner et al. "Geocarb Iii: A Revised Model Of Atmospheric Co2 Over Phanerozoic Time," *American Journal of Science*, Vol. 301, February, 2001, P. 182–204.
10 Michael Jerret et al. "Up in smoke: California's greenhouse gas reductions could be wiped out by 2020 wildfires," *Environmental Pollution*, Volume 310, October 2022.
11 Judd, Tierney, et al. "A 485-million-year history of Earth's surface temperature," *Science*, Sept. 20, 2024.

Chapter 14

1 Bjorn Lomborg, "The Climate-Industrial Complex," *Wall Street Journal*, May 22, 2009.
2 Mia Romare and Lisbeth Dahllöf. "The Life Cycle Energy Consumption and Greenhouse Gas Emissions from Lithium-Ion Batteries," Swedish Environmental Research Institute, May 2017.
3 Peter Lyon, "The Age Old Question Of Hybrids Vs EVs Is A Hot Topic At Toyota," *Forbes*, June 14, 2025.
4 Eric Wood et al. "The 2030 National Charging Network: Estimating U.S. Light-Duty Demand for Electric Vehicle Charging Infrastructure," National Renewable Energy Laboratory, June 2023.
5 See PBD Podcast Ep. 171, "The Truth About Greenpeace w/ Dr. Patrick Moore," July 14, 2022.
6 Jonathan Franzen, "Carbon Capture," *New Yorker*, March 30, 2015.
7 American Bird Conservancy, "How Many Birds Are Killed by Wind Turbines?" Jan. 26, 2021.
8 Auwahi Wind Farm Project Habitat Conservation Plan, 2012.
9 US Geological Survey, "Frequently Asked Questions about volcanic gas at Kīlauea."
10 Linda Bonvie, "What Will 357 Wind Turbines Operating off the New Jersey Coast Sound Like?" Badditives, October 16, 2024.
11 David Walker, "SNP cuts down millions of trees to build wind farms on public land in huge blow to environmental credentials," *Scottish Daily Express*, July 20, 2023.
12 Ione Wells, "Amazon forest felled to build road for climate summit," BBC News, March 11, 2025.

13 Hans Nicholas Jong, "Palm oil deforestation makes comeback in Indonesia after decade-long slump," Mongabay, Feb. 13, 2024.
14 ForoNuclear, "Germany's Chancellor Merz says the nuclear phaseout was a "huge mistake," March 17, 2026.
15 Melina Walling and Seth Borenstein, "In front of drowning nations, Trump calls climate change a 'green scam' at UN" KSAT, Sept. 23, 2025.
16 NOAA, "The Deadliest Atlantic Tropical Cyclones, 1492–1996."

Chapter 15

1 Lewandowski et al., "Climate emotions, thoughts, and plans among US adolescents and young adults: a nationally representative survey," *The Lancet Planetary Health*, Volume 8, Issue 11, November 2024.
2 NASA, "Why does the temperature record shown on your 'Vital Signs' page begin at 1880?."
3 Philip Shabecoff, "Global Warming Has Begun, Expert Tells Senate," *New York Times*, June 24, 1988.
4 Snejana Farberov, "Climate protester glues his head to 'Girl with a Pearl Earring,'" *New York Post*, Oct. 27, 2022.
5 Bill Gates, "Innovating to zero!" TED2010 Long Beach, California, February 20, 2020.
6 Ximena Bustillo, "Biden has a $369 billion climate plan—and new advisers to get the program running," NPR, Sept. 3, 2022.
7 IEA, Energy demand from AI.
8 Bill Gates, "Three tough truths about climate," GatesNotes, Oct. 27, 2025.

Chapter 16

1 David Tyrrell, *Cold Wars: The Fight Against the Common Cold*, (Oxford University Press, 2002).
2 Kristopher M. Curtis, Boyd Yount, Ralph S. Baric, "Methods for producing recombinant coronavirus," 2002-04-19, Application US10/474,962 filed by University of North Carolina at Chapel Hill. https://patents.google.com/patent/US7279327B2/en.
3 Cherry JD, Krogstad P., "SARS: the first pandemic of the 21st century." *Pediatr Res.* 2004 Jul;56(1):1-5. doi: 10.1203/01.PDR.0000129184.87042.FC. Epub 2004 May 19. PMID: 15152053; PMCID: PMC7086556. https://pmc.ncbi.nlm.nih.gov/articles/PMC7086556/.
4 "WHO announces discovery of virus that causes SARS," *UN NEWS*, 16 April 2003. https://news.un.org/en/story/2003/04/64992.
5 Ralph S. Baric, Curriculum Vitae, 57, "Synthetic Coronaviruses. Biohacking: Biological Warfare Enabling Technologies," June 2005, Washington, DC. DARPA/MITRE sponsored event. Invited Speaker, p. 28. https://media-speakerfile-pre.s3.amazonaws.com/documents/cc4e5e5d442320c20c7f76a0c3cadce51445358867.pdf.

6 Peter Daszak, "Understanding the Risk of Bat Coronavirus Emergence," NIH Grant Project No. 1R01AI110964-01, Project Start Date 01-June-2014, https://reporter.nih.gov/search/-bvPCvB7zkyvb1AjAgW5Yg/project-details/8674931.

7 Ge, XY., Li, JL., Yang, XL. et al. "Isolation and characterization of a bat SARS-like coronavirus that uses the ACE2 receptor." *Nature* 503, 535–538 (2013). https://doi.org/10.1038/nature12711.

8 Menachery, V., Yount, B., Debbink, K. et al. "A SARS-like cluster of circulating bat coronaviruses shows potential for human emergence." *Nat Med* 21, 1508–1513 (2015). https://doi.org/10.1038/nm.3985.

9 V.D. Menachery, B.L. Yount, A.C. Sims, et al. "SARS-like WIV1-CoV poised for human emergence," *Proc. Natl. Acad. Sci.* U.S.A. 113 (11) 3048-3053, 1517719113 (2016), https://doi.org/10.1073/pnas.

10 EcoHealth Alliance, "Project DEFUSE: Defusing the Threat of Bat-Borne Coronaviruses," 2018-03-27, p. 11 (PDF p. 13). Published on Document Cloud, https://www.documentcloud.org/documents/21066966-defuse-proposal/?mode=document#document/p13.

11 Forum on Medical and Public Health Preparedness for Catastrophic Events: Workshop Summary. Washington (DC): National Academies Press (US); 2016 Feb 12. 6, "Developing MCMs for Coronaviruses." Available from: https://www.ncbi.nlm.nih.gov/books/NBK349040/.

Chapter 17

1 Karl Laske and Jacques Massey, "The strange saga of how France helped build Wuhan's top-security virus lab." *Mediapart* 31 May 2020. https://www.mediapart.fr/en/journal/france/310520/strange-saga-how-france-helped-build-wuhans-top-security-virus-lab.

2 "'The Never Again Plan': Moderna CEO Stéphane Bancel wants to stop the next Covid-19—before it happens," Advisory Board, Dec. 22, 2020. https://www.advisory.com/blog/2020/12/moderna-ceo-covid-vaccine-bancel.

3 "DARPA Awards Moderna Therapeutics a Grant for up to $25 Million to Develop Messenger RNA Therapeutics™." Moderna Company Press Release, Oct. 2, 2013. https://investors.modernatx.com/news/news-details/2013/DARPA-Awards-Moderna-Therapeutics-a-Grant-for-up-to-25-Million-to-Develop-Messenger-RNA-Therapeutics/default.aspx.

4 "Coronavirus Vaccines and Prevention." https://www.niaid.nih.gov/diseases-conditions/coronavirus-vaccines-prevention.

5 Ikewaki N, Kurosawa G, Levy GA, Preethy S, Abraham SJK. "Antibody dependent disease enhancement (ADE) after COVID-19 vaccination and beta glucans as a safer strategy in management." *Vaccine*. 2023 Apr 6;41(15):2427-2429. doi: 10.1016/j.vaccine.2023.03.005. Epub 2023 Mar 8. PMID: 36906407; PMCID: PMC9992059.

6 Bancel S, Chakraborty T, De Fougerolles A, Elbashir SM, John M, Roy A, et al. "Modified Polynucleotides for the Production of Oncology-Related Proteins and Peptides." Cambridge, MA: US patent 9,587,003 filed on Feb. 4, 2016.

7 Ambati BK, Varshney A, Lundstrom K, Palú G, Uhal BD, Uversky VN, Brufsky AM. MSH3 Homology and Potential Recombination Link to SARS-CoV-2 Furin Cleavage Site. *Front Virol.* 2022 Feb;2:834808. doi: 10. 3389/fviro.2022.834808. Epub 2022 Feb 21. PMID: 39176223; PMCID: PMC11340822.

8 Fox Business, *Mornings with Maria*, February 24, 2022.

9 CEPI, Preliminary Business Plan 2017-2012, p. 7 (PDF p. 8). https://static.cepi.net/downloads/2023-12/CEPI-Preliminary-Business-Plan-061216_0.pdf.

10 "How Involved Was Epstein in Pandemic Strategies? What the Emails Do—and Don't—Tell Us," TrialSite News, February 19, 2026.

11 BioNTech SEC filings (U.S. Securities and Exchange Commission), Form F-1, 2019-2020. Exhibit 10.36, August 30,2019.

12 2019 Annual Report of the Global Preparedness Monitoring Board (GPMB), "A World at Risk: Annual report on global preparedness for health emergencies," September 2019, page 8.

13 David Cyranoski, "Inside the Chinese lab poised to study world's most dangerous pathogens," *Nature*, February 23, 2017.

14 Johns Hopkins Center for Health Security, EVENT 201, October 18, 2019. https://www.centerforhealthsecurity.org/event201/.

15 Material Transfer Agreement from NIAID/Moderna ("Provider") to Ralph Baric ("Research Recipient"), signed Dec. 12, 2019, pp. 105-107. https://embed.documentcloud.org/documents/6935295-NIH-Moderna-Confidential-Agreements/.

16 Jimmy Tobias, "Evolution of a Theory: Unredacted NIH Emails Show Efforts to Rule Out Lab Origin of Covid," *The Intercept*, January 19, 2023.

17 Joint WHO-China study: 14 January–10 February 2021.

18 Peter Daszak, "We Knew Disease X Was Coming. It's Here Now," *New York Times*, Feb. 27, 2020.

19 "NIH Clinical Trial of Investigational Vaccine for COVID-19 Begins," NIAID Press Release, March 16, 2020. https://www.niaid.nih.gov/news-events/nih-clinical-trial-investigational-vaccine-covid-19-begins.

Chapter 18

1 BIT CHUTE, "Dr. Zelenko Exposes How Dr. Rick Bright's Very Bad Move Sabotaged Early Covid Treatment Killing Masses," Sept. 2, 2021. https://www.bitchute.com/video/WHIktyjGEPcF.

2 New York State Department of Health, "Advisory: Hospital Discharges and Admissions to Nursing Homes," March 25, 2020.

3 "U.S. Government Engages Pfizer to Produce Millions of Doses of COVID-19 Vaccine," Department of Defense Press Release, July 22, 2020. https://www.defense.gov/News/Releases/Release/Article/2310994/us-government-engages-pfizer-to-produce-millions-of-doses-of-covid-19-vaccine/.

4 Matina Stevis-Gridneff, "How Europe Sealed a Pfizer Vaccine Deal With Texts and Calls," *New York Times*, April 28, 2021.

5 Christina Anderson and Henrik Pryser Libell, "In the Coronavirus Fight in Scandinavia, Sweden Stands Apart," *New York Times*, March 28, 2020.

6 Angelo M. Pezzullo et al., "Age-stratified infection fatality rate of COVID-19 in the non-elderly population informed from pre-vaccination national seroprevalence studies,"; originally published as a medRxiv preprint on October 13, 2022, later published in *Environmental Research*, January 1, 2023.

7 John Leake and Peter A. McCullough, *The Courage to Face COVID-19: Preventing Hospitalization and Death While Battling the Bio-Pharmaceutical Complex*, Skyhorse Publishing, 2022.

8 Wiegand et al. "Estimated SARS-CoV-2 antibody seroprevalence trends and relationship to reported case prevalence from a repeated, cross-sectional study in the 50 states and the District of Columbia, United States—October 25, 2020–February 26, 2022," *Lancet Reg Health Am.* 2022 Dec 2;18:100403. doi: 10.1016/j.lana.2022.100403.

9 Madeline Holcombe and Christine Maxouris, "Fully vaccinated people who get a Covid-19 breakthrough infection can transmit the virus, CDC chief says." CNN, August 6, 2021. https://www.cnn.com/2021/08/05/health/us-coronavirus-thursday.

10 Jenna Greene. "Wait what? FDA wants 55 years to process FOIA request over vaccine data," Reuters, November 18, 2021. https://www.reuters.com/legal/government/wait-what-fda-wants-55-years-process-foia-request-over-vaccine-data-2021-11-18/.

11 BNT162b2 5.3.6, "Cumulative Analysis of Post-Authorization Adverse Event Reports of Pf-07302048 (Bnt162b2)," Received through 28-Feb-2021, Report prepared by: Worldwide Safety Pfizer, p. 7. https://phmpt.org/wp-content/uploads/2021/11/5.3.6-postmarketing-experience.pdf?fbclid=IwAR0MtPA5vQ4wrubFmMO_QQS5eGQAV7feZ9RP8mRqniiZR7sD0CMeRGryWfg.

12 European Medicines Agency, "COVID-19 vaccines: update on ongoing evaluation of myocarditis and pericarditis," June 11, 2021.

13 Eric J. Rubin, Lindsey R. Baden, Rochelle P. Walensky, and Stephen Morrissey. Audio Interview: "Covid-19 Vaccines and Pregnancy—A Conversation with CDC Director Rochelle Walensky," April 21, 2021, *N Engl J Med* 2021;384: e73, DOI: 10.1056/NEJMe2106836, VOL. 384 NO. 16. https://www.nejm.org/doi/10.1056/NEJMe2106836.

14 Amanda K. Verma, Kory J. Lavine, Chieh-Yu Lin. "Myocarditis after Covid-19 mRNA Vaccination." *New England Journal of Medicine*, P. 1332-1333,

V 385 N 14 doi:10.1056/NEJMc2109975. https://www.nejm.org/doi/full/10.1056/NEJMc2109975.

15 Tom Kertscher, In Context: "Never going to learn how safe this vaccine is unless we start giving it," *Politfact*, November 1, 2021. https://www.politifact.com/article/2021/nov/01/context-never-going-learn-how-safe-vaccine-unless-/.

Chapter 19

1 Bill Gates, "What you need to know about the COVID-19 vaccine," Gates Notes, April 29, 2020. https://www.gatesnotes.com/meet-bill/save-lives/reader/what-you-need-to-know-about-the-covid-19-vaccine.

2 Matthew Cobb, "Who discovered messenger RNA?" *Current Biology*, Volume 25, Issue 13, R526 - R532.

3 Our History, "BioNTech—The Road to a New Era of Immunotherapy," https://www.biontech.com/int/en/home/about/who-we-are/history.html.

4 Morais P, Adachi H, Yu YT. The Critical Contribution of Pseudouridine to mRNA COVID-19 Vaccines. Front Cell Dev Biol. 2021 Nov 4;9:789427. doi: 10.3389/fcell.2021.789427. PMID: 34805188; PMCID: PMC8600071. https://pmc.ncbi.nlm.nih.gov/articles/PMC8600071/.

5 Collins, Francis S., *The Language of God: A Scientist Presents Evidence for Belief* (New York: Free Press, 2006).

6 Pascal Irrgang et al., "Class switch toward noninflammatory, spike-specific IgG4 antibodies after repeated SARS-CoV-2 mRNA vaccination" *Science Immunology* (2023).

7 OpenVAERS, https://www.openvaers.com/covid-data.

8 Electronic Support for Public Health–Vaccine Adverse Event Reporting System (ESP:VAERS) Inclusive dates: 12/01/07–09/30/10. Principal Investigator: Lazarus, Ross, MBBS, MPH, Team members: Michael Klompas, MD, MPH, Harvard Pilgrim Health Care, Inc. https://digital.ahrq.gov/sites/default/files/docs/publication/r18hs017045-lazarus-final-report-2011.pdf.

9 Stefan Oelrich, Statement at World Health Summit 2021, Berlin, October 24, 2021. https://www.youtube.com/watch?v=OJFKBritLlc&t=5375s.

10 Kevin Breuninger, "Fauci blasts 'preposterous' Covid conspiracies, accuses his critics of 'attacks on science,'" CNBC, June 9. 2021. https://www.cnbc.com/2021/06/09/fauci-blasts-preposterous-covid-conspiracies-accuses-critics-of-attacks-on-science.html.

11 20 Euros - Francis Treatment to prevent a pandemic. Numista Catalogue, Vatican City, 2022. https://en.numista.com/catalogue/pieces328913.html.

12 Tyler Arnold, "Pope names biochemist who contributed to COVID vaccine to Pontifical Academy for Life," Catholic News Agency, Feb. 12, 2024.

13 Jimmy Kimmel, Sept. 9, 2021. Video posted on Real Clear Politics.

14 Joe Rogan Experience #2099 - Aaron Rodgers. https://www.youtube.com/watch?v=c8rqfCDZlGc.

15 Novak Djokovic, "The twists and turns of his Australia mess." BBC, 15 February 2022. https://www.bbc.com/news/world-australia-59890943.
16 Madeline Holcombe and Christine Maxouris, "Fully vaccinated people who get a Covid-19 breakthrough infection can transmit the virus, CDC chief says." CNN, August 6, 2021. https://www.cnn.com/2021/08/05/health/us-coronavirus-thursday.

Chapter 20

1 Amy Choznick, "Trade Dispute Centers on Ukrainian Executive With Ties to Clintons," *New York Times*, Feb. 12, 2014.
2 Transparency International, Corruption Perceptions Index, 2016.
3 Anne Applebaum, *Red Famine: Stalin's War on Ukraine*, Doubleday, 2017.
4 Taras Kuzio, "Oligarchs Wield Power in Ukrainian Politics," Jamestown, July 1, 2008.
5 President of Russia press conference, "Vladimir Putin answered journalists' questions on the situation in Ukraine," May 4, 2014.
6 Vijai Maheshwari, "The Comedian and the Oligarch," *Politico*, April 17, 2019.
7 Josh Cohen, "In the battle between Ukraine and Russian separatists, shady private armies take the field," Reuters, May 10, 2015.
8 Tanya Kozyreva, "Ukrainian oligarch sanctioned following the FinCEN Files investigation arrested in Ukraine," International Consortium of Investigative Journalists, September 7, 2023.
9 "Ukraine ex-leader Poroshenko faces 'treason' charges," *Deutsche Welle*, Dec. 20, 2021.
10 'Foreign Affairs Issue Launch with Former Vice President Joe Biden," Council on Foreign Relations, January 23, 2018.
11 Federal Bureau of Investigation, CHS Reporting Document, "Summary of CHS's meeting with executives of Burisma Holdings."
12 Branko Macetic, "When officials say the quiet part about Russia and NATO out loud," Responsible Statecraft, Sept. 19, 2023.
13 Hillary Clinton interview, MSNBC, on or around February 28, 2022.
14 Camille Gus, "Zelensky: Ukraine ready to discuss neutral status to reach Russia peace deal," *Politico*, March 28, 2022.
15 Jake Johnson, "Boris Johnson Pressured Zelenskyy to Ditch Peace Talks With Russia: Ukrainian Paper," Common Dreams, May 6, 2022.
16 Samya Kullab, "Once a shadowy dealmaker, former Zelenskyy associate is accused in Ukrainian corruption scandal," AP, November 15, 2025.
17 Veronika Melkozerova and Jamie Dettmer, "Ukraine corruption scandal explained: The $100M plot rocking Zelensky," *Politico*, Nov. 12, 2025.
18 Valerie Insinna,"Pentagon fails (another) audit, restates 2028 goal to finally pass," Breaking Defense, Dec. 19, 2025.
19 Greg Myre, Stanislav Petrov, "'The Man Who Saved The World,' Dies At 77," NPR, Sept. 18, 2017.

Chapter 21

1 Cassius Dio, *Roman History*, Vol. IX, Loeb Classical Library edition, 1927.
2 Brandy Schillace, "The Forgotten History of the World's First Trans Clinic," *Scientific American*, May 10, 2021.
3 "Dr. Friedmann Here, Bringing His 'Cure'; Prefers to Call It Treatment, Says It's for All and Will Be Offered to Government," *New York Times*, Feb. 26, 1913.
4 Benjamin H. *The transsexual phenomenon* (New York: Julian Press; 1966).
5 *Diagnostic and Statistical Manual of Mental Disorders,* Fourth Edition, (America Psychiatric Association, Washington D.C., 1994).
6 John Colpinto, *As Nature Made Him: The Boy Who Was Raised as A Girl* (New York: Harper Collins, 2000).
7 Gooren, L., & Delemarre-van de Waal, H. (1996). "The feasibility of endocrine interventions in juvenile transsexuals." *Journal of Psychology & Human Sexuality*, 8(4), 69–74. https://doi.org/10.1300/J056v08n04_05.
8 Ibid.
9 Grigoria Betsi et al, "Puberty suppression in adolescents with gender dysphoria: an emerging issue with multiple implications," *Frontiers in Endocrinology*, June 2024.
10 J. A. Meerloo, "Change of Sex and Collaboration with the Psychosis," *American Journal of Psychiatry*, 1967; 124(2): 263–264.
11 Mia Hughes, "The WPATH Files Pseudoscientific Surgical and Hormonal Experiments on Children, Adolescents, and Vulnerable Adults," Environmental Progress, March 5, 2024.
12 Norman Spack Biography, posted on AAE Speakers website.
13 Jason Rafferty, MD, MPH, EdM, "Ensuring Comprehensive Care and Support for Transgender and Gender-Diverse Children and Adolescents" *Pediatrics*, Volume 142, Issue 4 (October 2018; online September 17, 2018).
14 Amanda Pretigiacomo, "Huge Money Maker': Video Reveals Vanderbilt's Shocking Gender 'Care,' Threats Against Dissenting Doctors," *Daily Wire*, Sept. 20, 2022.
15 Rose Kaplan, "Jennifer Pritzker's Foundation Gives $2 Million for Transgender Studies at Canadian University," *Tablet*, January 21, 2016.
16 AMA, Special Meeting of the House of Delegates, adoption of policy recommendations from Board Report 15 (prepared by the AMA's LGBTQ+ Advisory Committee and presented by Willie Underwood III, MD, MSc, June 2021.
17 Annie Tang et al. "Gender-Affirming Mastectomy Trends and Surgical Outcomes in Adolescents,' *Annals of Plastic Surgery* (2022).
18 Suarez, Trujillo et al. "Disparities in School Connectedness, Unstable Housing, Experiences of Violence, Mental Health, and Suicidal Thoughts and Behaviors Among Transgender and Cisgender High School Students—Youth Risk Behavior Survey, United States," CDC, Oct. 10, 2024.
19 CDC, Data and Statistics on Autism Spectrum Disorder, May 27, 2025.

20 David Smolin, "Suicide, Suicidality, and Pediatric Medical Transition in *United States v. Skrmetti* and Beyond," *Harvard Journal of Law & Public Policy*, April 4, 2025.
21 "Supporting Gender Expansive Students Guidance for Schools," Oregon Department of Education, January 5, 2023.
22 Asa Radix et al. "Standards of Care for the Health of Transgender and Gender Diverse People, Version 8, International Journal of Transgender Health," Sept. 2022.
23 BBC News, "Sydney axe attacks: Woman jailed for wounding 7-Eleven customers," Jan. 17, 2019.
24 KSTP Staff, "Robin Westman posted a manifesto on YouTube prior to Annunciation Church shooting," August 27, 2025.
25 Kieran Kelly et al. "Canada school shooter was transgender teenager," *The Telegraph*, Feb. 12, 2026.
26 Shakiel Mahjouri, "2024 Olympics boxing: Angela Carini concedes bout with Imane Khelif after 46 seconds, reigniting gender debate," *CBS Sports*, Aug. 1, 2024.
27 IBA News, "Statement made by the International Boxing Association regarding Athletes Disqualifications in World Boxing Championships 2023," July 31, 2024.
28 Chad de Guzman, "World Boxing Apologizes to Imane Khelif After Announcing New Sex-Testing Policy," *TIME*, June 5, 2025.
29 TAS press release, "Boxing Imane Khelif Appeals Against World Boxing at the Court of Arbitration for Sport (CAS)" Sept. 1, 2025.
30 The Cass Review, April 2024.
31 Office of the Attorney General, "Attorney General Labrador Challenges American Academy of Pediatrics to Disclose Gender Dysphoria Guidance and Methodology," Sept. 24, 2024.
32 See YouTube video recording interview, KGB defector Yuri Bezmenov's warning to America (1984).

Chapter 22

1 Chris Nesi, "Mystery bearded man who appeared to cheer shooting of Charlie Kirk claims he chanted 'USA' to create 'distraction'" *New York Post*, Sept. 12, 2025.
2 Amy Furr, "WATCH—VILE: Leftist Chants 'We Got Charlie in the Neck!' in Wake of Turning Point USA Founder's Assassination," Breitbart, Sept. 11, 2025.
3 Noam Fischman, "22% of Americans Under 30 Say Killing Charlie Kirk Was Justified," CloudResearch, Sept. 16, 2025.
4 Joshua Rhett Miller et al., "Tyler Robinson's Full Text Exchange with Roommate Lance Twiggs Revealed," *Newsweek*, Sept. 16, 2025.
5 Andrew Kolvet, post on X, Sept. 20, 2025.
6 Joe Kent, Interview with Tucker Carlson, March 18, 2026.

Chapter 23

1 Washington's Farewell Address to the People of the United States.

2 Richard A. *Stewart, Sunrise at Abadan: The British and Soviet Invasion of Iran, 1941* (New York; Praeger, 1988).

3 The National Security Archive, "CIA Confirms Role in 1953 Iran Coup," August 19, 2013.

4 National Security Archive, "The Battle of the Letters, 1963: John F. Kennedy, David Ben-Gurion, Levi Eshkol, and the U.S. Inspections of Dimona," May 2, 2019.

5 Antony Blinken, Bloomberg Big Take podcast, March 4, 2026.

6 Full Transcript: Omani Foreign Minister Badr Albusaidi tells "Face the Nation" a U.S.-Iran deal is "within our reach, CBS News, Feb. 27, 2026.

7 Patrick Wintour et al., "UK security adviser 'attended' US-Iran talks and judged deal was within reach," *The Guardian*, March 17, 2026.

8 Joe Kent, Resignation Letter, March 17, 2026.

9 Tulsi Gabbard, written opening statement for the Senate Select Committee on Intelligence's annual Worldwide Threats, March 18, 2026.

10 "The Spymaster: Meir Dagan on Iran's threat," *60 Minutes*, CBS News, Sept. 16, 2012.

Chapter 24

1 Carl Jung, *Collected Works*, Volume 10, "The Undiscovered Self," (Princeton University Press, 2024).

2 Email correspondence between Steve Bannon and Jeffrey Epstein, Sept. 19, 2018.

3 "Charlie Kirk, My Life Story: With Dr. Jordan Peterson." Quote begins at 23:00 on tape.

4 Email correspondence between Børge Brende and Jeffrey Epstein, Sept. 17, 2018.

5 Frédéric Bastiat's, *The Law*, English edition (Auburn, Alabama: Ludwig von Mises Institute, 2007).

INDEX